W9-AYI-245

The Complete Idiot's Reference Card

Ten Tips for Buying Your First Boat

1. Define the boat's "mission" first—how will you and your family use it most often? How much space do you need? Will you operate in protected waters or open sea?

2. Decide if you want (and can afford) a "name brand" boat. You pay more up front for the best-known, established brands, but you gain dependability, a long-term warranty from a company that hopefully won't go out of business, and much better resale value.

3. Give some thought to the engine if your first boat is to be a powerboat. Outboards are an all-in-one engine and drive system, light in weight and powerful for their size. Inboard/outboards combine the power and low-noise levels of automotive engines with outboard lower units or drive systems. Inboards are the best choice for larger boats.

4. Consider "package" boats. Many manufacturers now install the engine, electronics, and lots of other gear at the factory, rather than having the installations done by a dealer. You get a turn-key boat ready today rather than several weeks from now, and the price is usually better.

5. Opt for a trailerable boat if you have a vehicle large enough for safe towing. Trailering saves money on dock fees and also makes it possible to boat on a different lake, river, or bay every weekend.

6. Boats, like cars, have negotiable prices at most lots. Shop at several dealers, visit boat shows, and buy from the dealer who offers the best combination of price and the promise of dependable maintenance after the sale.

7. Don't overlook used boats. There are thousands of barely used boats sitting in garages and marinas nationwide, and these boats can sell used for as little as half the cost of new.

8. Decide how your boat will be stored before you bring it home. Ideally, it should be protected from weather to maintain its value and keep it clean and new-looking. Storage in a garage is best, but vinyl or nylon boat covers also work well.

9. Include the cost of insurance in your calculations on how much boat you can afford. Remember that boaters who pass a certified boating safety course often get reduced insurance premiums.

10. If you're considering a sailboat but don't know how to sail, take a sailing course before you go shopping. Once you know the basics, you'll have a better understanding of the type of sailboat that will make you happy.

alpha
books

Five Ways to Keep Your Crew Happy

➤ Start out with short trips if your family is new to boating. A couple of hours is plenty for a first voyage—and go only when the weather is perfect.

➤ Give your crew a short tour of the boat before you leave the dock. Show them where the life jackets are, bathroom facilities if any, where the cold drinks are stowed, and where they can safely sit.

➤ Remember comfort items including sunscreen and insect repellent in summer; warm, dry clothes for everyone aboard in spring, fall, and winter.

➤ Although the captain makes all decisions on navigation and boat handling, make sure to offer everyone a vote on what you do each day afloat, and try to do a little of a lot of different things—swimming, skiing, diving, fishing, and just relaxing—to keep everyone entertained.

➤ Make sure all aboard have sunglasses. Sun reflecting off water is much brighter than that absorbed by vegetation ashore. Polarized glasses are the best choice—they allow seeing through the surface glare to view fish and marine mammals, and also to avoid obstructions.

The Top Four Knots You Need to Know

➤ *Bowline.* The bowline is easy and quick to tie. The loop makes it easy to secure a line to a piling.

➤ *Half-hitch.* The half-hitch is the simplest of all knots and is the beginning of many other knots.

➤ *Two half-hitches.* Two half-hitches make a stout knot that won't slip and that can be tied by anyone quickly.

➤ *Clove hitch.* The clove hitch is a good temporary tie-up to a piling, but may slip down the pole if there's no strain on the lines.

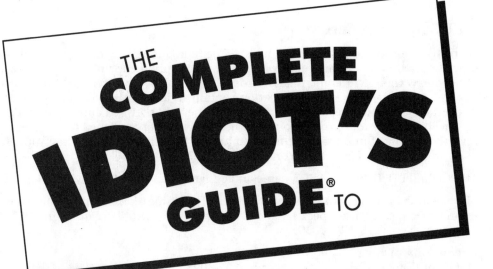

THE COMPLETE IDIOT'S GUIDE® TO

Boating and Sailing

by Frank Sargeant

alpha books

A Division of Macmillan General Reference
A Simon & Schuster Macmillan Company
1633 Broadway, New York, NY 10019

©1998 by Frank Sargeant

All rights reserved. No part of this book shall be reproduced, stored in a retrieval system, or transmitted by any means, electronic, mechanical, photocopying, recording, or otherwise, without written permission from the publisher. No patent liability is assumed with respect to the use of the information contained herein. Although every precaution has been taken in the preparation of this book, the publisher and author assume no responsibility for errors or omissions. Neither is any liability assumed for damages resulting from the use of information contained herein. For information, address Alpha Books, 1633 Broadway, 7th Floor, New York, NY 10019-6785.

THE COMPLETE IDIOT'S GUIDE name and design are trademarks of Macmillan, Inc.

Macmillan Publishing books may be purchased for business or sales promotional use. For information please write: Special Markets Department, Macmillan Publishing USA, 1633 Broadway, New York, NY 10019.

International Standard Book Number: 0-02-862124-7
Library of Congress Catalog Card Number: 97-80980

00 99   8 7 6 5 4

Interpretation of the printing code: the rightmost number of the first series of numbers is the year of the book's printing; the rightmost number of the second series of numbers is the number of the book's printing. For example, a printing code of 98-1 shows that the first printing occurred in 1998.

Printed in the United States of America

Note: This publication contains the opinions and ideas of its author. It is intended to provide helpful and informative material on the subject matter covered. It is sold with the understanding that the author and publisher are not engaged in rendering professional services in the book. If the reader requires personal assistance or advice, a competent professional should be consulted.

The author and publisher specifically disclaim any responsibility for any liability, loss or risk, personal or otherwise, which is incurred as a consequence, directly or indirectly, of the use and application of any of the contents of this book.

ALPHA DEVELOPMENT TEAM

Publisher
Kathy Nebenhaus

Editorial Director
Gary M. Krebs

Managing Editor
Bob Shuman

Marketing Brand Manager
Felice Primeau

Senior Editor
Nancy Mikhail

Development Editors
Phil Kitchel
Jennifer Perillo
Amy Zavatto

Editorial Assistant
Maureen Horn

PRODUCTION TEAM

Development, Production, and Copy Editor
Lynn Northrup

Cover Designer
Mike Freeland

Photo Editor
Richard H. Fox

Illustrator
Jody P. Schaeffer

Designer
Dan Armstrong

Indexer
Chris Barrick

Layout/Proofreading
Angela Calvert
Pamela Woolf

Contents at a Glance

Contents

Foreword

Many years ago, not too long after I'd given up professional seafaring for a job as a marine magazine writer, I exchanged a few complimentary words with Frank Sargeant at the Miami Boat Show. I'd never met Frank before, and he'd just won the prestigious National Marine Manufacturers Association Director's Award, an honor bestowed upon a marine journalist or scrivener each year for making a remarkable contribution to the world of boats and writing about them.

Frank was a guy I admired and envied. He wrote for all sorts of popular publications, from *Sports Afield* to *Boating*, and his name graced a whole raft of fishing how-to books I'd seen on bookstore shelves in Florida and elsewhere. Frank was, in fact, one of those guys who'd really made it in a realm I was only beginning to break into.

From the standpoint of personality, what most struck me about Frank at the time was the paradox he projected. While the man was having undeniable success with the written word, writing seemed to be rather secondary to him. Unlike many journalists who describe the experiences of others secondhand, Frank was a consummate boatman first and foremost, with his own experiences. He was one of those people who knows boats intimately and is passionate about them, with the requisite talent and intelligence to be able to simply and succinctly communicate to others his love for a rich, multifaceted sport.

In later years, as I honed my own writing talents at *Boating* and *Power & Motoryacht* magazines, I had the pleasure of working with Frank, editing his boat tests and stories, and deepening my appreciation for his expertise, knowledge, and humor. I'll never forget the time, down in the Florida Straits, when Frank and I spent a couple of uproarious, hair-raising hours in a high-powered, high-performance, 40-some-foot speedboat, leaping from the crest of one wave to the next, in sea conditions that were more like a washing machine's spin cycle than anything else. Frank's professionalism, knowledge, and humor that afternoon were both welcome and bolstering.

These same qualities are part and parcel of the volume you hold in your hands right now. *The Complete Idiot's Guide to Boating and Sailing* is an informed, cut-to-the-chase manual for recreational boaters that's written by a boatman who not only knows how to write, but knows his stuff, from the proper way to jibe a daysailer, to replacing a spark plug in an outboard, to navigating a runabout around a lake. Whether you're a boating beginner or an old hand, you'll find this book a great read and a fabulous resource.

Bill Pike
Executive Editor, *Power & Motoryacht* magazine

Introduction

As Ted Turner once said, "It ain't as easy as it looks." Turner, an accomplished boater and former America's Cup skipper, was not talking about boating, but about his success in business. However, an experienced skipper makes handling a boat look very easy, when in fact, it's a combination of knowledge and physical skills that takes a bit of preparation even to get started, and years of study and practice to master.

The Complete Idiot's Guide to Boating and Sailing offers that preparation, beginning with the basics and then wedding them to some of the more technical topics in the later chapters. For those who are not novices, skipping chapters is allowed and even encouraged—the convenient chapter outlines in the Contents at a Glance and the many subheads make it very easy to find your way around.

There will not be a test at the end of the semester, nor even pop quizzes along the way. However, if your state is one that requires you to pass a boating-knowledge test before acquiring a license, this book is designed to give you all you need and lots more.

Boating may not be as easy as it looks, but it's not all that difficult if you have a guide to direct you around the reefs and rough spots.

Most boating books are written as if they are military drill books, which makes sense if you're studying to be captain of a nuclear submarine—there's nothing funny about driving the Sea Wolf into the Bosporus Straits. But recreational boating is supposed to be fun, and I hope this book will be fun, too.

The design of this book means you don't have to read every chapter to make it useful. In fact, if you're a lake or bay boater who never intends to get out of sight of land, you can probably skip right over Part 3 on marine navigation. Ditto for Part 7 on sailing, if you're a confirmed powerboater. And sailors who wouldn't be caught dead in a "stinkpot" may chose to bypass Chapters 2 and 3 on engines and props.

With *The Complete Idiot's Guide to Boating and Sailing*, you can easily locate all the information you need—whether you're just getting started in boating, or you've had some experience on the water and want to know more about the arts of navigation, anchoring, or rough water handling. And although there's a very specific vocabulary in boating, I've taken care to define every term in everyday language that won't leave you guessing.

This book is a starting point to help you:

➤ Learn which boat is best for you and your family.

➤ Save you money when buying a boat.

➤ Understand the legal requirements for safety equipment aboard.

➤ Get through that unnerving first launch.

➤ Avoid problems afloat.

➤ Build your confidence for taking on longer voyages and bigger waters.

➤ Navigate like an old salt.

➤ Keep your boat shipshape.

➤ Understand basic engine troubleshooting.

➤ Master the basics of sailing.

How to Use This Book

The Complete Idiot's Guide to Boating and Sailing details all the important things you need to know to get started. Read the book and learn the basics, then take it with you on your first voyage and put them to work. The important details are covered in seven parts:

Part 1, "Getting Started in Boating," walks you through selecting a boat that will be right for your family, whether their idea of fun is a day on the beach, chasing the big ones, diving on a colorful reef, or simply enjoying a quiet day of sailing.

Part 2, "The Basics of Operation," helps you with the details of getting underway for the first time, handling a boat around the docks, anchoring your boat, tying proper boating knots, and moving a boat with both paddles and engine power.

Part 3, "Getting From Point A to Point B: Marine Navigation," covers the use of charts, the marine rules of the road, the tools of navigation, and making your first long cruise.

Part 4, "Nature's Triple Play: Wind, Weather, and Tides," teaches you to understand the signals that bad weather is coming and how to protect yourself. It also covers the ins and outs of tidal flows in coastal areas, and how they can work for or against you.

Part 5, "Staying Safe Afloat," reviews safety gear required by federal law for recreational boats, reminds you of some basic measures to avoid getting into trouble in your boat, and offers some tips on how to deal with emergencies that could someday occur aboard.

Part 6, "Boating Maintenance," gives a review of the tools you need to keep your boat running right, plus advice on keeping your boat clean, neat, and at maximum resale value. It also covers engine maintenance and fixing some common but simple problems.

Part 7, "Sailing, Sailing…," clarifies the sometimes confusing vocabulary of sailboaters; reviews the types of sailboats, rigging, and sails; and instructs in the basics of getting started in sailing in anything from an eight-foot sailboard to a 50-foot ketch.

Extras

Like your information in a nutshell—forget the verbiage and give you the facts? *The Complete Idiot's Guide to Boating and Sailing* does the job with lots of compact, easy-to-find, and quick-to-read tips. Look for these elements throughout the book:

Bet You Didn't Know

The devil may be in the details, but so is a lot of the interest. These segments give you added depth on topics that will help you navigate your way from being a boating novice to a seasoned skipper.

Boat Bytes

These are tips that make boating easier, more fun, or safer—a bit of advice from those who have been there and done that and can show you a better way.

Boater-ese

If you want to understand boating, you need to speak the language. Read these sidebars and your boating vocabulary will bloom.

Look Out!

You need to keep a sharp lookout when you go boating, and these sidebars will tell you exactly what to watch for when a situation can be difficult, expensive, or risky.

Acknowledgments

There have been so many people who have helped me along the way, both in learning boating and in becoming a writer, that it's hard to fit them all in a few paragraphs—but I'll try not to miss anyone.

Thanks to Marty Luray, who got me started in writing about boating when he bought my first story for *Rudder* more than 20 years ago. Thanks to Chris Caswell, who was my boss at *Sea* magazine for several great years; and to Harry Monahan, managing editor at *Sea*, who taught me lots of boating terminology, some of it printable in a family publication. (Harry, I finally learned to spell "accommodation"—two c's and two m's, right?)

Thanks to Paul Smith, my boss at the *Tampa Tribune*, who is tolerant of my ventures outside my "real" job at the paper—as long as I never miss a deadline! (So far, so good.) Thanks to Tom McEwen, who hired me at the *Tribune*, and who has been a guide and mentor to me and so many other sports writers for so many years.

Thanks to John Owens, Richard Stepler, and Randy Steele, my editors at *Boating* magazine over the last five years; and to features editor Jeanne Craig, who buried me with assignments in her tenure there; and to associate editor Lenny Rudow, who keeps me busy these days.

Thanks to Jay Cassell, who so ably edits my boating columns for *Sports Afield* magazine—I promise to write them shorter in future, Jay. Thanks to Larry Larsen of Larsen Outdoors Publishing, who convinced me to get into the book business for the first time almost a decade ago, and has now published 10 of my books.

Thanks to Dan Atwood at Pro-Line Boats, who put me up for the NMMA Award and be damned if we didn't win it.

At Trailer Boats, for which I used to do a great deal of work, thanks to former editor Randy Scott, managing editor Mike Blake, and the new editor-in-chief and my sometimes fishing buddy Jim Hendricks.

Thanks to Earl Bentz, former president of OMC Boat Group and now CEO of Triton, who backed two of my early boating books and has offered lots of encouragement. Thanks to Alex Leva of OMC/Hydra-Sports for countless assistances and advice. Thanks to the staff at Brunswick's Mercaibo Test Center for years of education. Thanks to Walker Agency and Yamaha, Bear Agency, and particularly tech wizard Dave Greenwood of Suzuki, and all the other boat and motor companies who have been so helpful on so many stories. BOAT U.S. was helpful in providing price data and other useful material from their excellent catalog, and Steve Colgate of the Offshore Sailing School got me interested in sailing for the first time more than 20 years ago.

Thanks to all the skippers and guides who have taken me under their wing all these years, glossed over my errors, and corrected my perceptions with their experience and good humor.

And finally, a special thanks to Lynn Northrup, my editor at Macmillan, who skippered me through the dangerous shoals (and deadlines) of book production—a somewhat longer and tougher voyage than either of us expected.

Special Thanks to the Technical Reviewer

The Complete Idiot's Guide to Boating and Sailing was reviewed by an expert who double-checked the accuracy of what you'll learn here, to help us ensure that this book gives you everything you need to know about choosing and operating a boat. Special thanks are extended to Bill Pike.

Bill Pike is former senior editor of *Boating* magazine. He spent years piloting ships and driving tugs around the oceans of the world before he became a writer, and is one of the most respected authorities on pleasure boats in the nation. He's written hundreds of articles on recreational boating of all kinds, and is currently executive editor of *Power & Motoryacht* magazine.

Trademarks

All terms mentioned in this book that are known to be or are suspected of being trademarks or service marks have been appropriately capitalized. Alpha Books and Macmillan General Reference cannot attest to the accuracy of this information. Use of a term in this book should not be regarded as affecting the validity of any trademark or service mark. The following trademarks and service marks have been mentioned in this book:

Ad-Tech	Dexter	Hydra-Skiff
Bass Footwear	Draw-Tite	Hydra-Sports
Bearing Buddy	Easy-On	Iosso
Chevrolet	Evinrude	Johnson
Clorox Clean-Up	Ford Explorer	Land & Sea Props
Coleman Corporation	Golden Rod	Leatherman Tools
Corrosion-X	Gore-Tex	Lexan
Dacron	Grady White	Lysol
Damp-Rid	Honda	Mylar

Monza

Nissan

No Damp

Polyform

Rain View

Rain-X

Reese

Soft Scrub

Star-Brite

Sterns

Styrofoam

Suzuki

Swiss Army knife

Thermax

Tohatsu

Topsiders

Transom-Saver

U-Haul

Unepoxy

Wal-Mart

The Weather Channel

WD-40

Windsurfer

Yamaha

Ziplock

Zodiac

Part 1
Getting Started in Boating

Help! Where do you start?

Right here. Part 1 helps you and your family decide which boat will best meet the needs of the things you'd like to do on the water.

Prefer to cruise, ski, dive, fish, or simply relax on a secluded beach? There's a boat that's just right for each of these activities. Ditto if you're into sports that use your muscles as power, or your technical skills to harness the winds.

And if you'd prefer to "dock" your boat in your garage, I'll tell you how to do that too, as well as give you details on which trailer is right for your boat and how to handle it—and maintain it.

Chapter 1

Welcome to the Wet and Wonderful World of Boating!

You've looked at the boating magazines and mooned around the boat shows long enough. Now it's time for *you* to be the guy or gal next to that smiling, Florida-tanned model with the mirrored sunglasses and the wind-rippled hair, cruising across that emerald sea toward adventure, romance, and a monthly payment book.

Or maybe your vision is a bit more domestic: the spouse, the kids, the Boston terrier, a jug of Gatorade and a picnic basket full of pastrami on rye, off for a visit to a sandy beach. Sailing, water-skiing, snorkeling, a visit to the next port down the river, or maybe a cruise to that island over the horizon—*you* are the skipper; you decide.

Maybe it's that sense of being in command in a world where there are no yellow lines and no traffic jams, where fish and birds and wonderful marine mammals like porpoise and manatees are frequently part of the scenery, and where you can find true solitude when you want it. But people love boats and boating.

And although there's an aura of mystery to handling a boat, cultivated in part by the arcane language of the old salts of the sea, getting started is a lot easier than you might imagine, and learning the basics for competent, safe operation takes a minimal investment of time and energy.

But what type of boat is really best for you and your family? Read on.

Start at the Bottom Line

Whatever your boating dream, realizing it starts with facing the realities of affordability, space, affordability, seaworthiness, affordability, comfort, affordability, and affordability.

It's the money, friends. Everybody knows that.

Boat Bytes
If you can manage just $100 per month, you can go boating in style. In fact, if you enjoy "people-powered" boats such as canoes, you can be a boat owner for under $50 per month!

With boating, as with everything else in life, you will soon find that you always want just a bit more than you can actually afford. And unfortunately, as yachtsman J.P. Morgan once said, if you have to ask how much it costs...you can't afford it.

Nevertheless, it *is* possible to go boating at some level on just about any budget that features discretionary income. I currently own a 14-foot Sears aluminum jon boat with a 4-horsepower Johnson outboard, which I can afford, and a $25,000 Hydra-Skiff fiberglass tunnel-hull with a 175-horsepower Johnson, which I can't. (If a man's reach does not exceed his grasp, what are second mortgages for?)

Because boats last a long time and don't go out of style rapidly, you can get long-term financing, up to 15 years, on most models. This makes the payments easy for anyone steadily employed to handle. You can get a rough estimate of five-year payments at 8–10 percent by multiplying the number of thousands by $20—that is, a $5,000 boat will have payments around $100, a $10,000 boat will run around $200, and a $20,000 boat will cost around $400 per month. Check out the following table for examples.

What Kind of Boat Will Your Money Buy?

Payments on a $1,000 Canoe at 10 Percent Interest

Term	Monthly Payment	Interest Over Full Term
60 months	$21.25	$275.00
120 months	$13.22	$586.40
180 months	$10.75	$935.00

Payments on a $5,000 Bass Boat at 10 Percent Interest

Term	Monthly Payment	Interest Over Full Term
60 months	$106.24	$1,374.40
120 months	$ 66.08	$2,929.60
180 months	$ 53.73	$4,671.40

As you can see, longer payments mean lower payments. But they also add up to lots more interest—an amount almost equal to the principal in the case of the 15-year term.

Cash is usually the best buy on any depreciable asset, but if you can't manage, the long-term payments make it possible to enjoy the boat of your choice within your budget.

Bet You Didn't Know

I own two boats because, for me, one is never enough, and sometimes two are not enough. I have owned as many as seven boats at one time, until the zoning people came knocking.

The problem, as you soon discover when you get into boating up to your chin, is that the boat that's just right for a solitary paddle into a yard-wide tidal creek where the scarlet ibises nest is a bit overwhelmed when you try to cross a 25-mile-wide bay with four or five aboard. That's why many long-time boaters wind up with a backyard that looks like a boat basin.

However, there are lots of single boats that will meet the needs of most beginning boaters. The problem is, out of all the thousands of designs and sizes, which one will be the best fit for you and your crew?

If the Sloop Fits, Buy It

The trick to buying a boat that's right for you is to get a rig that has enough space for everybody you'd normally bring aboard, and one that fits the "mission" you and your crew envision.

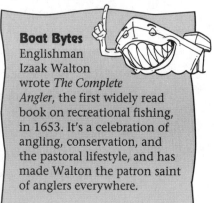

Boat Bytes
Englishman Izaak Walton wrote *The Complete Angler*, the first widely read book on recreational fishing, in 1653. It's a celebration of angling, conservation, and the pastoral lifestyle, and has made Walton the patron saint of anglers everywhere.

If you want silence and communion with nature, you're probably going to be sailors, or perhaps paddlers of your own canoes. If you want the thrill of mile-a-minute speeds, big-engined muscle boats may be for you. If you have budding Izaak Waltons in the family, a fishing boat will do the trick, while if you like boats so well you want to live aboard, a trawler or houseboat may be in your future.

What to Call the Pointy End (and the Rest of a Boat)

Before delving into what type of boat you want, you need to learn a bit of "boater-ese"—the language of boaters. You'll see some of the basic definitions in the following figure. You'll find more definitions scattered throughout the coming chapters as "Boater-ese" margin notes. Once you learn the lingo, you'll sound like an old salt when you talk about boats!

The following two figures show you the various parts of the boat. (Sailboats have their own terminology, which we'll discuss in Part 7.)

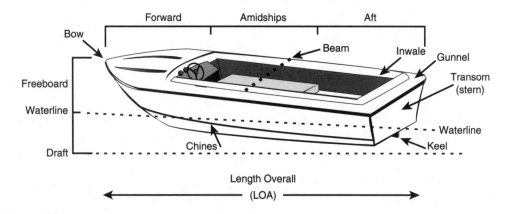

The vocabulary of boaters can be as confusing as Russian at first, but it becomes more familiar after some time aboard.

Here are the basic terms to describe the various parts of most boats—use them as often as you can, and soon they'll be second nature:

➤ *Aft.* Toward the back part of the boat.

➤ *Amidships.* The middle part of the boat, between aft and forward.

➤ *Beam.* The width of a boat, usually measured at its widest point.

➤ *Bow.* Pronounced like "ow," this is the pointy front end of a boat. (Canoes have two pointy ends. The one in front is the "bow.")

➤ *Chines.* Where the bottom of a boat meets the sides.

➤ *Draft.* The distance from the waterline to the lowest point of the hull—the shallowest depth in which a boat will float without any part touching bottom.

➤ *Forward.* Toward the front part of the boat.

➤ *Freeboard.* The distance from the waterline to the gunnels. (A taller freeboard makes a boat more seaworthy.)

➤ *Gunnel.* The top of the hull, where the inner liner joins the outer hull. (It's also spelled "gunwale," but still pronounced "gunnel.")

➤ *Inwale.* The inner side of the gunnel.

➤ *Keel.* The part where the two halves of the bottom meet. Structurally, the main center frame member of the hull. In sailing, the fin projecting from the bottom to reduce leeway.

➤ *Length overall (LOA).* The distance from the tip of the bow to the end of the stern.

➤ *Stern* or *Transom.* The squared-off back end of the boat.

➤ *Waterline.* Where the surface of the water meets the hull.

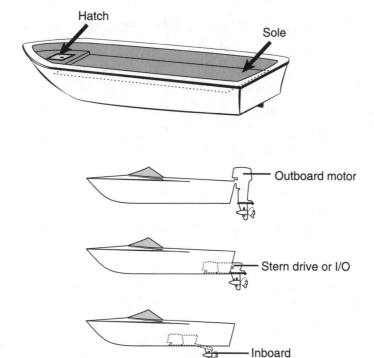

Even the floors and doors have special names aboard a boat.

Here's the rundown on each of these terms:

➤ *Hatch.* A horizontal door, usually on a storage compartment.

➤ *Sole.* The part of the boat you stand on, the floor.

➤ *Outboard motor.* A self-contained engine and propulsion system that mounts on the stern. Most are two-cycle and burn oil along with gasoline to make power.

➤ *Stern drive.* Also known as an "inboard/outboard" or "I/O," this system combines a four-cycle automotive type engine inside the boat with a drive unit on the transom.

➤ *Inboard.* A four-cycle gas or diesel engine mounted amidships, which drives the boat through a shaft in the bottom.

What Kind of Boat Are You Looking For?

Boats can be broadly classified into "power" and "sail," according to their forms of propulsion. In addition, there are many divisions within the classes.

Powerboats generally have large engines and depend entirely on fossil fuels for propulsion. Sailboats may or may not have auxiliary engines, but they always carry a mast and sails that allow them to harness the wind.

Power to the People—Boats With Motors

For most families, that first boat is a powerboat that is 14 to 16 feet long and powered by a two-cycle outboard motor of 50 to 90 horsepower. Powerboating takes less study and requires less physical work than sailing, so it's a quick, easy way to get started.

Powerboats range from slow as a turtle to fast as a flying fish. They can be broken into many subclasses, including:

➤ Runabouts, ski boats, and performance boats

➤ Fishing boats

➤ Live-aboards—cruisers, trawlers, and houseboats

➤ Pontoon and deck boats

➤ Personal watercraft (PWCs)

➤ Inflatable boats

Powerboat prices range from under $2,000 to millions of dollars, and sizes range from diminutive eight-footers powered by 1-horse electric motors to stately 150-footers driven by multiple diesels with thousands of horsepower.

Many powerboats in the popular 14- to 17-foot class are available at prices from $5,000 to $14,000, including a trailer that allows you to "dock" them in your garage and tow them to the ramp each weekend. These are great starter boats.

One Model Fits All: The Runabout

This range includes the ubiquitous "runabout," which is what most of us think of when we think of a one-model-fits-all family boat. It's sort of the Honda Civic of boats, with a closed bow, a windshield, back-to-back seats that fold down into a sun lounge, and space to store water skis and life jackets under the sole or main deck.

Runabouts offer versatility, comfort, and economy in a package that fits in most garages. This variation, known as a bow-rider, offers added seating in the bow and doubles as a fishing boat due to the large cockpit aft. (Photo credit: Grady White Boats)

A variation on the runabout is the "bow-rider," which has the same hull and aft layout, but with seats replacing the closed bow and a walk-through door in the windshield to allow passage forward. An advantage of the bow-rider is that there's more seating space—you can carry six or eight passengers, depending on the depth and beam of the boat and your tolerance for close company.

The front section of a bow-rider creates a great "kiddie-pen" where you can keep little sailors under your watchful eye with just a bit of separation provided by the windshield. It's no place for kids once the boat is underway, however—the ride is rough, and they'll be safer back in the cockpit.

Dedicated ski boats are a specialized form of runabout. They're usually inboard-powered, 18 to 22 feet long, and have fairly flat bottoms so that they plane easily when pulling several skiers.

Boat Bytes
The National Marine Manufacturers rating, listed on a sticker placed on the dash of all powerboats, gives the safe load capacity in terms of persons estimated at 150 pounds each, plus gear. It also lists the safe power rating of any powerboat.

They feature special fins on the bottom that allow them to turn very sharply, a ski pylon or post near the center to attach the tow rope, and a rear-facing seat so that one passenger can keep an eye on the skier without turning around. Ski boats tend to be fairly expensive for their size, ranging from $20,000 to $50,000.

The Need for Speed: Performance Boats

Performance boats also share the general configuration of runabouts, but there's a difference in the engine room. They're also called "muscle boats" for their powerful engines relative to their weight, and they're dedicated to white-knuckle speeds. While a runabout might be powered by as little as 70 horses, muscle boats sport engines of 225 to 500 horsepower.

Performance boats usually have a deep vee bottom to provide a soft ride at speed, but the aft several feet of the keel may be flattened into a planing pad. (When a boat *planes*, it lifts near the surface, increasing speed and decreasing drag.) This pad functions like a slalom ski as speed increases, elevating the boat very high in the water and allowing it to reach speeds of 60 mph and higher.

It's not uncommon for performance boats only 20 feet long to wear outboard engines of 250 horses. Those in the 30- to 35-foot range may have twin 500-horsepower stern drives and run close to 100 mph in the hands of a highly skilled driver! Because of the cost of high-powered engines, these boats are also expensive, ranging from $30,000 to well over $150,000.

Look Out!

Sixty miles an hour is fairly sedate cruising down the interstate in your Chevrolet, but on the water, mile-a-minute speeds are exciting, challenging, and possibly dangerous. The rapidly changing contour of the surface, unmarked shoals, and the unique handling forces that develop as a boat accelerates demand added caution and skill from the driver.

Something Fishy: Boats for Anglers

Fishing can be as frustrating and expensive as golf and slightly more addictive than cigarettes. Consequently, fishing boats of all sorts are top sellers.

Of course, many "fishing boats" are also used regularly as ski boats, dive boats, and casual day-cruising rigs. One variety known as the "Fish 'n Ski" includes a ski pylon, walk-through windshield, and bow-rider seats, as well as fishing seats, rod boxes, trolling sockets, and live wells. It serves double-duty.

Fishing boats can be divided into those suited for fresh water, which include rigs specifically designed to chase largemouth bass, walleyes, crappies, and other species, and those designed for coastal use.

Boater-ese

A *walk-through windshield* has a hinged section in the middle that swings open to allow easy access to the bow.

Up the Creek: Freshwater Fishing Boats

Bass boats, so called because they're popular in fishing for bass, are often high-performance hulls designed to travel across big reservoirs at speeds better than a mile a minute. (Fast fish, those bass!) Bass boats tend to be javelin-shaped and powered by big V6 outboards producing 150 to 225 horses. Most run on a narrow "pad" near the transom, which causes them to plane up on top of the water much like a slalom ski, increasing speed and reducing fuel use (but not reducing it much!). They're usually equipped with a silent electric trolling motor at the bow to provide low-speed maneuvering as the angler probes cover for his quarry (see the following photo). Prices range from $8,000 to $35,000.

Smaller boats, some with squared-off bows known as "jon boats," are popular for pursuit of all sorts of finny critters from catfish to sturgeon. Most of these boats are lightweight aluminum, which means they can be pushed with motors from five to 40 horses. Overall prices are affordable, starting as low as $2,500 including a trailer but without a motor. (The motors are portable and can be added or removed as needed.)

Boat Bytes
According to the National Marine Manufacturers' Association (NMMA) statistics, the most popular boat sold in the U.S. is the outboard-powered rig, which accounted for 215,000 of the 604,750 powerboats sold in 1996. A close second? Personal watercraft or jet skis, which tallied 191,000 in 1996.

Raised casting decks at the bow and stern make for easy fishing in a bass boat. Swivel seats add comfort as the angler tries his luck in all directions. The trolling motor at the bow provides silent power while fishing. (Photo credit: Champion Boats)

Monsters of the Sea: Saltwater Fishing Boats

Coastal fishing boats fall into three general divisions determined by size, seaworthiness, and price.

Most seaworthy are the biggies designed for fishing well offshore. They range in length from 22 to 55 feet and are priced anywhere from $25,000 to several million dollars. These boats have lots of freeboard, lots of beam, and usually twin engines. They can be center consoles, with the wheel in the middle of the boat and fishing space both fore and aft—the preferred arrangement for those who cast to their fish.

Cuddy-cabin boats have a low cabin under the bow—usually space for bunks and a dinette, but not enough head room to stand up. Full-cabin boats have standup head room, usually a full bath or "head," and a kitchenette or "galley." If you dream of catching marlin bigger than a pickup truck, this is your boat.

The "walk-around," shown in the following photo, is a popular variation of the cabin boat. It has space around the sides of the cabin to allow anglers to walk to the bow to fish, thus giving it some of the advantages of the center console, yet preserving the amenities of the full "house."

Walk-around cabin boats have full cabins, but also provide walkways to the bow for easy fishing and anchor handling. This model, from Grady White, includes a built-in motor bracket at the stern. (Photo credit: Grady White Boats)

Cabin rigs make it possible to spend the night afloat. Camping out on the water has a special charm (if the mosquitoes aren't too thick) and cabin rigs make it possible to extend the range of your cruises beyond the distance you can travel in a day-fisherman.

Bay boats have moderate vee bottoms, moderate freeboard, and usually a single engine. Lengths of 17 to 24 feet are common, and prices range from $15,000 to $50,000. They're usually center consoles or walk-arounds. These are boats designed to take on sizable waters, and they're often used along the ocean and gulf beaches in moderate weather.

For the Shallow-Minded: Flats Boats

"Flats boats" are designed to pursue trophy saltwater species in depths of one to four feet. Some of these boats float in only eight inches of water and can run in as little as a foot. Elusive, metallic creatures known as bonefish spend a good part of their time in water barely deep enough to float a tadpole. They are as neurotic as turkeys the day before Thanksgiving, ready to speed for deep water at the bump of an oar against a gunnel, very difficult to fool, and inedible when caught. In the perverse way of anglers, they are considered wonderful game fish. Similarly obnoxious species include the permit and the six-foot-long tarpon, also avidly chased by trophy anglers.

Flats boats are stealth fighters devised to sneak up on these species. Most have a nearly flat bottom (the boats, not the fish) to give them a shallow draft.

Flats rigs have low freeboard so that they don't catch the wind and drift excessively. Lengths range from 15 to 21 feet. Center or side consoles are common, although some are simply operated from near the transom via a tiller. Prices range from $7,000 to as much as $35,000 for special lightweight models with particularly shallow draft.

Boat Bytes
The NMMA is both a boating industry booster and watchdog. It includes thousands of companies that build boats, motors, and accessories, and it also helps to set boating standards for construction and safety. Their address is 200 East Randolph Drive, Suite 5100, Chicago, IL 60601; (312) 946-6200.

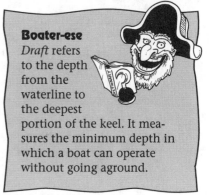

Boater-ese
Draft refers to the depth from the waterline to the deepest portion of the keel. It measures the minimum depth in which a boat can operate without going aground.

Leisure Afloat: Cruisers, Trawlers, and Houseboats

For those who can afford them, these floating houses turn boating into a much more leisurely, even luxurious, affair that those not into salt in the hair and sardines in the swimsuit can appreciate.

Cruisers and trawlers differ from houseboats in that they have deeper-draft hulls and are more suited to taking on offshore waters and big inlets. They also usually have more power and more seaworthy fittings. Consequently, they're expensive, with prices starting at about $1,500 per foot and going into the stratosphere.

Cruisers have planing hulls, which means they offer speeds not possible with displacement hulls. They're often equipped with twin engines and can cruise at better than 20 mph, reaching maximum speeds, with adequate power, of near 40 mph. The level of interior finish can be superb in these boats, and the prices reflect the quality fittings. Lengths from 30 to 55 feet are common, with prices from $80,000 to several million dollars.

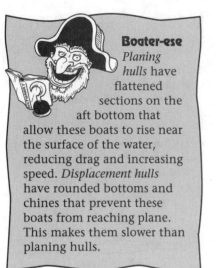

Boater-ese
Planing hulls have flattened sections on the aft bottom that allow these boats to rise near the surface of the water, reducing drag and increasing speed. *Displacement hulls* have rounded bottoms and chines that prevent these boats from reaching plane. This makes them slower than planing hulls.

Trawlers nearly always have displacement hulls, rounded bottoms where speed is limited by the waterline length. No matter how much power you put on a round-bottomed trawler, it still chugs along at a speed of somewhere south of 10 knots. Cruising speeds of up to 10 mph are typical, so you need to have plenty of time to go anywhere in a trawler. However, the round hulls are extremely seaworthy, and displacement speeds are very fuel-efficient. This is the reason that many long-distance travelers choose trawlers. Equipped with a small diesel inboard, some can travel over 1,000 miles between refueling. Lengths range from about 28 to 50 feet, with prices from $100,000 to $300,000.

Houseboats are the camper-trailers of the watery world—slow, unlovely, and unexciting, but with all the comforts of home for those who do most of their boating in protected waters. And they're amazingly affordable.

Many houseboats ride atop a pair of aluminum cylinders known as pontoons, although some models have fiberglass vee hulls. Lengths range from 25 to 100 feet. Power is usually an outboard of 30 to 100 horses, although the larger rigs have inboard power. Prices range from $25,000 to $200,000. You get actual conventional rooms aboard—kitchens, dining rooms, living rooms, bedrooms, and bathrooms, all on one level. Houseboats feel like a home ashore, but you can take a swim off the back porch.

Bet You Didn't Know

The largest boat-owners' association in the world is BOAT U.S., which frequently lobbies for boating causes in Washington. It offers special insurance packages and maintains its own mail-order catalog. The association also offers Web sites for the computer literate: Type **www.boatus.com** to get a menu. Their address is 880 S. Pickett Street, Alexandria, VA 22304; (703) 461-2864.

Houseboats Without the House: Pontoon and Deck-Type Boats

Pontoon boats and deck-type boats feature couches, dinettes, sinks, refrigerators, and usually portable marine toilets, but no sleeping areas and no permanent roof. Weather protection is usually from a convertible top known as a Bimini. It's tall enough to stand under, but with no side panels to prevent air circulation. A pontoon with a front deck for fishing is shown in the photo on the next page.

Pontoon boats ride on aluminum or fiberglass "logs" or cylinders filled with foam. These boats are inexpensive, roomy, and comfortable, although not quite so graceful in appearance as other boats. (Photo credit: Jerry Martin & Associates)

Pontoon boats ride on the same sort of aluminum cylinders as many houseboats. They can be powered by motors as small as 10 horsepower but rarely more than 60 horsepower, and they're cheap to buy and operate. Because of the great amount of floor space and comfortable seating, pontoon boats are a favorite with families. Prices are surprisingly reasonable, starting at around $12,000 for an 18-footer and ranging up to $25,000 for a 30-footer.

Decked boats look much the same as pontoon boats from the deck upward, with couches, lounge chairs, tables, and maybe even a portable TV and barbecue grill. But below the deck is a semi-vee hull that allows full planing operation with adequate power. They can handle motors of 50 to 150 horses and speed along at 30 to 50 mph, making them good ski boats. Decked boats range in length from 18 to 24 feet. They cost considerably more than pontoons, with prices of $15,000 to $35,000 common.

Motorcycles on the Water: Personal Watercraft

Personal watercraft, also known as PWCs, are the newcomers in the boating world, but have rocketed to near the top of the fleet in sales since their introduction in the mid-1980s. They're also the motorcycles of the boating world, designed for thrills and speed rather than comfort. They offer special appeal to the young and the young at heart who want excitement in their boating.

Most PWCs are under 10 feet long. The seats are saddles, just as in a Harley-Davidson, and you steer via handlebars. The power for these boats is via a water-jet instead of the open-bladed propeller found on conventional boats—a safety measure that also makes the craft capable of spectacular end-for-end turns.

The power ranges from 40 to 110 horsepower. Given the light weight of these boats, this results in speeds to 70 mph or more with some models. Prices begin at around $5,000 and go to a bit over $10,000.

Boating in a Balloon: Inflatable Boats

Inflatable boats are basically waterborne balloons, but they're a lot tougher. Multiple air chambers and very stout skins on modern inflatables make them extremely durable. In fact, some of the heaviest-duty boats used by the Coast Guard are inflatables, and they take these boats through outrageous weather where lesser boats with conventional hulls wouldn't stand a chance.

Inflatables have incredible buoyancy for their weight and can carry many times the load of conventional boats of equal size. Let the air out of them and you can carry them in the trunk of the family car and stow them in the hall closet.

Inflatables like this Zodiac are favorites as yacht tenders because their light weight makes it easy to get them aboard and they can be stored deflated to save space. The soft sides also don't mar a yacht's finish as a hard-sided dinghy might. (Photo credit: Zodiac of North America)

Add a fiberglass bottom, as many larger inflatables have, and you have a boat within a boat—a vee bottom to soften the ride and the giant sponsons to provide that remarkable flotation and capability to bump into things without scratching or bending. Some inflatables have twin outboards so they can really fly.

The downside is it's expensive to make a really good inflatable—the good ones cost about as much as a fiberglass boat of equal size. Lengths range from seven to 22 feet, with prices from $300 to $12,000.

Powered by the Wind: Sailboats

Boats powered by the wind are a totally different genre than those powered by machinery and seem to appeal to an entirely different group. In sailing, the voyage is often as important as the destination.

The basic configurations of sailboats range from the tiny, flyweight sailboards to majestic double-masted ketches capable of crossing all the world's oceans. Sailboats vary in price from as little as $1,000 to millions of dollars, and their designs vary as much as the price.

We'll delve into the basics of selecting a wind-powered craft that fits both your budget and your interests, and take a closer look at the categories of these boats, based on their mast and sail arrangement, in Part 7.

Single-masted sailboats like this one are known as "sloops." They're the most common sailboat, more economical to buy and easier to sail than two-masted ketches and yawls. (Photo credit: Pearson Yachts)

Muscle-Powered Boats: Canoes, Kayaks, and Rowboats

Also in a class of their own—but increasingly popular—are boats that depend on you to supply the power. "Human-powered" boats, including canoes, kayaks, and rowboats, are the boat of the 1990s—environmentally friendly, physically challenging, easily stowable in a suburban garage, and relatively affordable. They can be transported on the top of a compact car. However, it takes a bit of practice and some conditioning to get the most from them. We'll go into detail in Chapter 10.

These boats range in length from eight to 18 feet and prices start at under $400 for basic models. Lightweight custom versions designed to take on white water and fly-weight rowing sculls may cost thousands of dollars.

Look Out!
Some dealers price rigs without trailers to get you in the door. But unless you're going to store the boat at a marina or the dock in back of your house, you're going to have to have a trailer. This adds $1,200 to $2,500 to the base price—ask about the trailer, right away.

Boat Bytes
It's a good idea to have a marine mechanic take a look at any used boat you're con-sidering. They can tell you in an hour what you couldn't fig-ure out for yourself in weeks—or until the engine stranded you. The fee might be $100–$200, but it's well worth the price.

Buy New or Used?

Boats, like cars, have negotiable prices. Nobody pays the sticker price. You can get 10 percent off the sticker price for sure, and maybe more if the dealer needs to make a sale to pay the rent. If you buy used, you can save lots more. Here's a look at the advantages and disadvantages of buying new versus buying used.

Buy new and:

➤ You can order exactly what you want, including a special engine, electronics, and interior trim.

➤ You get a full warranty—the dealer has to worry about the repairs.

➤ Some companies offer special package deals with lots of extra equipment at bargain prices.

➤ You pay new-boat prices and take the initial depreciation hit of 10 to 25 percent.

Buy used and:

➤ You save big money—25 to 50 percent!

➤ You get lots of extra gear added by the first owner, at no extra cost.

➤ There may be hidden faults that will have to be fixed—and you have to pay to fix them.

Not only that, but there's more "wiggle room" in the price of a used boat than in the price of a new one. The difference between the wholesale price, what the dealer gives you for your used rig, and the retail price, the price he wants to charge the next buyer, is usually 20 to 30 percent.

You can talk him out of some of that difference, particularly if you're interested in a boat that's not a hot property. It's not uncommon, after some negotiation, haggling, arguing, and sometimes begging—to buy a two-year-old boat in excellent shape from stem to stern for 60 percent of the original price.

"Trader On-Line" is a valuable Internet site that lists thousands of used boats (and cars and trucks) for sale by owners. It's the electronic version of a weekly catalog of boats for-sale-by-owner, and it's free. Even if you don't use it to buy your boat, use it as a way of checking prices on boats available in your area. It's available at **www.traderonline.com**.

The Least You Need to Know

➤ No one boat is perfect for all families or all applications. Choose a boat that suits most of your needs, but be aware that it has limitations.

➤ Boaters have a vocabulary specific to watercraft. Learning what to call the parts of a boat makes operation simpler for all aboard.

➤ Boats, like cars, have negotiable prices. If you don't haggle, you don't get the best deal.

➤ New boats may give the dealer headaches, but you don't have to worry about them.

➤ Used boats save you money, but any headaches that come with them belong to you.

Chapter 2

Power to the People—Marine Engines

In This Chapter

➤ Bolt one on—outboard motors

➤ Inside-out and outside-in—stern drives and inboard engines

➤ Petro-dollars and how to save them

➤ Do you need twin engines for your boat?

➤ The advantages of diesel engines

Most boats on the water today are powerboats. Good thing, too, or a lot of people wouldn't be boating—oars don't do the job when it comes to heading 20 miles offshore, and sailing is an art not learned in the 10-minute attention span some have for recreational pursuits these days.

The power in a powerboat comes from many sources. In this chapter, I'll tell you about the types of motors used in boats and discuss the costs both for their purchase and operation.

Portable Power—Outboard Motors

The first boats of most boaters are powered by outboard motors, so let's look at those first. Outboards are engines featuring an integral drive system including a drive shaft and propeller, all in a single unit that can be moved from boat to boat. All of them still look more or less like the motor designed by Wisconsin inventor Ole Evinrude and patented in the U.S. on September 16, 1910. Evinrude went on to found Outboard Marine Corporation (OMC), one of the world's largest manufacturers of outboards.

Boater-ese
The propeller on a boat is commonly referred to as the *prop*. The shaft that connects it to the drive shaft from the powerhead is called the *prop shaft*.

An outboard motor includes a gasoline engine mounted at the top of a long shaft and a prop mounted at the bottom. The motor clamps on the stern of a boat, and the whole thing—motor, shaft, and prop—pivots to steer the boat.

The outboard concept was particularly useful in the early years when mostly smaller boats were used in the recreational industry, and a single motor could easily be moved from one boat to another. An individual who owned one of these light, portable motors could carry it to boat rental operations anywhere in the trunk of his car, and in the booming economy before 1929, lots of folks had spare cash to spend. Thus they made Ole Evinrude and his offspring quite wealthy.

Boater-ese
In nautical parlance, an *engine* is the power unit itself without the drive train and propeller. A *motor* is a complete power unit including a drive shaft and prop. Thus, inboard and stern-drive power plants are usually referred to as engines, while outboard power plants are usually called motors.

Outboards today offer the advantages of high performance, low weight, and push-button trim and tilt of the lower unit, which makes it easier to control the running attitude of a boat—the angle of the boat bottom to the surface of the water—and makes it easier to operate in shallow water. Outboards are also easy to steer due to the "vectorable" thrust—that is, the propeller itself can be angled to push the stern to one side or the other.

The following figure shows the lower unit of an outboard.

The lower unit of an outboard and a stern drive are identical. This section couples the power put out by the engine to the prop, which causes the boat to move through the water.

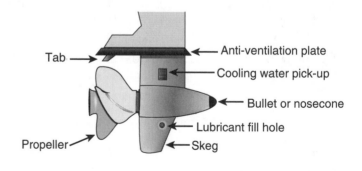

Tab
Anti-ventilation plate
Cooling water pick-up
Bullet or nosecone
Lubricant fill hole
Propeller
Skeg

The lower unit of outboards and I/Os are streamlined to reduce drag. The entire section can be trimmed up or down to change the running angle of the boat.

Let's run through the parts of the lower unit of an outboard:

➤ *Tab.* The tab offsets the tendency of a prop to "walk" sideways slightly at some trim positions.

➤ *Bullet or nosecone.* The bullet or nosecone houses the forward and reverse gears and prop shaft.

➤ *Propeller.* The propeller grips the water and propels the boat. Three-bladed props are most common.

➤ *Skeg.* The lowest extension of the lower unit, the skeg protects the prop from striking obstructions, and also helps the boat track straight.

➤ *Lubricant fill-hole.* The lower unit is full of oil to provide lubrication. This hole allows draining and refilling.

➤ *Anti-ventilation plate.* This flat plate helps prevent the prop from drawing in surface air and losing its grip on the water.

➤ *Cooling water pick-up.* This small vent allows the water pump to pull water through the lower unit and up into the cooling passages of the powerhead. It must be kept free of debris at all times.

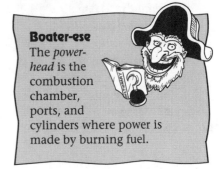

Boater-ese
Power trim is an electrical and hydraulic system for moving the lower unit of an outboard or stern drive in or out relative to the transom. Trim is used for minor adjustments while underway to help improve the running attitude of the boat. *Power tilt* is part of the trim system. It allows the motor to be tilted to almost 90 degrees while at the dock or on a trailer.

Boater-ese
The *powerhead* is the combustion chamber, ports, and cylinders where power is made by burning fuel.

Tabs on outboards and stern drives are usually made of zinc, which acts as a "sacrificial anode" in salt water. The "sacrifice" it makes is to literally be eaten up by electrolysis in order to protect the more important aluminum and steel parts of the motor. The tab can be replaced by loosening one bolt after it becomes severely depleted.

Outboard Motor Brands

For many years, there were only two outboard companies that mattered in the U.S. market. Outboard Marine Corporation (OMC) was the company formed by uniting Evinrude with Johnson Outboards, creating the largest outboard manufacturer in the world. Mercury, founded by Carl Kiekhaefer, was the chief competitor. Mercury later spun off a second company, Mariner, to assist in adding new dealerships. Boat owners were either OMC people or Merc people. There was no third alternative, although a number of smaller companies came and went over the years.

In the early 1980s, Japanese manufacturers entered the boating industry in a big way, and from that point on the U.S. companies were in a serious dogfight. Just as U.S. automakers were forced to change their thinking and improve their products due to international competition, the arrival of Yamaha, and later Suzuki and Honda, forced the whole industry to lift itself up by the boatstraps (er, make that bootstraps).

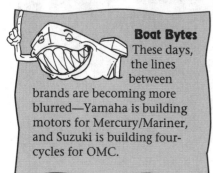

Boat Bytes These days, the lines between brands are becoming more blurred—Yamaha is building motors for Mercury/Mariner, and Suzuki is building four-cycles for OMC.

These days, you can buy any of the mainstream engines with confidence. These include the OMC brands Johnson and Evinrude, the Brunswick brands Mercury and Mariner, and Yamaha. They range in price from as little as $800 for the smallest to over $17,000 for the largest.

This V6 outboard from Mercury puts out 225 horses but weighs only about 450 pounds. An excellent weight-to-horsepower ratio is the major advantage of two-cycle outboards. (Photo credit: Mercury Marine)

Suzuki also builds a very good motor but somehow manages to sell it for quite a bit less than the other manufacturers. And if you don't need a really large motor, the four-cycles from Honda are wonderful. (At this writing there are none larger than 130 horses, however.)

The Low-Priced Spreads—Economy Outboards

There are economy motors made by Tohatsu (identical motors are also sold under the Nissan brand) and by Force, a Brunswick subsidiary. These motors have fewer bells and whistles than the top-of-the-line stuff—no oil injection on the Force motors, for example, and no models over 120 horses for Force or 140 for Tohatsu. But they sell for 15 to 25 percent less, horsepower for horsepower, than the full-featured motors. Tohatsu has been a popular commercial motor overseas for over 40 years and offers a two-year warranty. If you need to keep the price to a minimum, they're worth a look.

You can also save money by buying the economy version of the prestige motors. Yamaha's "C" version does not have oil injection, and so it sells for a lot less than the standard motor.

OMC calls their low-end motors the SPL series. They have less efficient fuel-air systems than the full-price engines, and power tilt and trim is an extra-cost option on most. They are not offered in power greater than 112 horses. But these motors are widely used by commercial fishermen who run them eight to 12 hours a day, so you know they're durable.

Carry-Out Outboards—Mini-Motors

The mini-outboards offer portable power in weights as light as 23 pounds. They're easily carried by kids (which I strongly recommend), and most have the same quality as the larger motors except that they don't offer oil injection, power tilt and trim, or electric start. We're talking motors from two to about eight horses here, with the 2-horsepower motors weighing just over 20 pounds, and the 8-horsepower motors weighing about 60 pounds in most makes. Prices range from just under $1,000 to about $2,000.

My youngest son has had years of enjoyment on the Little Manatee River with a Johnson 4, which scoots his 100-pound aluminum jon boat along at about 20 mph, full speed with only him aboard. You can fish two or three days on a three-gallon tank of fuel, another big plus of the mini-motors.

Compact Motors

Compact motors are like compact cars, big enough to get you from point A to point B, but not big enough to

Look Out!
Make sure when you look at a low-priced rig that the dealer is not trying to sell you one of these economy motors for the same price the dealer across town is offering for a full-featured motor. The economy motors are good products, but the price should reflect the reduction in features.

Boat Bytes
A big plus of the 2- and 4-horsepower motors is their light weight—their power is very modest, but you can lift them off a dock with one hand.

Boat Bytes
Many small motors have the fuel tank built right into the cowling. These little tanks don't hold a lot of gasoline, but they're adequate for short trips and fishing outings, and you don't have to tote a separate fuel tank.

Look Out!
Portable outboards come with portable gas tanks, either three or six gallon. The tanks have a hose that connects to the engine. Most are clip-on, and they only go on one way. Try putting them on upside-down, and fuel will come shooting out the ball valve in the connector.

provide much in the way of comfort or performance. A 100-pound motor is more than most people want to carry down the dock, and this weight kicks in at about 10 to 15 horsepower in most brands. Prices range from $2,200 for a 9.9 to about $7,500 for a 50.

Anything over 15 is definitely not portable, and will require you to either have a motor cart, or to put the boat on a trailer and leave the motor in place. (I know, those big husky fishing guides sometimes manhandle 125-pound, 30-horse motors onto the back of their big square-ender freighter canoes, but the rest of us may find that a bit much.)

Some very inexpensive portables are air-cooled rather than water-cooled. An air-cooled engine is cooled by air passing over aluminum fins on the cylinders. A water-cooled engine is cooled by water passing through molded water passages around the internal parts of the powerhead. The powerhead looks and sounds like a lawnmower motor. These tend to be hard on the ears, but they are also very light and very cheap. If you must pinch every penny, they're okay, but you'll definitely be happier in the long-term buying a small water-cooled motor.

Jet Power

Jet drives are available from all the major outboard builders, and are also used on all personal watercraft or jet-type stern drives. They are not nearly as impressive as they sound. In the first place, they are not true jet engines—only the drive system operates on the jet principle, creating propulsion by shooting a condensed stream of water out a nozzle. The powerhead is a conventional gasoline piston engine, either two- or four-stroke. Two-cycle engines fire at the peak of every upward cycle of each piston, while four-cycle engines fire at the peak of every other upward cycle of the piston.

The lower unit of a jet outboard has an "impeller" inside the housing, rather than a propeller on the back of a prop shaft. Water is drawn through the square intake on the bottom and jetted out the back at great speed, driving the boat forward. (Photo credit: Frank Sargeant)

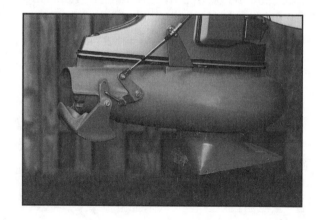

Jet drives waste horsepower and fuel—the horsepower rating is automatically reduced by about 25 percent on all these motors by the maker to account for their lack of performance. That is, when you buy a 100-horse jet, you get the performance of a 75-horse prop engine—but you burn fuel like a 100! Jets are also much noisier than prop engines and extremely hard to steer at low speeds—docking one is like playing bumper cars.

So why does anyone buy one? For operation in extremely shallow, rocky water, these motors are unbeatable. They can bounce off rocks and shoals and skip over water that's only inches deep—they're a favorite for river-running in the Pacific Northwest. And for personal watercraft, the fact that there's no dangerous propeller spinning along under the rider is a huge safety factor. Jets are also capable of making 180-degree turns in a heartbeat, a big plus for those who enjoy the thrills of personal watercraft riding.

In most other venues, though, jets are not the ticket. (I tried one in the shallows of Florida for a time. The motor skimmed over the flats beautifully, but every time we stopped, it sucked weeds into the impeller and couldn't get back on plane without a major cleanout.)

Two-Cycle Outboard Oils

With two-cycle motors, the oil is mixed with the fuel and burned in the firing chamber. It's critical that the oil maintains its lubricating capabilities right up to the moment it's fired off, and then that it burns cleanly, leaving behind little carbon, which can foul the plugs or gum the rings.

These days, most motors from 40 horses up have automatic oiling systems, which means you put the oil in a separate tank and the motor meters just the right amount for various speeds, ranging from as little as 200:1 (200 parts gasoline to 1 part oil) at idle up to as much as 50:1 at full throttle.

This results in less oil consumption and less fouling than with the old way of doing things, which was to pour the oil directly into the gas tank at a ratio of 50:1 and hope it mixed adequately with the fuel to keep the motor from frying.

Look Out!
Automatic oiling systems work great—as long as you remember to keep the oil reservoir filled. Keep an eye on the warning light on the dash, and as a safety measure refill the oil tank each time you fill the fuel tank. (A warning horn will tell you if you're dangerously low on oil, but by the time it goes off, damage may have already occurred.)

Bet You Didn't Know

The outboard companies would love you to buy their particular brand of oil at $15.00 a gallon. It's top-flight stuff, to be sure, but any oil that is rated TCW-3 by the Society of Automotive Engineers meets the requirements of the warranty, and you can go down to your Wal-Mart store and get no-name oil for about half that price. Particularly with larger motors, the savings can be huge over a year of running.

Or, if you'd prefer the quality spread but at a reduced price, take your own clean gallon container to the nearest dealership and have him pump it full from his 50-gallon stock drum. The price will be about two-thirds to three-quarters of the price of buying it off the shelf.

Innies and Outies—Inboard/Outboards

Inboard/outboards (I/Os) or stern drives have become the second-most popular form of propulsion for recreational boats. Their advantages are several:

➤ Automotive-type engines are available in larger sizes than outboards, up to more than 500 horsepower.

➤ Four-cycle inboard/outboard engines are more economical on fuel than two-cycle outboard engines and don't require oil to be mixed with the fuel.

➤ Because the lower unit can be steered, trimmed, and tilted like an outboard, maneuverability and performance are better than with most conventional inboards.

➤ Inboard/outboards are usually quieter than outboards.

The inboard/outboard combines an inboard engine with the lower unit of an outboard. Advantages include better maneuverability and control of trim than found in inboards, more power, and quieter operation than found in outboards. (Photo credit: OMC)

The Volvo Penta DuoProp system is a special kind of stern drive that features two propellers that counter-rotate on a single shaft. This system gives outstanding performance and cuts steering wheel torque. (Photo credit: Volvo Penta Corporation)

Inboard Engines

Inboards are primarily automobile and truck engines, slightly modified to fit the marine application. They supply power to the prop via a shaft through the bottom of the boat. The inboard power system allows the use of engines much larger than those available in outboard power, so they're the universal choice for big sportfishing boats and yachts.

Inboards like this Crusader are modified versions of auto and truck engines. They provide lots of power for larger boats. (Photo Credit: Crusader Corporation)

The disadvantage of inboards is that the prop and shaft are fixed in place, straight ahead. They can't be adjusted or trimmed to improve the running attitude of the boat, and they require more draft, or water depth, to operate without touching bottom. Also, steering is less positive at lower speeds because a rudder is used for directional control, rather than moving the prop thrust to one side or the other as in outboards and I/Os.

Bet You Didn't Know

Got a noisy inboard or inboard/outboard motor? You can quiet it by adding a high-density foam to the inside of the engine box. Standard material for this job includes a soft foam sheet sandwiched between Mylar metallic outer skins. The stuff can be glued or stapled into place. It acts like the insulation in the hood of your car to trap noise and heat inside.

Power Without Spark Plugs—Diesel Engines

Boat Bytes
Diesels are available in power to more than 1200 horses, which makes them the only reasonable choice for large yachts. Very small diesels of 50 horses or less are sometimes the engines fitted to ocean-going trawlers because of their extreme stinginess with fuel—there are no fuel pumps in the middle of the Pacific Ocean!

In 1892, a German engineer named Rudolph Diesel invented an engine that required no spark plugs to set off the fuel charge—heat caused by compression caused the fuel to go off.

Most diesels have four cycles, like the gasoline engines used in automobiles. However, on the intake stroke, the diesel sucks in only air. And the compression stroke will squeeze that air charge down to at least $1/14$ of its initial size, making it very hot. A fuel injector at the top of the cylinder then shoots in a small amount of fuel, generally kerosene-like light oils, and the heat ignites it immediately. The power and exhaust strokes are like that of gasoline four-cycles.

Diesels burn less expensive fuel than gasoline engines, and they burn it more efficiently. They must be built heavier than gas engines due to the forces of compression, but they last longer—in fact, a well-maintained diesel may outlive three or four gasoline engines before requiring a major rebuild.

Diesels like this Caterpillar are available in sizes large enough to power even 200-foot yachts. They're heavy but very durable, normally outliving gasoline engines. (Photo credit: Caterpillar Corporation)

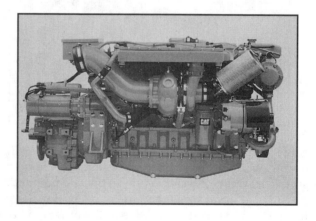

Fuel Economy

Gasoline outboards put out about 10 horses per gallon of fuel burned at full throttle. For example, a 200-horse motor will consume somewhere near 20 gallons an hour, while a 150-horse motor will eat somewhere around 15 gallons an hour. It's not uncommon for motors to be a couple of gallons over on this, with a 150 taking, say, 18 gallons an hour at 5800 rpms.

Top-End Performance

While all gasoline motors of a given horsepower are similar in top speed at maximum rpms, they're not the same. Some do better on fuel and still manage excellent performance. The test results run in magazines such as *Boating*, for whom I work, give you exact numbers for comparison.

Better at Cruising Speed

What we find is that, true to the operating manual, most outboard motors get their best fuel economy— that is, their best miles per gallon—somewhere between 3500 and 4500 rpms, with most gas inboards best between 2500 and 3500. For diesels, the economy range is likely to be around 1800 to 2400 rpms. (Big diesels are never run as fast as gasoline motors—most redline at 2200–2700 rpms. However, some of the smaller models may be run close to 4000 rpms without damage.) The most fuel-efficient speed for a given boat is called its "cruising speed."

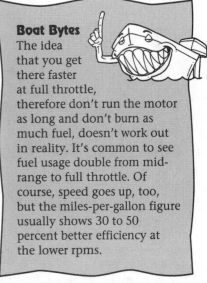

Boater-ese
Rpms, or "revolutions per minute," refers to the number of times an engine's output shaft rotates in 60 seconds.

Boat Bytes
The idea that you get there faster at full throttle, therefore don't run the motor as long and don't burn as much fuel, doesn't work out in reality. It's common to see fuel usage double from mid-range to full throttle. Of course, speed goes up, too, but the miles-per-gallon figure usually shows 30 to 50 percent better efficiency at the lower rpms.

The range of most boats is longer if you keep the rpms somewhere around the 60 to 70 percent level. Most wise captains allow a 10 percent safety margin on fuel. Here's the basic math a captain might work out to estimate his range at various speeds with a 100-gallon fuel tank:

Safety margin or reserved fuel: 10 percent × 100 gallons = 10 gallons

Reserve minus total tankage: 100 – 10 = 90 gallons

Range at best cruising speed: 90 gallons × 4.0 mpg = 360 miles

Range at full speed: 90 gallons × 2.25 mpg = 202.5 miles

Note that in this case, you can travel more than 100 miles farther at cruising speed than at full speed. (I have seen one or two lightweight performance rigs that came close to matching their mid-range numbers at top end or full speed. These boats ride so high in the water at full speed that friction is reduced, greatly increasing their efficiency.)

Running your engines at moderate speeds gives the best fuel economy. Higher speeds can nearly double fuel usage on some boats. (Photo credit: Mako Marine)

Low-Speed Fuel Gobblers

Boat Bytes
What's the best way to keep fuel use minimal? Plane off quickly at full power, trim up the motor as soon as you're on full plane, and reduce power to about 60–75 percent of full throttle. You'll get a nice, brisk ride but maximize your miles per gallon.

It's common for boats to get good mileage at idle speed, then very bad mileage as they "squat" or drop into the hole before planing. This is because they are pushing uphill—there is a lot of friction with the water as the bottom is pushed forward at an angle of up to 10 degrees from the horizontal. Even though you're going slow, the fuel gauge is going fast, toward empty.

When the boat planes off, this angle drops rapidly to one or two degrees, which greatly reduces friction. Fuel economy and speed increase. Thus, if you want to save fuel, the *worst* thing you can do is what many first-timers do: get the boat into a bog at somewhere between 1500 and 2000 rpms and motor along, blissfully sinking all boats tied to the docks with their enormous wakes as they pass.

One Engine or Two?

Redundancy is bad in writing, but good in boat motors. People like dual engines on boats because they can't pull over to a service station if one quits. That's a big reason for having two motors, particularly on offshore boats. However, the redundancy factor has to be weighed against a lot of other factors when you decide whether to have one engine or two.

The most obvious factor is cost. Outboard motors are outrageously expensive, averaging from $10,000 to $14,000 for a V6 of 150 to 225 horsepower. Buying two motors instead of one can add 30 percent to the price of a boat. Inboards and stern drives are similarly costly. Two engines also burn a lot more fuel—basically twice as much, although you may go faster.

If you go with two motors, choose them so that *each* motor can plane your boat. You may have to buy somewhat larger motors to have this capability, but it's money well spent when you really need that extra power 50 miles offshore and want to come home at 25 mph instead of 5. Twin engines have the added advantage of making for easy steering around the docks (see Chapter 6 for details).

> **Look Out!**
> With two motors, the same redundancy that's good in terms of dependability is bad in terms of maintenance. If you run aground, there are two props and two lower units to repair. There are 12 spark plugs instead of six, two batteries to keep charged instead of one, and so on.

Twin engines provide security when you head offshore. If one breaks down, the other will bring you home. However, if you're pinching to buy a boat in the first place, that second engine may put you way over the top. (Photo credit: Mako Marine)

Is one big engine better than two small ones? Could be, if you're interested mostly in speed. A pair of 90s won't usually match a single 200 and maybe not even a 175, because the single has less drag due to there being only one lower unit. It's also much less expensive to buy one big single rather than two smaller motors that put out an equivalent power combined.

The power you choose for your boat depends on the "mission" you hope to pursue. Balance the initial costs, fuel economy, and dependability factors when you make a selection. Fortunately, nearly all modern engines are far more dependable and more fuel-efficient today than they were just a few years back.

The Least You Need to Know

➤ Two-cycle outboards are the usual motor for most beginning recreational boaters.

➤ Outboards, stern drives, and inboards are suited to different boats and boating needs.

➤ Most motors deliver their best economy at three-quarter throttle.

➤ Single engines are more economical than twin engines, but twins provide more security.

Good Prop

Bad Prop

Picking a Proper Prop

The propeller, known by almost everybody in boating as a "prop," is the tires of your boat, the part that hooks up to the medium through which you travel—water—to convert motor power to propulsion. If the prop isn't right, it can make a dog out of the finest hull and motor combination. (And we're not talking a greyhound—a basset, more likely.)

A prop functions in water like a screw passing through wood, drawing the boat forward as the motor, connected via the prop shaft, causes it to rotate. Also like a screw, the pitch determines the performance of the prop. (Get the wrong prop and it's you who will be screwed, however.)

In this chapter, you'll learn how a propeller functions, and how to select the best one for your particular combination of boat, motor, and preferred boating activity. We'll also take a look at some of the difficulties having the wrong prop can cause.

Gay Blades—and Serious Ones

The most obvious difference between one prop and another is the number of blades. The blades are the part that do the work, and the number, size, angle, and shape of the blades determine how the prop performs. The more blades a prop has, the less vibration there is. That's why a complete disc would be vibration-free—but it wouldn't move your boat an inch!

Here's a look at the characteristics of some popular designs:

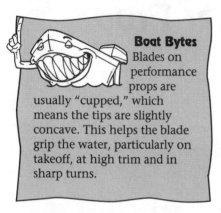

Boat Bytes
Blades on performance props are usually "cupped," which means the tips are slightly concave. This helps the blade grip the water, particularly on takeoff, at high trim and in sharp turns.

➤ *Two-blade props* have the least resistance and highest vibration. They are used mostly for smaller outboards and electric trolling motors.

➤ *Three-blade props* are the most popular design, offering good performance with moderate vibration at a reasonable cost.

➤ *Four-blade props* have very low vibration, good takeoff, and good performance, at a higher cost.

➤ *Five-blade props* have the lowest vibration, excellent takeoff, and some reduction on top-end speed, at a very high cost.

Barrel Onward

The *barrel* or *hub* is the central structure of the prop, the cylinder to which the blades attach. Most props on outboards and stern drives feature a "through-hub" design, which means the hub is large and hollow, allowing the exhaust from the motor to pass through the center. It's a convenient spot to let the gases exit, and because they come out underwater, there's a considerable muffling effect.

Here's a closer look at the parts of the propeller, which are shown in the figure on the following page:

➤ *Blade.* Thin, curved sections that grip the water as the prop rotates.

➤ *Hub.* The central barrel to which the blades attach.

➤ *Prop nut.* The nut that holds the prop to the prop shaft.

➤ *Prop shaft.* The stainless-steel rod that couples the prop to the drive shaft and gears.

➤ *Diameter.* The width, in inches, of a circle made by a blade tip in a complete rotation.

An "over-the-hub" prop, shown on the following page, is less common except on performance boats. The hub is much smaller and is solid on these. They create less drag and consequently can run faster. The motor makes more noise, but if you're after maximum speed you don't care, do you?

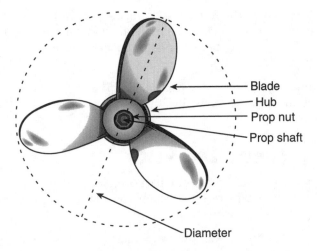

The typical three-blade propeller includes a tubular barrel or hub through which the engine exhaust passes.

Blade
Hub
Prop nut
Prop shaft

Diameter

Over-the-hub props are designed for high-speed boats. They feature a smaller, solid barrel compared to through-the-hub models.

Most props have a rubber or composite core pressed into the center of the hub that acts as a shock absorber should the prop strike bottom. It gives a bit and springs back into shape on light strikes, but tears in a hard strike—you have to get a new hub core pressed in, but you don't destroy the very expensive gears and shafts in the lower unit. The stripped hub will usually get you home at idle speed, but won't move the boat at higher rpms.

Diameter and Prop Performance

Just as the diameter of your waist determines whether you are a fast or slow runner, the diameter of a prop determines its performance. The measure of prop diameter is the width, in inches, of the circle made by the blade tips.

In general, large-diameter props grip the water better and are particularly effective in low-speed maneuvering and in pushing heavy loads. Smaller-diameter props can "wind up" faster, and are often good choices for high-performance boats because they go through the water with less resistance.

Typical diameters on V6 outboard props range from 13 to 15½ inches. Typical diameters for 10-horse props are around eight inches, while 20- to 40-horse motors carry props with diameters of 10 to 11 inches.

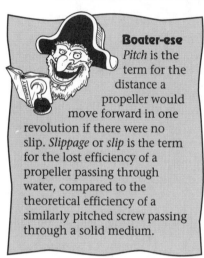

Boater-ese

Pitch is the term for the distance a propeller would move forward in one revolution if there were no slip. *Slippage* or *slip* is the term for the lost efficiency of a propeller passing through water, compared to the theoretical efficiency of a similarly pitched screw passing through a solid medium.

Here's the Pitch

Diameter is only one part of the prop equation. The other is pitch, which is the distance a prop would travel through water in one revolution if there were no slippage.

A prop is a water screw, remember: If it were screwing through wood, a 21-inch-pitch prop would travel forward 21 inches in one revolution due to the angle of the blades. In water, because of slippage, it might only go 19 inches due to the slip in the liquid medium. A slip of 4 to 15 percent is common.

Pitches for V6 outboard props typically range from 15 to 25 inches. Smaller motors will require lower pitches, down to as little as four inches for a 2-horse.

If there were no slip, a prop would move forward a distance exactly equal to its pitch in one revolution. However, a slip of 4 to 15 percent is common on most props.

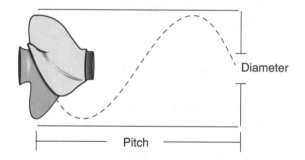

Putting It Together

The diameter is always listed first on a prop, usually stamped on the barrel or on the hub inside of the barrel. A 14 × 17-inch prop would have a 14-inch diameter and a 17-inch pitch. A prop of these dimensions is very common on runabouts in the 17- or 18-foot range, powered with a 120- to 150-horse outboard.

The higher the pitch, the faster the boat can travel, if power is unlimited and weight limited. But power is always limited, so the pitch must be matched to the weight and power of the boat/motor combination.

The right combo when the boat has five gallons of fuel and one passenger might be completely overwhelmed when there are 500 pounds of gasoline (gas weighs around six pounds per gallon), 800 pounds of people, and 500 pounds of ice, food, and gear added. It's a commonly made mistake when setting up boats. Instead, you want to get the motor running in its peak horsepower range at full throttle, usually somewhere around 5000 to 5800 rpms for large and mid-size outboards, 4500 to 5000 for stern drives and inboards with its typical load.

An inch of pitch increases or decreases rpms about 150 to 250 rpms. But props are offered by most manufacturers in only two-inch increments, which vary rpms 300 to 500 rpms.

So, if your rig turns up 5000 rpms with a 19-inch-pitch prop and the motor is rated for 5500, you might drop down to a 17-inch to get it running at the max.

The lower pitch would also give better takeoffs or "hole shots"—the hole being the hole left in the water when a planing boat takes off. The stern squats and there's a big hole pushed down for a moment before the hull squirts forward like a cake of soap to race along on top.

> **Boat Bytes**
> Larger-diameter props drop rpms and increase holding power and lift, but the diameters are limited by the space between the prop shaft and the anti-ventilation plate on outboards and stern drives, so there's not much variety offered.

When One Goes Up, the Other Goes Down

For a given boat/motor package, the diameter and prop are inversely related: The larger the diameter, the lower the pitch; the smaller the diameter, the higher the pitch.

This is also true in relation to the number of blades. A three-blade prop can be pitched a little higher than a four-blade prop used on the same boat/motor combination, because the four-blade has more gripping surface to "load" the motor.

Propping is a science, and it's best left to a dealer who has plenty of props to play with and is willing to do the job right for you. Particularly in performance boats, the wrong prop can not only cut into speed, but also make a given boat difficult or even downright dangerous to drive, while the handling problems may go away completely with the right prop.

> **Boat Bytes**
> Boat props turn at only about half the speed of the engine rpms due to gears where the prop shaft meets the drive shaft. The 2:1 gears cut the prop rotation speed but increase the torque or twisting force. More powerful engines sometimes have lower gear ratios of around 1.85:1, and some racing engines are direct 1:1 drive.

Four-blade props offer more lift for a quick hole shot and run smoother than three-blade props. However, they're more expensive and a bit slower on top end. (Photo credit: Stiletto Props)

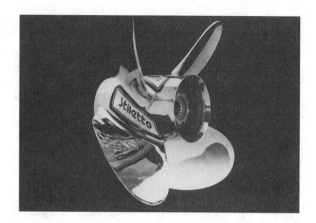

Bet You Didn't Know

How do you swap props? Props are held in place by a prop nut, which is sometimes secured by a cotter pin. To remove the prop, you first straighten the bent end of the cotter pin, then remove it by inserting a flat screwdriver or punch into the rounded end and tapping lightly until it slides free.

When you try to take off the prop nut, you'll find that nut, prop, and prop shaft all turn happily together—there's no resistance to allow you to torque off the nut.

To secure things, place a pine 2 × 4 between one of the prop blades and the cavitation plate of the motor. This holds things in place so you can get the nut off. The nut secures a washer and a spacer—make sure to set them aside in the order they came off so you don't get confused later.

The prop should slide off easily once all the fasteners are removed. You may need to lightly tap the prop with a rubber hammer to get started, especially if it hasn't been removed in a long time. The prop can't be twisted off the shaft—it's splined in place, so you have to pull straight out.

Before you put on a new prop, rub a light coating of waterproof grease on the splines of the prop shaft. This will help the prop to come off more easily next time.

Replace the spacer and washer, grease the nut, and reinstall it to torque specifications, again using the 2 × 4 to hold the prop in place. And don't forget to use a *new* cotter pin, and only one made of stainless steel. Many a $400 prop has been lost due to use of an old 25¢ pin.

Right Hand or Left?

When the engine is in forward gear, single-engine props usually rotate clockwise, viewed from astern. This is called *right-hand rotation*. On dual-engine installations, it's standard procedure for the left or port engine to rotate counterclockwise, and thus it must be equipped with a counterclockwise-rotating prop. This is called *left-hand rotation*. A right-hand prop won't work on a left-hand rotating engine, and vice versa.

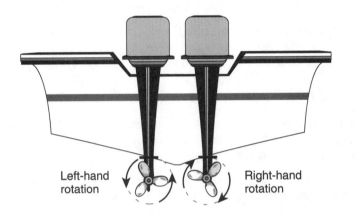

Left-hand
rotation

Right-hand
rotation

On dual-engine installations, it's common for the engines to rotate their props in opposite directions to counteract torque and make for easy steering.

The idea is that when you're going straight ahead, the opposite rotation of the blades helps to steady the boat and causes it to steer straight easily. If both blades rotated in the same direction, the back end of the boat would want to "walk" in that direction, forcing the bow in the opposite direction. (For more on how prop torque or rotating force affect handling, see Chapter 6 on docking.)

What Props Are Made of

The materials used in making props are a compromise between durability, performance, and price. Props are usually made out of one of the following:

➤ Aluminum

➤ Stainless steel

➤ Bronze

➤ Plastic

Let's take a look at each of these materials in more detail.

Light, Cheap, and Bendable—Aluminum Props

Chances are that your first boat will come rigged with an aluminum prop. Aluminum is not the best prop material, but it is one of the cheapest, and that's the reason you see it on most package rigs designated "entry-level" or "value-priced."

But, as I must occasionally remind my wife, just because something is inexpensive doesn't mean it's bad. (She in turn reminds me that "cheap" is not a synonym for "good.") Prices range from as little as $45 for an aluminum prop fitted to 6–10-horse motors up to about $150 for props matched to the larger V6 outboards in stern drives. For the right application, aluminum is just fine. Used on engines with moderate horsepower in areas where bottom contact is unlikely, it's the most common prop material, and survival can be good—as long as you don't hit bottom, an aluminum prop can last for as long as you keep your boat.

Where you may hit rocks, shell bars, or even hard sand, an aluminum prop will soon begin to look a bit worse for the wear. Also, aluminum props don't have the required stiffness in thinner castings to give maximum performance on large motors.

Stainless-Steel Reputation

Stainless steel is the material of choice for most seasoned boaters. It's extremely tough and rustproof, and the high strength allows it to be cast into very thin blades that slice through the water more efficiently than the thicker blades required in aluminum castings.

Steel also holds its shape at extreme speed and load, while aluminums tend to flex, slightly but enough to lose efficiency at maximum rpms on big motors.

Fishermen like stainless steel because it can bounce off a submerged stump or oyster bar without turning into origami. And if the prop does get slightly bent, you can often straighten it out yourself with a hammer and pliers. Aluminums that get cobbled up have to make a trip to the heli-arc welding shop. However, because stainless is so tough, a hard strike on rocks can be transmitted to the prop shaft or gears of the lower unit and cause damage there, which is much more expensive to repair than the prop.

Stainless-steel props are relatively expensive, but are so tough that they may outlast your motor. They're also best for high-performance boats. (Photo credit: Mach Propellers)

Stainless props ain't cheap. Prices start at around $300, and some of the high-performance models cost over $600. But one stainless prop will outlast a half-dozen aluminums in tough duty.

Bronzed Warriors

Bronze props are rarely seen on small boats, but they're the choice for many large yachts. Bronze offers good strength, but not so much that it will snap off the stainless drive shaft and make a hole in the bottom of an inboard boat, which is one of the reasons that it's a preferred material for big inboards.

Small bronze props cost about the same as stainless. Big-yacht props, usually four-bladers measuring up to 36 inches across, can cost thousands of dollars. Bronze props have an indefinite life span and in many cases will last as long as stainless.

Plastic Props

Plastic is...well, plastic. Plastic is a nice thing to make computer disks from. It's good for fishing lures, coolers, and a lot of other things. But plastic is not the best material to put on the end of the prop shaft of an internal combustion engine that can generate a couple hundred horsepower.

Plastic props are very inexpensive, which is the only reason they have any chance at all in the market. They are like the little wheelbarrow-type tires put in modern cars as spares—adequate to get you home in an emergency, but not really up to the rigors of daily use in anything much beyond a 10-horse kicker.

Prices on typical plastic props for V6 motors run around $50 to $75, a good deal as insurance for the day your stainless-steel prop falls off (sob!) in deep water due to a loose prop nut.

Boat Bytes
There are high-performance plastic props out there, but most never stack up to steel props in head-to-head performance tests, and when it comes to durability, the slightest touch on an oyster bar makes them vaporize.

Props for Electric Motors

The plastic, nylon, or Lexan props supplied with electric trolling motors do a good job due to their low speeds and modest horsepower. I've chewed several of them up pretty badly, but they still hold their blades and keep on functioning.

Trolling motor props are available in three- or four-blade "weedless" models with large barrels and small blades, which are designed to cut through the thick weeds found where largemouth bass, pike, and other species live.

Weedless props are not quite as efficient as standard or "power" props in open water. Power props are usually

Look Out!
When installing a plastic trolling motor prop, tighten the lock nut with your fingers only. Tightening the nut with pliers may distort the hub or even cause it to crack.

43

two-bladed and have a smaller hub. They're a better choice for those who have to deal with strong currents or wind in open water.

Both weedless and power props for trollers are inexpensive, ranging from about $10 to $30.

Counter-Rotating In-Line Props

It sounds like Engineering 101, doesn't it? But two props on a single engine make sense for many boats. The concept, first perfected by Volvo Penta in 1983, combines a right-hand and left-hand prop on the same shaft, one rotating each way. Mercruiser now markets a version, and Yamaha has outboard models.

In-line systems provide a sort of "four-wheel drive" for boats, with amazing traction in hole shots, blazing acceleration, white-knuckle cornering, torque-free steering, and very positive reverse. With nearly twice the blade area of a single prop unit, these systems do everything except top end speed better.

The systems work via a prop shaft within a prop shaft, allowing the counter-rotation off a single main engine shaft. They cost more than conventional drive systems, but for those who can afford it, the advantages are well worth the price.

These Props Are Not Shiftless

Most props are shiftless, sitting there without ambition, mindlessly doing the job designated by their designers. But there are a few mechanical wonders that actually do show some unique capabilities to shift for themselves.

Shifting props use moveable blades that change position based on centrifugal force to adjust their pitch while underway. Why would you want this? Because boats, unlike cars, don't have shifting transmissions. The prop that starts you off well in low gear is somewhat of a compromise when it comes to top speed.

Boat Bytes
Which boats are most likely to benefit from shifting props? Usually those with a minimal power-to-weight ratio; that is, a small engine relative to the weight of the boat. Heavy stern drives are the best candidates.

Particularly in heavy or underpowered boats, it sometimes takes such a low pitch to start planing that the engine over-revs after the boat planes off. (Remember, the lower the pitch, the faster the motor can turn it.) The shifting props solve the problem. They start out in a lower pitch, say 10 inches or so, and then as prop speed builds up after the boat jumps up on top, springs and cams force the blades to rotate slightly and become more aggressive, up to a pitch of 17 or 19 inches.

When one of these props shift, it feels like an automatic transmission in your car—a quick surge and you're on your way. As you slow down, powerful springs rotate the blades back to the lower starting position so that you're ready for the hole shot again.

Shifting props like this one from Land & Sea can help heavy boats plane easily yet perform very well at top end. They're more expensive than standard props, but solve a problem for some rigs. (Photo credit: Land & Sea)

Sounds great, huh? But these props are not for everyone. For one thing, a shifting prop has dozens of moving parts, while a conventional fixed prop has one. Guess which prop gives you more maintenance problems, breaks more easily, and costs more?

Not only that, but no shifting prop currently on the market can quite match the top-end performance of a well-designed single-pitch when used in performance rigs.

Problems of the Improper Prop

Problems with the prop are one of the primary woes of beginning boaters. Both initial selection and maintenance can cause difficulties.

If Your Prop Is Too Tall...

If your boat doesn't want to take off, it probably has a prop that's pitched too "tall" or too high. The available power of the engine can't force the boat forward at the high rate of incline of this particular water screw, so it bogs down.

If you ever get this rig on plane, it may be very fast on top end, because resistance drops once the boat jumps up on top.

Boat Bytes
Some boats designed for top-end speed are purposely "over-propped" to squeeze out the last tenth of miles per hour at full throttle, even though this makes them real dogs at the takeoff. If you have to be the fastest skipper on the lake, you may want to select a prop that is "taller" than is best for all-around use.

For the usual recreational use, a prop that provides a good hole shot with the typical load is much preferred, even if it's a couple miles per hour slower at full throttle.

Some boat dealers will assist you in finding the best prop for your rig by swapping to achieve the best combination of hole shot and top end. (Photo credit: Frank Sargeant)

If Your Prop Is Too Short...

Props that are too "short" or pitched too low may just about smoke the tires on the hole shot, but they soon allow the engine to wind up into the stratosphere once the boat gets on top. It takes real care not to over-rev the motor and break something expensive inside with a prop that's several steps below the needed range.

When Your Prop is Just Right...

The idea is to choose a prop that will take you and your entire crew and all their food, drinks, and diving gear up on plane quickly and without a lot of bow-rise, and then give an effortless performance in the cruising range of the engine, about 3000 to 4500 rpms for outboards and 2500 to 3500 for most inboards and I/Os.

Bad Vibrations

Vibrations from a prop usually mean there is some sort of debris on the blades or barrel. An easy way to clear it is stop the boat, shift the engine into reverse, and let the boat slide backwards for a boat-length or so. This often unwinds the plastic bags, weeds, or whatever has gotten into the prop. If this doesn't work, you may have to shut off the engine, tilt up the lower unit, and pull out the stuff by hand.

Used fishing line is a chronic problem these days on many waterways. If you run through a nest of this stuff, it will wrap around the prop hub and then work its way down around the prop shaft. On larger motors it's usually chopped up and spit out, but on smaller motors it often stays put and gradually cuts its way into the seal around the prop shaft. Water eventually gets in, and the first thing you know you're looking at a four-figure repair bill.

The cure is to check your prop shaft after each trip to make sure there's nothing on it that shouldn't be. Line wrapped on the shaft can usually be unwound or cut away, but in extreme cases you may have to take off the prop to get it all cleared.

> **Look Out!**
> Fishing line lasts forever, and it's not only a death trap for shorebirds, but an accident waiting to happen to your lower unit. Make sure you dispose of all fishing line on shore.

Care and Feeding of Your Prop

Props don't require much care. The paint that comes on many will wear away, but it has no effect on performance. However, over years of service the blade tips of aluminum props are sometimes worn away by "cavitation" or high-speed air bubbles that form as the prop races through the water. These rough edges can reduce performance over time. Any chip in the blades or even the slightest bending away from the factory-set pitch can also cause a prop to lose performance or to vibrate.

> **Boat Bytes**
> Vibrations can also mean that the prop is bent from hitting something. The prop will get you back to the dock, in most cases, but don't keep operating the motor with the gimpy prop because the vibration will soon ruin the bearings, making the repair a whole lot more costly than it would be to simply fix the prop.

It's a good idea, every year or so, to drop your prop off at a prop shop and have the pitch checked and any nicks repaired by welding and/or sanding. Not only will your boat perform better, but you'll assure longer life from your lower unit with a vibration-free propeller.

The Least You Need to Know

➤ Props are selected for a particular combination of load and power.

➤ Variables including pitch, diameter, and number of blades determine prop performance.

➤ Stainless steel is the most dependable material for recreational boat props, although it's more costly than aluminum.

➤ Props need occasional care to maintain performance.

Chapter 4

It Follows You Anywhere— Trailering Your Boat

In This Chapter

➤ The right stuff for hauling your boat

➤ Getting hitched

➤ Trailer towing tips

➤ Let's do launch—loading and unloading your boat at the ramp

➤ Keeping your trailer in top shape

The great thing about putting wheels under your boat is that you no longer have to leave it in one particular body of water. Trailering your boat gives you access to lakes, rivers, and bays across the state and across the nation—you can even change oceans if you like!

Another plus is that you don't have to pay those monthly dock rental fees. You don't have to worry about little creepy-crawlies clamping themselves to the bottom of your boat or boring through the hull as it sits week after week afloat. And when it storms, you know your boat is not going to sink because it's sitting in your garage, as snug as the family cat.

In all states, boats up to eight feet wide can be trailered without a special permit, and many allow trailer/boat widths up to 10 feet without requiring any flashing lights and wide-load signs. Thus, the size of boats that can be trailered reaches up to more than 30 feet, although the larger boats require proportionally larger tow vehicles.

In this chapter, you'll learn how to select the proper trailer for your boat and what sort of hitch you'll need for your tow vehicle. I'll also offer some tips on driving while towing—it's different, but not that difficult.

Get Fit

It's important that trailers and boats fit together. A trailer designed for a 17-foot aluminum skiff will be flattened into twisted metal if you load it down with a twin-inboard cruiser, even if that cruiser is also exactly 17 feet long. On the other hand, you can spend a lot of money needlessly if you buy a trailer that's bigger than required for your boat. The bottom of a deep vee boat won't fit a trailer designed for a flat bottom. A catamaran won't begin to fit on a trailer designed for a monohull.

Your boat dealer will usually fix you up with a matched rig, but not always—trailers come in a variety of quality levels, and some fly-by-night operations occasionally try to get away with a light-duty trailer under a heavy boat to put a little extra profit in their pocket.

The following figure gives you a look at the parts of a trailer. Note that the one shown is for a typical monohull powerboat. Those made for catamarans and keeled sailboats look quite a bit different.

Boat trailers make it possible to visit distant lakes, bays, and rivers with ease, and also allow you to store your boat in your garage rather than at a marina.

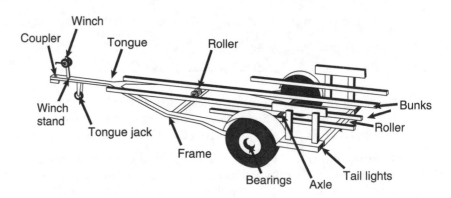

Like everything else in boating, the parts of a trailer have specialized names. Here are some of them:

➤ *Coupler.* The fitting that attaches to the hitch ball to secure the trailer to the towing vehicle.

➤ *Tongue.* The extension from the main frame members forward to the coupling.

➤ *Tongue jack.* A lifting device that allows raising and lowering the tongue to fit easily on the hitch ball.

➤ *Winch.* A winding device used to pull the boat into place.

➤ *Winch stand.* The supporting frame for the winch.

➤ *Frame.* The main support members of the trailer.

➤ *Axle.* The solid-steel member on which the wheels turn.

➤ *Roller.* A rubber cylinder that allows the boat keel or hull to roll into place on the trailer.

➤ *Bearings.* The friction-eliminating devices between the axle and the wheel hub.

➤ *Tail lights.* Red lights mounted on the rear of the trailer so that it can be seen by other drivers after dark.

➤ *Bunks.* The boards on which the boat bottom rests.

Keep in mind that trailers have both length and load ratings, listed on the tag on the tongue. The length of the trailer must match the length of your boat—and it must fit so that the transom is fully supported, not hanging over the back of the bunks even a half-inch. Too big is better than too small here.

Weight Wisdom

It's wise to buy more load capacity than you think you need. That rig that weighs 2,500 pounds on the day you buy it will, like you, tend to get a bit more portly with age. Add anchors, ice chests, fuel, water, and all the fishing, skiing, and diving gear you might accumulate aboard and you can boost the load by 50 percent. Allow for enough leeway for the add-ons.

> **Boat Bytes**
> It's a good idea to get a trailer with full-sized tires, 14- to 15-inchers. These run cooler than smaller tires, roll over potholes better, and give your boat a smoother ride. They also last a lot longer—the little donut jobs get hot and blow out at a distressingly high rate.

Two Wheels or Four?

Trailer tires are not car tires. Trailer tires are made of more layers or plies and have a higher load rating, which is why you can often carry a boat on two tires instead of four.

Two-wheel trailers (see the photo on the next page) are easier to back and maneuver than four-wheelers. However, if you have a flat tire on a two-wheeler, you must stop immediately and fix the problem. With a four-wheel trailer, you can continue to a station at reduced speed (*very* reduced—no more than 20 mph) if you have a flat, because the second tire on that side will support the load.

With many boats, there's no choice—big weights require two-axle trailers, period. However, four-wheelers cost more and are heavier, so they add to the towed weight. They may add enough to require a larger tow vehicle. There are always trade-offs.

Two-wheel trailers like this Calkins are lightweight and strong enough to haul most small- to medium-sized recreational boats. (Photo credit: Calkins Trailers)

The Right Stuff

Painted steel trailers are inexpensive and have reasonable durability if always used in fresh water. Baked enamel finishes that match the boat make them the best-looking of all trailers. Put them in salt water even once, though, and you'll soon see the rust streaks start to form. If you plan to use your boat in coastal areas, don't buy a painted steel trailer.

Trailers made of galvanized steel are rustproof, tough, and probably the best value on the market, although they're more expensive than painted steel.

Aluminum may be the best of all trailer materials. It's light but strong, corrosion-resistant, and looks good without paint for years. Aluminum trailers are somewhat more costly than galvanized, but are worth the price in easy towing and years of service. (Some aluminum trailers are so light that the air in the tires will cause them to float once the boat is unloaded!)

Stainless steel is the most expensive trailer material, but it's exceptionally strong and durable. Stainless trailers are made by only a few companies nationwide—you're much more likely to find galvanized or aluminum.

How Winches Work

Winches multiply rotary force and enable you to crank a 3,000-pound boat into place with only enough effort to start a couple of hernias. The winch sits on a winch stand, a stout brace that elevates it to about the height of the bow eye on the boat. The assembly can be adjusted up or down by loosening the U-bolts that hold it in place, and the entire stand can be moved forward or backward to make the boat balance and fit properly on the trailer.

The winch works because you're turning a long handle attached to a tiny gear, which meshes with a gear about the size of a CD. The ratio or mechanical advantage gives you the power to move the load.

There's a three-way ratchet on the winch gear that allows it to go only forward, only backward, or to freewheel. It's controlled by a small lever next to the gears.

You back off on tension on the gears slightly with the handle and you can move this lever where you want it, to allow the cable or strap to pay out to launch the boat, or only to wind on when you're retrieving it.

Boat Bytes
An electric winch that draws on the power of your tow-vehicle battery takes the work out of loading a heavy boat, although it may cost about 10 times as much as a manual winch—$300 for a model that can handle up to 10,000 pounds. A nice feature is that you can turn the power winch on remotely by pulling on a cord, which allows you to push your boat into position and at the same time activate the winch—very handy if you have to load your boat yourself.

The gears in winches multiply effort, making it possible to crank heavy boats into place with ease. Note the spare tire bolted to the frame. (Photo credit: Frank Sargeant)

Tongue Jacks

Look Out!
Failing to raise the jack wheel is a common oversight. Always double-check that the wheel is well clear of the ground before you take off, or the jack assembly will be bent into a paper clip as the rig moves forward.

The jack is the assembly that allows you to raise or lower the trailer tongue to fit the height of the hitch ball on your tow vehicle. It's bolted to the tongue a foot or two behind the hitch coupling. Most have a caster or wheel on the bottom that allows you to roll the trailer around manually when it's unhitched.

Once the trailer coupling is attached to the hitch, the jack is cranked to the "up" position so the wheel doesn't hit the roadway. This usually takes a lot of cranking—the gear ratios are low. A much handier type of jack is the "swing-away" model that allows you to pull a pin on the shaft and swing the jack up to lock parallel with the tongue, rather than cranking and cranking to get the thing up out of the way.

Do You Need Brakes?

If the rig weighs more than 1,500 pounds, trailer brakes are a good idea. They're particularly important if you tow with a small or mid-size vehicle, because the weight of the boat pushing against the hitch can actually overpower the stopping capabilities of the tow rig.

Some states require trailer brakes if the towed weight is above a certain level. Nearly all rigs big enough to require two-axle trailers are equipped with brakes. However, brakes are a real headache around salt water, and may have to be reworked as often as once a year to keep the actuating mechanisms inside the wheel from rusting solid.

Washing your brakes with dishsoap and fresh water after each trip to a salt water ramp will significantly improve their longevity. If possible, order your trailer with a built-in hose coupling and wash-down tubes, which pipe fresh water to the inside of the brake drums when a garden hose is attached.

Trailers with brakes have a special coupling that includes a manual brake cable. If the coupling fails, the cable activates the brakes. (Photo credit: Frank Sargeant)

Getting Hitched

The hitch is the connection between the trailer and your tow vehicle. The best place to buy a hitch is at a trailer rental company such as U-Haul or a shop that specializes in hitches. Hitches are very particular about which cars and trucks they're fitted to, and sometimes the hitch for a 1994 model won't fit a 1995 model of the same vehicle. The specialized shops have hitches on hand to fit all makes, models, and years.

Have the shop do the wire hookups, too. Trailer wiring is notorious for causing problems because it can be difficult to sort out where the yellow and green and brown and striped wires go.

U-Haul, Reese, and Draw-Tite are probably the best-known national hitch makers, and all have franchised shops nationwide. It takes only 30 minutes to an hour for most installations by the dealer, including tail-light hookup.

> **Boat Bytes**
> Can you install a hitch yourself? Yes, if you have some large drill bits and don't mind getting dirty. However, you'll spend a lot of time under the frame, scrape your knuckles, and maybe punch a hole in the gas tank while you're at it. The fee for having a shop install a hitch you bought from them is so modest it makes no sense to do the work yourself.

Matching the Load—Hitch Ratings

Hitches have load ratings, just as trailers do. One size does not fit all. Standard hitches put all the weight on the point of contact with the tow vehicle. Weight-distributing hitches use spring-tension bars to put some of the tongue weight onto the suspension of the tow vehicle—therefore, they're more suitable to very heavy loads, but they cost more and are more troublesome to hook up.

Here are the hitch ratings:

➤ *Class I.* This is the standard bumper hitch, cheap and easy to install. However, the load limit is 2,000 pounds and the tongue weight a maximum of 200 pounds, so it's suitable only for lightweight rigs.

➤ *Class II.* These can be either bumper hitches or frame hitches, rated for up to 3,500 pounds and a tongue weight of 300 pounds.

➤ *Class III.* This includes frame hitches that can handle up to 7,500 pounds and that distribute some of the tongue weight to the tow vehicle frame.

➤ *Class IV.* This includes frame hitches that can handle up to 10,000 pounds and that distribute some of the tongue weight to the tow vehicle frame.

Have a Ball—Hitch Balls

Hitch balls come in several sizes, and the ball has to fit the coupler on your particular trailer. The most common are $1^7/_8$ inches in diameter, which is suitable for weights up to 2,000 pounds, and 2 inches, which is used for boats up to about 3,500 pounds.

If you pull a really big boat, you might go to a $2^5/_{16}$-inch ball, which is rated for 10,000 pounds. You won't find these big babies at Wal-Mart, but hitch dealerships like U-Haul have them.

It's a good idea to select a hitch ball with a predrilled hole in the shaft for a cotter pin. Because the trailer puts a lot of twisting force on the ball during turns, it's very common for the nut to work loose. Without a cotter pin, it can actually come off, and as a result the ball pops out, leading to potential disaster.

Look Out!
If you have trailer brakes, make sure you don't get spray oil anywhere near the brake shoes or pads. Even a trace of oil on the brake pads can ruin them permanently—and you may only find out you have a problem when you really, *really* need to stop quickly.

Boat Bytes
The best way to get waterproof grease off your hands is to wipe them thoroughly with paper towels, then use hand cream and more towels to eliminate the residue. Soap and water alone won't do a good job.

Keeping Your Trailer on the Trail—Maintenance

Your trailer must be washed after use in salt water, even if it's galvanized, aluminum, or stainless. The wheels, nuts, and other parts may be carbon steel and subject to rust. Spray the trailer with a dish-soap solution and then rinse with fresh water. Once it's rinsed clean, coat the springs and bolts with a rustproofer like Corrosion-X or WD-40.

Wheel and Tire Maintenance

The bearings, which cut friction between the wheel and the axle, must be greased before and after each long trip. Bearing Buddies are spring-loaded grease fittings that hold grease inside the wheel hubs. They're cheap and easy to install and eliminate lots of bearing headaches. You simply tap them into the wheel hub. Grease can then be added through a fitting in the center of each Buddy. When filled, the devices keep pressure on the grease, forcing it into both inner and outer bearings. The fittings are available at most dealers.

To get grease into the hub at the bearing fittings, use a grease gun and waterproof grease. It's messy (stow the gun in double-Ziplock bags) but essential. Make sure you wipe off excess grease from the fitting, or centrifugal force will toss it all over the wheel, trailer, and boat.

Let There Be Lights

Functioning trailer tail lights are critical because cars behind you can't see the stop or turn lights on your tow vehicle when you're pulling a boat and trailer.

When trailer lights don't light, it's due to either a short or a burned-out bulb. Check the bulb first. Remove it from the socket and check it for corrosion. Coat the socket with Corrosion-X before putting the bulb back—the stuff conducts electricity, so it won't interfere with the current.

If the bulb is okay but the lights still don't work, there's a short in the wire. You'll need a circuit tester to check this. These are available at Radio Shack and other electronics stores for less than $20, and worth hundreds in the money they'll save you over a few years.

Getting Wired

The trailer connection to the hitch ball forms the ground or negative connection on many hookups, so you can't test trailer wiring unless you actually couple the ball to the tow vehicle, or unless your harness has an extra ground wire running back to the tow-vehicle battery.

One wire controls the lights, one the left signal and brake light, and one the right signal and brake light. So, if the turn signal works, you know the brake light also works—you don't need somebody stepping on the brake to check.

Avoid any breaks in the wire run. If you get a nick in the insulation, you can be sure the wire will soon corrode there and quit working. Cut it and clean it immediately.

Take special care when repairing wire that will be submerged in water. Follow these steps:

1. Cut back bad wire until you see bright, uncorroded wire.
2. Bare about one-half inch of wire on each end.
3. Securely wrap the wires over each other.
4. Solder the junction.
5. Place a "heat-shrink" plastic fitting over the junction and heat it to seal the wires, then follow up with silicone sealer or electrical tape.

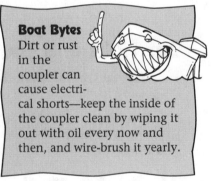

Boat Bytes
Dirt or rust in the coupler can cause electrical shorts—keep the inside of the coupler clean by wiping it out with oil every now and then, and wire-brush it yearly.

Look Out!
Many galvanized trailers attach the wiring with unpainted raw steel clips. These last about as long as paper clips would around salt water. Replace them with nylon tie-wraps or other non-rusting clips.

Boat Bytes
If you have a four-wheel or six-wheel trailer, carry a "jack-ramp." This can be three 2 × 6s that are nailed together to form a small stairsteps. You pull either the front or back wheel on these ramps and it raises the other one on the same side, without a jack or without any work on your part. It's safer than a jack, too, because it can't slip out and let the trailer crash down.

Inflation Is Good

Check the side of trailer tires carefully for the recommended inflation and top them off once a month. If you don't, the tires will inevitably overheat during a long pull and blow out. Under-inflation allows the sidewalls to flex, which builds up heat. You've seen the sad trailer waifs along the side of the road, waiting until Dad comes back with a spare. Don't put your kids among them.

Winch Maintenance

Check the cable hook, eye, and winch regularly and tighten the nuts on the gear mechanism. The one on the winch handle is notorious for coming off, causing the handle to be lost. Put a second nut on behind the first to act as a locknut, or coat the threads with a silicone sealer—it's firm enough to keep the nut in place, but can be stripped off if you ever need to replace the handle.

Get Tight and Load It Right

Make sure the hitch is locked to the ball and that the ball nut is securely tightened in place—it will work loose with some frequency due to turning forces from the trailer.

Trailer loading can be a factor in handling and safety. You need about 10 percent of the weight of the load on the hitch, or up to the limit of the tow vehicle. This can be any-where from 100 to 300 pounds.

Wandering Trailers

Having a mind of your own is good if you're a human but bad if you're a boat trailer. Less weight on the hitch makes the trailer pull up on the back wheels of the car, making it hard to steer. Put some weight on the hitch by loading ice chests or other heavy gear forward in the boat or by moving the winch stand forward. Don't overdo it—just a couple of inches at a time will do it. Secure all bolts after this change.

Conversely, if the back of your tow vehicle squats and the front tires barely touch the ground, either you are driving a low-rider or you have too much weight on the hitch. Sliding the boat aft on the trailer bunks an inch or two should rebalance the load.

The fore and aft adjustment of the boat is controlled by the location of the winch stand. The transom should just fit onto the bunk—don't let it hang over even a half-inch or you're headed for trouble. The stress on the transom created by the lever action of the motor will eventually cause damage.

Factory-matched boat, motor, and trailer packages like this Sea Nymph assure that the trailer has the right load capacity and is properly fitted to the hull. (Photo credit: Sea Nymph Boats)

It's a good idea to use transom tie-downs so that the boat doesn't hammer itself against the trailer on rough roads or railroad crossings. The ratchet type are best, with strong nylon straps for security.

A motor support for outboard motors is another good idea. Most newer motors have a trailering brace that flips into place and is secured by the weight of the engine. If your rig doesn't, use a "Transom Saver," a metal bar that fastens to the lower unit and to the aft member of the trailer frame, to support your motor. They're available at most marine dealers.

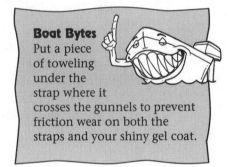

Boat Bytes
Put a piece of toweling under the strap where it crosses the gunnels to prevent friction wear on both the straps and your shiny gel coat.

The Chain Gang

Trailer chains are used as a security factor should the hitch ball or the hitch itself break or come loose. They won't do much good, though, if they're not big and stout. Welded chain is best.

The chains should be crossed several times to help them catch the trailer tongue before it can hit the ground. Leave just enough slack so that you can make a sharp turn without binding with the chains.

Towing Tips

Towing a big rig at highway speeds looks scary, but with a properly matched rig and a little practice, there's nothing to it. Just remember that it takes longer to stop, and that you have a "tail" hanging behind the car that's longer than the car.

Some people advise that you shouldn't tow in overdrive, but according to Chevrolet Trucks, there's no problem with using overdrive with automatic transmissions as long as the weight of your rig doesn't cause continual shifting at highway speeds. If it does, it's better to drop down to third gear or even lower on a long mountain grade. (Some other companies do advise against towing in overdrive—it's best to follow the manual for your specific rig. With manual transmissions, the advice is accurate—it's tough on the engine to tow in fifth gear.)

Watch Where You Tow

There are some places that even the most experienced trailer-boater will not take his rig. There's no sense causing yourself problems by trying to fit the rig into a tight, 90-degree parking spot when you can pull straight ahead into several empty slots. Watch out for these potentially hazardous situations:

➤ *Using a drive-thru.* Never go through the drive-thru of a fast-food restaurant or store unless you're sure the boat is not much wider or taller than your towing vehicle. The overheads are particularly hazardous because we tend to forget about them.

➤ *Making a U-turn.* If you need to make a U-turn in heavy traffic, the best advice is *don't make the U-turn.* Choose a light with a turning lane if possible, turn left into the cross street, make another left into the alley, then another to bring you back to the highway—and now you've got an easy right to get back where you need to go. That's better than risking an accident—or these days, a gunshot—by pulling across traffic.

Secure It All

Sargeant's Law says that anything that can blow out of a boat will blow out of a boat when it is being trailered. The last step before you head down the driveway should be to climb aboard the boat and look things over.

Hatch lids are notorious for disappearing if they're not hinged in place. Loose cushions also take wing, never to be seen again. Life jackets and cooler tops, or even whole coolers if empty, also disappear regularly.

Tie everything down or stow it in a secured box to avoid any problems. (Bungee cords are great for this—buy a dozen of them and keep them on board your boat.) Even heavy objects like anchors can leap right out of the boat on a rough road. Don't give things a chance to go wrong—make sure everything is secure before starting out.

Maneuvering Your Trailer

Backing a trailer is a challenge almost equivalent to docking a boat. The way to learn it is to practice—at home, not at a crowded boat ramp late on a Sunday afternoon.

The basic thing to remember about backing a trailer is that the trailer goes in the *opposite direction* of the back end of the tow vehicle. The no-brainer way to remember this is to grip the bottom of the steering wheel with one hand. (Not that hard! No need for white knuckles here.)

To make the trailer back left, move your hand left. To make it back right, move your hand right. Make these movements small unless you're trying to back around a corner (not recommended for beginners).

If things get completely out of whack, simply pull forward, get the trailer and the tow vehicle in a straight line again, and try once more. You can also make small adjustments by stopping, pulling forward a bit, and then backing up again, during your approach to the ramp or garage.

With practice, you'll be able to back the rig around sharp corners, but beware of getting "jack-knifed," which is when the angle between the trailer tongue and the car becomes so sharp that the vehicle bumper starts to push the trailer sideways. Keep an eye on how close you're getting through the side-view mirrors (if your vehicle doesn't have them and you trailer your boat frequently, invest in a pair of large ones).

Highway Trailering

Pulling a trailer down a highway is fairly straightforward except you have to remember you have less acceleration than normal, so taking off takes longer. You also have more weight to stop, particularly if the trailer does not have brakes, so it will take longer to stop.

Air blast from passing trucks can make a trailer swerve. If this happens, hold your course and speed and don't hit the brakes, and the trailer will straighten out.

When trailering a boat, you also have to change lanes more gradually and allow twice as much room when passing before you pull back in. Getting up to passing speed may take three times longer, too. Remember not to cut corners too close. The trailer will go over the curb or hit the fire hydrant on the corner if you don't go around the corner wide.

Look Out!
If you can't keep up with traffic and it's stacking up behind you, do other motorists a favor and pull over to let them pass!

Keeping Your Cool

The added load of trailering can be hard on your tow vehicle. Make sure the cooling system is full and working properly before you start a long tow. If the system starts to overheat, turn off the air conditioning. In a worst case, turn on the heater until the engine cools—it makes it miserable inside the car in the summer, but the heater acts as a mini-radiator that helps throw off heat in a hurry.

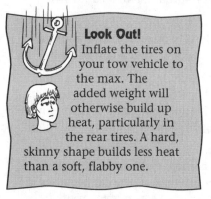

Look Out!
Inflate the tires on your tow vehicle to the max. The added weight will otherwise build up heat, particularly in the rear tires. A hard, skinny shape builds less heat than a soft, flabby one.

If you tow a big boat, you'll need a transmission cooler. It's a radiator for the transmission, and sits in front of the regular radiator. Without it, you can boil the transmission fluid or fry it—neither is good for your transmission, and I speak as one who spent $1,400 a few years back for a rebuild on my Explorer tranny.

If you're buying a new tow vehicle, opt for the tow package—transmission cooler, larger cooling system, larger battery, trailer harness and sometimes a hitch, and a lower gear in the rear end. You won't have any towing problems and you'll be glad you spent the extra bucks.

Pushing Off

It's wise to tow the first 10 miles, then stop and check out the rig. Touch the bearing housing and the trailer tires to check for excessive heat. (They're dirty, so have a paper towel handy to wipe your hands afterward.) Both will be warm, but if they're hot to the point that they're uncomfortable to touch, something is wrong—check bearing grease and tire pressure.

Make absolutely sure that your hitch is secured and the ball is tight. A friend of mine had his hitch ball come loose while he was traveling a four-lane highway in south Florida. The trailer tongue dropped on the pavement and sent out a mighty shower of sparks as the rig swerved into the left lane and passed the slowing truck at flank speed. It then went across the median, dodged two lanes of traffic coming south, and ran down an embankment to neatly deposit the boat into a river. The trailer was ruined, but the boat was miraculously unscathed!

Had my buddy used safety chains, properly wound around each other to snub the tongue in the event of hitch failure, he wouldn't have lost his rig.

Don't forget to attach the trailer's emergency brake cable to the hitch, if the trailer has surge brakes—it's a small cable with a hook, coming out of the trailer brake mechanism on the tongue. If things come apart, pressure on the cable will apply the trailer brakes.

Let's Do Launch

Once you've arrived safely at the ramp, get the boat ready to launch in a parking area away from the actual launching zone. This saves time and avoids jamming the ramp for those who are ready to go.

Get your lines untangled and secured to a cleat, remove the tie-downs on the boat and the motor support, make sure the boat key is in the ignition, and *be sure the drain plug is in place*. This is a biggie that's often forgotten. Many a boat has sunk because the intrepid skipper didn't put that little $2 plug in place. Put it in, and then check it again just before you put the boat in the water.

Then it's time to back down the incline of the ramp, utilizing the lessons practiced at home. Have a crewperson stand on the dock, holding a bow line attached to the boat.

If your trailer has Bearing Buddies to keep water out of the bearings, you can back right in until the boat floats free. The crewperson then pulls it in and ties it to the dock while you go park the car. Some experienced boaters simply put a driver at the boat wheel and have him or her back it off and move it to the dock under power.

With break-frame trailers or trailers without sealed bearings, you back in until you're just short of sinking the wheel bearings, then pull the pin on the trailer frame and push upward on the boat bow. This causes the trailer to tilt backward and allows the boat to slide free.

Boater-ese

A *cleat* is a clever but simple device that eliminates the need to tie a knot in securing a boat. The two-horned prongs, usually metal but sometimes fiber-filled plastic for smaller boats, allow quick tie-ups and avoid the jamming of knots common under stress. To use a cleat, you take a full wrap around the base, make a half-hitch over one of the horns, and then another couple wraps around the horns.

Look Out!
Don't forget to attach a bow line before you push the boat off the trailer, or you'll have to swim to recapture it!

Up-Loading

Once your day on the water ends, don't make the mistake of sinking the trailer out of sight as you try to reload the boat. Back in just far enough to wet the bunks completely, then pull forward so that only the last foot or two of the bunks is underwater. Even though this looks like the trailer is too far from the water to ever load the boat, this is the way to do it. Resist the temptation to sink the bunks. If you do, the boat can't possibly center itself on them because it won't even touch them!

Place wheel chocks made of foot-long 4 × 4s behind your tow vehicle's back wheels—this prevents turning your car into a boat—and you're ready to load.

Power Loading

Power loading is using the boat motor to push the boat onto the trailer. It's fast and easy: Get the boat lined up squarely with the trailer, ease forward until the keel makes contact with the center roller, and then advance the throttle a little so that the boat climbs right up onto the trailer bunks. It should stop a few inches from the winch hook.

Hook up the winch and use the ratchet to snug up the boat against the bow roller. Shift the winch lock to the "on" position, add a safety chain from bow to trailer, and you're ready to pull out.

Break-Frame Loading

If you don't have a drive-on trailer, you probably have a "break-frame" that tilts up when you pull a pin on the tongue. These are suitable for light, small- to medium-sized boats, up to about 17 feet. Your partner slides the boat bow onto the back roller of the trailer (What, you don't have a partner? Then get a drive-on trailer!), then you walk the plank, teetering your way along the frame as you pull out the winch cable to hook onto the bow eye. Then you teeter back.

You may have to use a stern line to keep the back end of the boat aligned with the trailer in the early going, particularly if there are winds or a current from the side. Once the boat is in place, chain it down as described previously.

Look Out!
Although you don't want to take off the emergency brake before putting the car in gear, you *must* take it off before trying to pull forward. Sounds too obvious for you to possibly ever forget, doesn't it? I did it again just a week ago, and couldn't figure out why my truck suddenly had lost power.

Pulling Out

Remove wheel chocks, put the car in low gear, take off the emergency brake *only then*, and pull out steadily. If you take off the emergency brake first, the car will rock back against the transmission park pin, making it difficult to shift into drive. Or, even worse, it may rock back and break the pin and proceed rapidly down the ramp into the water.

Trouble at the Ramp

There are times when you can't pull out. Slippery, steep, or potholed ramps or dirt or gravel can make it difficult. So can a boat that's too big for your tow vehicle. The best thing to do in a situation like this is get a tow from a nearby vehicle, if possible.

You can also try to improve traction by scraping away moss or loose gravel in front of the drive wheels. Mats laid in front of the drive wheels may help—carpet, plywood, or anything that will provide traction can work.

Sometimes, you may have to offload the boat, pull the trailer out, and put it in again at another location on the ramp where traction is better.

In an emergency, you can use your boat engine's power to give you a push those first few critical feet. You need a helper for this—one person drives the tow vehicle, the other the boat. Make sure the boat is completely tied down with both winch strap and safety chain. Lower the lower unit, make sure the propeller and water pickup are underwater, and start it up.

As the vehicle driver applies power, you put the boat in gear and give a power assist. Sometimes it only takes a nudge, sometimes a more authoritative push. In either case, a quick hand is required to cut back power as soon as the vehicle wheels begin to grab. The best way to shut it down is pull the kill switch lanyard, which cuts off the ignition.

A word of warning: You MUST shut off the motor before the water intake clears the water or you may wind up with a fried engine. Over-revving is also possible if the propeller clears the water. And of course, if you apply too much power and the hold-downs are not adequate, you could wind up turning your car into a boat trailer. Clearly, this is no remedy for the faint of heart, but it's highly effective and one that the experts use when necessary.

A Tail-Light Cure

Trailer tail lights are chronically ill because they're so often submerged. One cure is to put the tail lights atop PVC plastic tubing made into guide poles. These poles help steer the boat onto the trailer during reloading, but they also keep the lights out of the water. U-clamp brackets will hold them in place.

Run the wires through the hollow interior of the pipes. The pipes are also a good place to mount your trailer license—the low mounts on the trailer expose the license to being scraped off on rough ramps.

Trailering seems daunting the first time you pull up to a ramp, but after a few successful launches and retrievals, you'll find it's the easiest part of boating.

The Least You Need to Know

➤ It's important to buy the right trailer for your boat.

➤ Hitches are load-rated and must be matched to the towed package.

➤ Practice learning how to maneuver a trailer at home before you try it at the launch ramp.

➤ Trailer maintenance is critical to long life.

Part 2
The Basics of Operation

Okay, now you've got a boat, so how do you run it? Part 2 gives you the nitty-gritty on powerboats—getting the crew aboard, starting the engine, handling the boat around the harbor, and keeping your crew happy.

Not only do you learn how to make your boat move in this part, but also how to make it stay put. There's also a surprising amount to know about anchoring, which we'll explore in Chapter 8. The use of ropes aboard—don't forget, that boaters call them "lines"—is also in this section.

And if you're into pollution-free propulsion that's good for the cardiovascular system as well as the soul, don't bypass the chapter on "paddle-power."

Getting Underway for the First Time

You don't have to know much to make a powerboat move. Turn the key, shift into "forward," and away you go. However, there are a few basics of operation without which you will definitely prove yourself a duffer.

It starts with getting yourself and your crew safely from the dock into the boat.

In this chapter, we'll cover the safe way to get aboard, how to get even a temperamental engine started, how to get underway, and how to get the boat trimmed out for the best ride. We'll also look at a very important safety topic, refueling the tanks.

All Aboard!

Getting aboard the boat is usually pretty straightforward, but it's not quite as simple as stepping into your car. There is a delicate moment when going aboard that invites disaster. Getting into a small boat requires a positive but not hurried motion. He who hesitates with one foot on the bank and one in the boat is assuredly lost—the boat moves seaward due to the push from the foot, and the boarder falls between boat and dock. I know this to be true because I have done it in moments of inattention, several times. Avoid doing as I have done, and do as I say.

Look Out!
Particularly early in the morning, all walking surfaces aboard a boat are likely to be covered with dew. Be very cautious when stepping onto a wet surface—it can be slippery as ice.

With a small boat, step as nearly amidships as possible, near the center rather than on the gunnels. Stepping on the gunnels of small, light boats leads to rather spectacular reverse flips. You may earn a 9.9 from the judges, but you won't be happy.

In larger boats, things stay put much better, and there's usually a broad step on the transom or aft gunnel to make things fairly easy. Don't expect a boarding ramp like they have on the *Love Boat* unless the boat you are boarding is more than 50 feet long.

Keep Your Hands Handy

Always step aboard with unfettered hands—if you step on the boat with your hands full and the boat shifts, you may fall, hard. (Even if you intend to honeymoon aboard, don't try to carry your bride over that nautical threshold.) Instead, lay your gear on the dock, step aboard the boat, and then reach back up for the gear or have someone hand it to you.

It's a good idea to pull the boat in close to the dock before trying to board. Cleat the lines short and then step aboard. Don't start to go out, change your mind, and leave the boat with the lines tied short, because the tides may drop and leave your boat suspended in midair!

Starting the Engines

This is supposed to be very simple—turn the key and the boat runs. But many engines are temperamental. Here's a basic procedure that will get most engines going—you may have to customize it a little to suit your particular motor:

Boater-ese
A *kill switch* is a safety switch attached to a lanyard that shuts off the motor if the driver leaves his or her seat.

1. Turn on the key or the electrical power switch to make sure there's fuel in the tank according to the fuel gauge. If there's a kill switch, make sure it's in the "run" position.

2. Pump up the fuel bulb (shown in the figure on the following page), if there is one. Most outboards have fuel bulbs about the size of an oblong tennis ball placed in the fuel line, either in the motor well or in a compartment near the stern. Just follow the fuel line and you'll find it. Squeeze the bulb until it's firm. This means that there's a solid charge of fuel from the bulb into the engine.

The primer or fuel bulb is a small pumping device that pushes fuel into the carburetor when squeezed. It's usually found within a foot or two of the motor.

3. Make sure the drive gears are in neutral. On single-lever systems like most outboards and stern drives, this will be when the lever is straight up. There's a detent or slot in the shifter housing so that the throttle lever clicks as it goes into neutral. Wiggle the lever around until you feel this click. Most motors will not crank unless the gears are in the neutral position.

4. On inboards and some performance boats, the throttle or fuel lever is separate from the shifting lever. The fuel lever has a red knob, the shifting lever a black knob. Advance the red knob slightly to start, but keep the black one centered for neutral.

5. Prime or choke the motor if needed. On fuel-injected motors this won't be necessary. Otherwise, push the choke or prime button. Sometimes it's built into the ignition key and you prime by pushing in on the key as you turn it. Choke or prime as you crank the engine for about five to 10 seconds.

6. Some motors start best if the throttle is advanced slightly. On single-lever controls, you do this without putting the motor into gear by pushing a lockout button on the throttle base and then advancing the throttle. Move it only an inch or so—don't push it all the way forward or the motor will start at 5000 rpms!

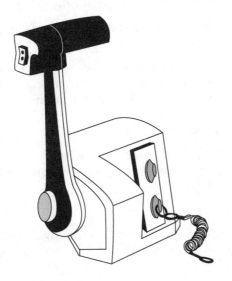

The throttle lever and shift controls are combined in one handle on most outboards and stern drives. The rocker switch on the handle controls the trim of the lower unit, which adjusts the running attitude of the boat.

7. Normally, the motor starts, or at least coughs, within the first 10 seconds. Once it coughs, there's fuel in the cylinders—don't prime or choke it again right away or you'll flood it (that is, you'll get an excessive amount of liquid fuel into the firing chamber and make it tough for the spark plugs to touch it off).

8. Once the motor starts, you may have to give several short bursts of choke to keep it running, particularly on chilly mornings.

9. After about 20 seconds, you can pull the throttle back to idle speed. The motor should now run normally. If it stumbles and quits after it's been running a minute or two, don't choke it again. Simply put it in neutral and restart it.

In twin-engine boats, follow the same routine for the second engine. However, if one of the engines is hard to start, start that one first. It's difficult to hear what the second engine is doing once the first one is running, so get the troublemaker out of the way first. Keep an eye on the tachometer of the first engine to make sure it keeps running once the second one fires up—it's not uncommon for one to go back to sleep.

Leaving the Dock

Getting away from a dock is usually less challenging than returning to it, but there are a few tricks. First of all, make sure everybody is seated or at least in a safe spot. Kids, in particular, have a way of getting their hands between the dock and the boat at just the wrong moment.

Boat Bytes
In some states, children age 12 and under are required by law to wear PFDs any time they're in a boat. And the jackets must be child-sized, so that they fit snugly and will stay in place in the water.

In small boats, personal flotation devices (PFDs) should be worn by all aboard, and *must* be worn by non-swimmers and children. In cold weather or when facing rough weather, everyone should automatically put on a life jacket.

In larger craft, tell everyone where the jackets are, and show novices how to put one on.

If the boat has been attached to shore electrical power to recharge batteries or to operate accessories, make sure the power cord is disconnected and stowed. The dock fenders—plastic bumpers you hang over the side of your boat—can also be put away at this time.

Normally, you simply cast off the dock lines and put the boat into gear to leave the dock. But sometimes it can be more complicated—see the next chapter for details.

Keeping Trim Afloat

The trim system on a stern drive or outboard controls the angle of attack of the prop to the water, and also affects the running angle of the boat. Small motors have manual trim, adjustable only at the dock by moving a pin on the mounting bracket to shift the lower unit in or out relative to the transom.

But most motors larger than 50 horsepower have power trim, an electrical/hydraulic system controlled most often by a rocker switch on the throttle lever, or sometimes by a separate rocker switch on the dash. You push the button to activate a pump in the hydraulic tube, causing the lower unit to tilt in or out relative to the transom.

Time to Trim In

Push the bottom of the trim button when you want to take off or begin planing. This tilts the bottom of the lower unit closer to the transom. Most lower units will trim to a "negative angle," which means the lower section tilts beyond vertical toward the transom. This boosts the transom up and pushes the bow down, which is what you want for a quick takeoff or hole shot.

You also trim in to make a series of tight turns at speed. This holds the stern better, preventing it from sliding sideways, because there's more of the "foot" of the motor in the water.

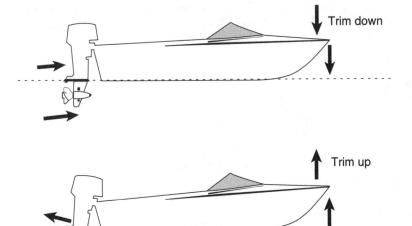

Trim down

Trim up

Trimming the motor closer to the transom forces the bow down, while trimming it away from the transom pushes the bow up.

Those Are the Brakes

Trimming in can help you slow down quickly, as well. Rapidly dropping the lower unit creates drag to slow the boat, and also drops the boat off the optimal running angle, further reducing speed. It's the only "brakes" on a boat until you drop off plane.

Look Out!
Never shift the motor into reverse at high speed—it can damage the gears.

Once your boat is at a speed of under 10 miles per hour, the reverse gear becomes your brake. Just like reversing the engines on a landing jet, kicking the gears into reverse quickly pulls the boat to a halt. This doesn't work at higher speeds—the prop simply ventilates or grabs air and makes a lot of noise, but the boat keeps on going.

Softening the Waves

Because it drops the bow, trimming in brings the sharp forward vee of the keel (the "entry") into first contact with the waves, splitting them and softening the ride.

All vee and semi-vee boats have a sharper bottom at the bow than they do near the stern. If you get this sharp vee into the water, the ride is improved, like a knife going through the water instead of a rounded spoon slapping down on the surface. This slows the boat a bit, but it greatly improves passenger comfort.

Trimming down too much at high speed may cause the boat to "bow steer," meaning the bow digs in while the transom slides around on turns. You can tell if you've trimmed down too far because the steering starts to feel heavy and the white water rushing out the sides of the boat moves forward beyond amidships. Trimming down too much also lowers freeboard at the bow, decreasing the distance from the water to the gunnels, which you want to avoid in high waves.

Time to Trim Out

Trim out (push the top of the trim button) when the boat is on plane and you want to go faster. This causes the lower unit to tilt away from the transom. Trimming out raises the bow and rocks the boat back onto the aft third of the bottom, the surface designed for most efficient high-speed running in a planing hull.

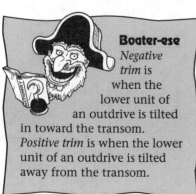

Boater-ese
Negative trim is when the lower unit of an outdrive is tilted in toward the transom. *Positive trim* is when the lower unit of an outdrive is tilted away from the transom.

This reduces what engineers call the "wetted surface," the section of bottom in contact with the water, and consequently cuts drag and improves speed and fuel economy.

In the extremes, as in high-performance bass boats and racing boats, the front half of the boat is actually out of the water. On family boats, the front may just touch the surface, but it's not plowing along as it would under zero or negative trim.

With the bow forced upward by trimming out the twin outboards, this Monza can get anglers offshore in a hurry. (Photo credit: Haber & Quinn)

It Ain't Flipper—Stop Your Boat From Porpoising

The higher you trim the bow, the faster the boat will go until you overtrim, at which point the prop and speed can't support the bow and it falls off, or drops the bow back to the surface.

This creates fore-and-aft rocking called "porpoising." In the extremes, it's a bit like riding a bucking horse. You stop it by trimming in a bit, or by giving more throttle, because the faster you go, the more weight the combination of engine power, prop, and hull design can support.

The Art of Cornering

Lots of trim makes steering light and easy and adds speed, but it also makes the boat more inclined to skid in sharp turns. So if you're faced with running through a narrow, winding creek or making sharp turns, the lower unit needs to be trimmed down. Otherwise, you may wind up like the bad guy in *Miami Vice*, boating on dry land.

Don't trim in too much or the boat may "bow steer," with the front section of the keel grabbing the water and pivoting the aft section so sharply that gear and passengers may be endangered.

> **Boat Bytes**
> What if your boat porpoises all the time? Chances are you have too much weight forward, making it impossible for the prop to adequately lift the bow. A quick fix is to move passengers, ice chests, or other heavy gear aft. Or you may want to switch from a three-blade prop to a four-blade—the added blade area sometimes helps in giving more lift.

Ventilation: Good in Motel Rooms, Bad in Props

Excess trim can lead to "blow out" or prop ventilation, in which the prop sucks in surface air as it breaks the surface. This is most likely to occur on turns as the boat heels or leans into the turn. The prop loses its grip on the water and the motor howls, winding up very fast while the boat slows quickly. This sometimes happens when a fast boat jumps over a large wave, as well.

You know you're at maximum trim when rpms go up but speed does not. On most performance boats, this can be quite high, to the point where the motor howls and there's a healthy "rooster tail" or white-water spray upward from the prop. (This looks cool, but it wastes fuel.)

Some performance props are what are called "surface piercing," which means that at the top part of the stroke, each blade pops free of the water. Since it takes less power to turn out of the water than in, the prop load decreases and the engine winds higher.

This can result in more speed on very light boats with the right bottom design. On heavier vee boats, it results only in lots of noise, white water, wasted gasoline, and sometimes a blown motor from over-revving.

Bet You Didn't Know

The redline is the upper limit in revolutions per minute (rpms) recommended by the engine manufacturer. It's indicated on the tachometer, the dash instrument that indicates rpms. Most motors are redlined at well below the rpm that will destroy them, but exceeding the redline regularly or for prolonged periods will definitely cause the powerhead to start making noise—or even worse, no noise at all.

Most outboards are redlined between 5000 and 5800 rpms, although some high-performance versions are designed for sustained speeds in excess of 6000 rpms, and motors used in racing sometimes rev up to 10,000 (but they don't have to live very long between rebuilds). There is actually a red line on many tachometers indicating the line beyond which you should not go if you don't like spending time and money in the company of mechanics.

Shallow Water Trim

You also trim up at idle speeds when crossing shallows or grassy areas—it gets the prop higher and avoids bottom contact. Many times, when you think you're stuck on a shoal, you can get off by trimming up the lower unit of an outboard or stern drive to the point where the water pickup is barely below the surface and the prop is actually breaking the surface.

You lose a good bit of your propulsion with the prop in this position, but the blades grab enough to ease you off the obstruction—usually. If not, it's time to step over the side and put your shoulder to things. (You can't back up very well with the prop in this position, though—better to go forward.)

Boating in a Bog

Avoid trimming up much at speeds between 1000 and 2000 rpms in the shallows because this pushes the stern down. The boat actually runs deeper in the water than if you had the motor in the full down position.

Remember that at about 1500 to 2500 rpms on outboards, many boats will "plow" or bog severely. You'll go slow, but you'll actually make a much larger wake and burn more fuel than if you went fast.

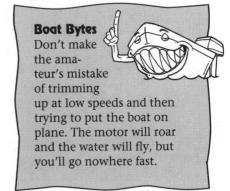

Boat Bytes
Don't make the amateur's mistake of trimming up at low speeds and then trying to put the boat on plane. The motor will roar and the water will fly, but you'll go nowhere fast.

This sort of slow-down infuriates skippers tied to the docks when you pass, and marks you as a real amateur. (You're legally responsible for any damage your wake does, don't forget!)

The boat's running angle or attitude also makes it very difficult to see over the bow in some models. You're driving blind! Avoid the plow!

Refueling Your Boat

Gasoline is very dangerous in boats because the bowl shape of the hull interior traps any spilled or leaking fuel. The closed decks and compartments hold in leaking vapors, creating a fuel-air bomb that is only lacking a spark to turn your boat into a Roman candle.

Diesel fuel is less explosive than gasoline, but still highly flammable. Thus, fueling is a business that requires your undivided attention.

Most trailer boats get gassed up at a filling station on the way to the ramp, and this is a good idea because it saves you big on fuel costs. Buying fuel from a marina is usually 15 to 20 percent more expensive than buying it from a filling station. However, at times you will need to refuel on the water, even with a trailered boat. With larger boats stored at the marina or in the water, this is always standard operating procedure. Follow these steps to do it right:

1. Make sure your boat is properly tied to the fuel dock. Nothing is more distracting than having the boat begin to leave the docks with the fuel hose in the filler! Incompetent cleating can make it happen, so if you let Uncle George handle the lines, make sure he knows how to make things stay put.

2. Make sure you put fuel only into the fuel tank. Where else could you possibly put it? On some boats, the water filler cap looks exactly like the fuel filler cap—gasoline shower, anyone? There have even been instances of people pumping fuel into trolling rod holders! How do you know which cap leads to the fuel tank? It has a code on the cap. It says "F-U-E-L."

3. Avoid careless spills, which are both dangerous and bad for the watery environment. Any spilled gas aboard should be wiped up with paper towels, which should then be disposed of at the marina in a metal barrel, *not* in the nearest plastic trash can.

4. It goes without saying neither you nor anyone aboard should smoke during fueling. That is, it goes without saying unless someone tries it. Better to warn everyone ahead of time. Even if it means putting out that freshly lighted, $10 Macanudo.

5. Have someone keep an eye on your gallonage, and slow down the flow rate on the fuel as you get near what you think should be full. Some marina hoses have an extremely high flow rate so that they can fill yacht tanks quickly, but this can mean your smaller tank fills a lot faster than you think it will. Fuel can come shooting back up the fill pipe and drench you.

6. Open all hatches, particularly the engine compartment on inboards and I/Os, after fueling. This is also a good time to check your fuel hoses for tight connections and for deterioration. The slightest seepage should be investigated and corrected immediately.

7. Turn on the blower and let it operate for several minutes. It's a little exhaust fan down in the bilge that sucks out any fumes, pushing them out vents usually located near the transom.

8. Secure the fuel cap. Make sure it's tight enough so that rain and spray won't get into the tank. Some fuel fill caps require a "key" (shown on the next page), which is a tool that fits into detents in the cap, allowing you to open or close the cap. Can't find the key? Often, the back of the blade of a closed folding knife will fit into the slot and allow you to turn the cap. A quarter can also be substituted on some caps.

9. Sniff for fumes. You can buy $200 fuel fume detectors, but they don't work as well as your own nose. (Just don't do this too much, or it will lower the SAT scores of any potential offspring.)

10. Start the engine. Only when the cap is secured and you're sure there are no fumes should you touch the ignition key.

All of this is not to say that your boat is likely to explode at any moment. Fuel fires afloat are extremely rare. But they do happen, and the results can be catastrophic. You can't simply run out in the street and wait for the fire department.

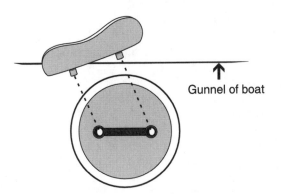

Gunnel of boat

The fuel key allows opening fuel caps that may be too tight to open with your fingers alone. Caps must be tightened securely to prevent water from getting into the fuel.

In 30 years on the water, I've never had a serious fire, but I've been close. Once a searchlight wire shorted out across both battery terminals. The wire turned red hot instantly and the rubber insulation caught fire. Fortunately, a quick shot from an extinguisher stopped the problem.

All powerboats with enclosed fuel tanks are required to carry one of the various classes of fire extinguishers at all times. See Chapter 17 for details on selection and use.

The Least You Need to Know

➤ Boarding a boat can be tricky—make sure your passengers use care.

➤ Starting the motor is easy if you follow the proper procedure every time.

➤ The trim button is the key to efficient boat operation.

➤ Use special care when refueling and ventilate the boat afterwards.

Chapter 6

The Art and Science of Docking

> ## In This Chapter
>
> ➤ Leaving home—undocking your boat
>
> ➤ Coming back—the landing is everything
>
> ➤ Picking up a mooring
>
> ➤ Securing your boat in a slip

Handling your boat in and around a marina or boat ramp is not all that difficult. In fact, after a few months afloat, you'll find there's nothing to it. But learning how to handle a boat around a marina or ramp can be a challenge, not because it's really dangerous, but because it's potentially embarrassing if you goof. And you can also do some damage to your boat's gel coat if you're really careless.

There are "ramp ghouls" who entertain themselves on Sunday afternoons at the marina by sitting in lawn chairs, sipping a cold one, and laughing at the errors of boaters allegedly less skilled than themselves.

The good news is that with a bit of practice, you won't give them anything to laugh about.

In this chapter, you'll learn how to leave the docks and how to return smoothly. I'll also cover the art of picking up a mooring and how to tie up the boat in a slip—a special art where tides can vary the water height several feet.

Slip-Sliding Away: Maneuvering Out of a Slip

Like everything else in boating, the ropes used to tie up and maneuver a boat around a dock, which are always referred to as *lines*, have special names. A *bow line* is attached to a cleat on the front of the boat. A *stern line* is attached to a cleat on the back end of the boat. A *spring line* is attached to a forward cleat and run aft to the dock, or attached to an aft cleat and run forward to the dock.

A *slip* is a boat's home, a spot where docks and pilings allow the boat to be tied securely. Leaving a slip when the boat is backed in is simply a matter of going straight forward until the stern clears the outside piling or the end of the dock.

With a single-engine boat, prop torque may walk the back end of the boat very slightly to starboard, which can bring your port bow too close to the pilings—you may have to give a bit of right rudder to compensate.

Keep the boat moving straight ahead until the stern is clear of the slip and the pilings. If you start to turn too soon, the stern will pivot into the pilings.

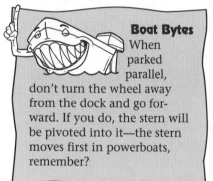

Boat Bytes When parked parallel, don't turn the wheel away from the dock and go forward. If you do, the stern will be pivoted into it—the stern moves first in powerboats, remember?

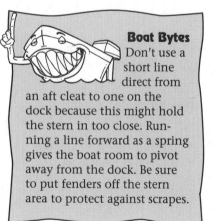

Boat Bytes Don't use a short line direct from an aft cleat to one on the dock because this might hold the stern in too close. Running a line forward as a spring gives the boat room to pivot away from the dock. Be sure to put fenders off the stern area to protect against scrapes.

If the boat is bow-on in the slip, back out straight until the bow is clear of the last piling, then turn. The stern may work slightly left—a crewperson may have to fend off the starboard bow. (The rudder doesn't help much at extremely low speeds in reverse with inboard boats. Reverse steering is more positive with outboards and I/Os.)

The Easy Way Out

If your small boat is tied parallel to a dock and pointed toward the channel, and there's no wind or strong current, all you have to do is push off the bow and go. Keep the wheel dead ahead and put the boat into gear at idle speed. Hey, you're boating!

With twin-engined boats too big to push around, the standard technique is to put the outside engine into reverse for a moment, then pop it back to neutral. The burst of thrust pulls the bow away from the dock, and you can then go straight ahead to get clear. Once the bow has swung well out, you might give a short burst of forward to the inside engine to help it. All this is done with the rudder dead ahead, so don't touch the steering wheel.

If there's another boat or an L-section of dock behind your boat, you add a spring line running from an aft cleat well forward to a dock cleat. Then, that same burst of reverse works to pivot the stern in place with no backward movement at all, and thus no unkind words from your neighbor to the rear.

If there's wind or a current off the dock, pushing off is even simpler—just untie the lines and wait until the natural forces carry you a couple yards away from the pilings before going ahead. Again, don't turn the wheel sharply away from the dock or you may force the stern right back against the pilings. Wait until you're well clear before turning.

Wind Into the Dock

When a strong wind or current is blowing into the dock, it can be a handful. I once saw a 40-foot cruiser pinned against a dock by a 20-knot wind, and the inexperienced skipper couldn't figure out how to get clear. The shouts and conflicting advice of a half-dozen bystanders didn't help, even though they upped the volume each time he crashed back into the pilings.

Look Out!
If you have inexperienced crew aboard, make sure that all the lines are actually untied and stowed before you try to leave the docks. It's not uncommon for a spring line to be overlooked, and this definitely puts a cramp in your style when you try to pull out.

You can't get away from a dock by turning away and going forward in this situation, because the back end of the boat will pivot first, locking itself against the dock. No matter how much power you apply, you can't force the bow out. (You might knock down the dock, if you work at it, though.)

The trick here is to get the stern of the boat into the wind and back away. Tie a long spring line to the bow cleat. Then run the spring line aft on the dock to somewhere near the stern (see part A of the figure on the next page). Hang a couple of fenders off the bow quarter to protect it from scrapes as you pivot.

Now, when you put the outside engine into forward, the rudder dead ahead, it walks the stern away from the pier, pivoting on the spring (see part B of the figure on the next page). The same thing works with a single outboard or stern drive, but you may want to turn the wheel slightly toward the dock to give the stern an assist. (This works best if you're docked port-side to, because the clockwise rotation of the prop when going ahead will want to walk the stern to the right or starboard.)

Once the stern is straight into the wind, cast off the bow spring line from the dock and back up the boat far enough to give *plenty* of working room to turn around. It's not a problem with twin engines, but with a single, you may be blown right back to the dock by the time you can spin unless you give yourself *many* boat lengths. Go out twice as far as you think you could possibly need, then double that, until you get more salt in your hair.

Boat Bytes
A boat likes to keep spinning the way it's backing. If you're backing to starboard, spin the wheel to port before putting it into forward. This encourages bow and stern to keep doing what they're doing, and will spin the boat smartly.

When the wind pins your boat against a dock, a bow spring line can help get the stern out into the wind so that you can back away.

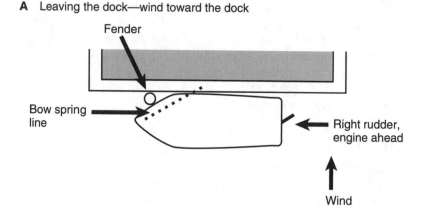

A Leaving the dock—wind toward the dock

Fender

Bow spring line

Right rudder, engine ahead

Wind

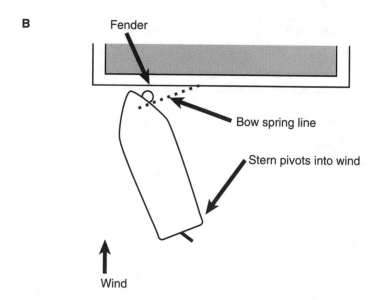

B

Fender

Bow spring line

Stern pivots into wind

Wind

Spring Ahead, But Don't Fall Back

With the wind blowing parallel to the docks, all you have to do is cast off the upwind end of the boat first, give it a push, and the wind will quickly get either the bow or the stern pointed where you need to go. If the wind is off the bow, take in that line first, let the bow swing completely clear, and then go ahead slowly.

If there's another boat behind you, you'll have to put out an aft spring line (see part A of the figure on the next page), running from a stern cleat forward to the dock, so that the boat doesn't slide back and bump into it as the wind pushes on the bow. Don't forget to position a fender between the dock and the boat.

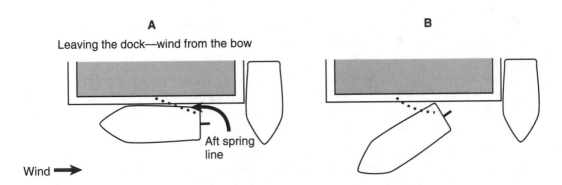

Leaving the dock—wind from the bow

Aft spring line

Wind ➡

With the wind parallel to the docks and another boat close behind you, it's best to put out an aft spring line, then push off the bow and let the wind swing the front of the boat clear.

You Can Go Home Again—Docking Tactics

In boating, as in flying an airplane, the landing is everything. Whatever mistakes you make out on the water are between you and your crew and the seagulls, but when you come into a busy marina, you'll feel that everybody is watching you.

The bad news is, they will be, if you start banging into things.

The Best Plan Is to Have a Plan

Go over with the crew exactly what you want to do, and exactly what you want them to do, long before you get near the docks. Then things can proceed step by step as you instruct in a calm voice.

Before you begin, look over the situation. What is the wind doing? Is it high or low tide? Is there any other traffic? Are there any unusual problems, tight squeezes, or shallow areas? Consider all of these things before you speak to the crew.

Practice, Practice, Practice

It's best to learn the basics in a quiet backwater where forces of wind and tide are minimal. Go slowly at first as you study what happens when you apply a short burst of power in forward, then reverse.

As you'll notice, a single-engined boat does not simply go straight ahead or straight back in this situation. The torque of the prop makes it walk sideways a little, the stern kicking

> **Boat Bytes**
> Every docking situation can be different, but in general it's best to work *into* the wind when possible—that gives you a natural brake if things don't line up just right. Going with a strong wind can make the job twice as difficult because the boat will move toward the dock—and other boats—even when you don't do anything.

slightly right (with right-hand or clockwise rotation, as most motors have) and the bow left when you go ahead. It's exactly the opposite when you put it in reverse.

You can use this tendency in your favor. If you need to ease the bow left, giving a quick burst of forward *without turning the wheel* will often be all that's needed. If you need to make the bow go right, a burst of reverse may accomplish it—again, without turning the wheel at all. (This is particularly true on large props with cupped blades, which tend to "paddlewheel" sideways more than other prop designs.)

However, if you want to back up straight with a single-engine rig, the paddlewheel effect can be a problem, particularly in reverse where the rudder doesn't help much. You may have to give lots of starboard rudder, or in outboards and stern drives, turn the lower unit a bit to starboard, to make the boat back straight.

Avoiding Slip-Ups

Twin-engine steering around the docks is usually accomplished with the wheel straight ahead—if you want to go left, you put the starboard motor into gear for a few seconds, and right, the port motor. It's much more effective than using the wheel or rudder.

Making use of the thrust of two engines rather than one eases handling around the docks, often without turning the wheel at all. (Photo credit: Frank Sargeant)

With one engine, it's more difficult—you have to turn the wheel and be quick with the gear shifting. Again, be aware that the prop can walk your stern sideways a little if you use short bursts in either forward or reverse.

When going into a slip you should have one crewperson on the bow and one at the stern. If you only have one other person aboard, put him on the stern to start. As you back in, the crewperson should pick up one of the bow lines off the post (a boathook helps!) and walk forward.

For example, let's say you've got twin engines, and your helper grabs the port line first. You stop the boat with a short burst of forward as the bow comes even with the bow post, and the crew ties off that side, allowing some slack for maneuvering. Now you bump the port engine into gear for a second or two and it will magically walk the bow over to the starboard post, where your crew can pick up that line and tie it fast. Then you apply a bit more reverse on both engines, stopping it with a shot of forward within a foot or two of the docks, where the aft man can jump up on the dock and complete the securing process.

Parallel Parking

Arriving at a parallel dock is usually less challenging, unless other boats are blocking the ends of the parking spot. If there are no complications, you simply motor toward the dock at a 30-degree angle at idle speed, then take the prop out of gear, turn the wheel away from the dock, and let the momentum start to carry the stern toward the pilings.

This is easiest with a single, clockwise-rotating engine if you go in port-side to. Straighten the wheel and give a burst of reverse and the boat stops, but also magically crawls sideways to barely touch the dock—man, you look cool!

You can do the same thing with twin engines, leaving the port engine in neutral and giving the starboard engine a shot of reverse. Since the starboard engine has more leverage to turn the stern to port in reverse, you only need a second or two of power to do the job. Is this easy or what?

Of course, there are often complications. One more little test life puts in your way.

Current Events

If there's a strong wind or current pushing off the dock, you may have to ease the bow in and get a bow line on a cleat either with a helper ashore or by having a crewperson step down on the dock (see part A of the figure on the next page). Then you would dock by going ahead slowly, the wheel turned away from the dock, as the bow line acts as a bow spring to walk the stern right to the dock (see part B of the figure on the next page). This is also the tactic for getting in between two other boats against the docks.

When the wind or current is off a parallel dock, a bow spring line is used to pivot the boat close to the pilings. The wheel is turned away from the dock and the engine put in forward idle.

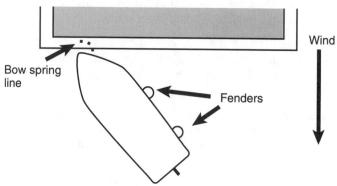

A   Returning to the dock—wind off the dock

Wind

Bow spring line

Fenders

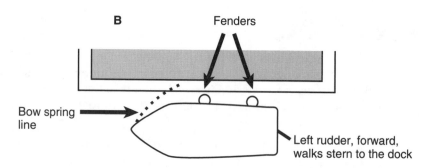

B   Fenders

Bow spring line

Left rudder, forward, walks stern to the dock

Again, with a single engine, it's easier if you go port-side to. With twin engines, use the inside engine in forward to do the job. In either case, have a crewperson on the stern ready to get the line ashore as soon as you touch or you'll have to go through the procedure all over again.

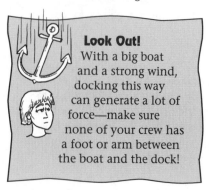

Look Out!
With a big boat and a strong wind, docking this way can generate a lot of force—make sure none of your crew has a foot or arm between the boat and the dock!

If the current or wind is toward the dock, it's easier—you simply pull up parallel to the spot where you want to land and put the engines in neutral. Let nature dock you, shifting in and out of gear briefly if you need to adjust by a foot or two. Get your dock fenders over the side in advance.

Currents or winds parallel to the docks are usually less problematic. The only trick, if you come in bow-on to a current, is to get a bow line on the dock quickly (see part A of the figure on the next page). The force of wind or current will then cozy you up to the planks (see part B of the figure on the next page).

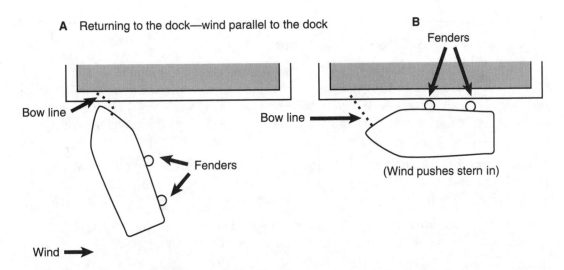

A   Returning to the dock—wind parallel to the dock

B

Fenders

Bow line

Fenders

Bow line

(Wind pushes stern in)

Wind ➡

The wind does the work when blowing parallel to the docks if you simply drop a bow line on a cleat and slip the fenders over the gunnels.

Shoehorn Maneuvering

If there are boats ahead of and behind the spot you need to fit into, the best plan is to pull up parallel to the dock and toss your lines to somebody ashore. If there's no one there, nose the bow in and put a crewperson on the dock. With a small boat 25 feet and under, the crew can then manhandle you in, even in moderate winds or currents.

With larger boats, fitting into a spot like this requires using spring lines and judicious maneuvering—it's not something to try until you've seen a lot of water pass under the hull.

Slow Is Good

Things can go badly wrong when docking at anything other than dead slow. A few years ago I was standing on the dock at Southwest Pass, Louisiana, as a brand new 50-footer was being brought briskly to its slip by a seasoned skipper. All went well until one of the hydraulic lines on the gear box let go just as the captain needed reverse, and lots of it, to stop the boat's momentum. The bow plowed about three feet through the railroad-tie dock. Damage to the boat was about five grand.

That sort of accident is rare, but it's not at all uncommon for an engine to die just when you're depending on it to brake your hull. Keep that in mind, be cautious, and go slowly.

Bet You Didn't Know

There may be a time when you have to turn around in an area that's too small for your boat to turn in while underway—for example, the space between main piers. Managing this with a twin-engine boat is easy—with the engines idling, put one in forward and one in reverse, steering dead ahead, and the boat rotates like it has eyes.

But how about with one motor? With an outboard or stern drive, you do it much as you would with a car, spinning the wheel hard to port as you go forward a few feet, then back to starboard as you reverse a few feet, until the turn is complete.

With single inboards, though, it's a different deal. The best procedure to rotate to the right is to put the wheel over hard right and then leave it there as you alternately shift the engine into forward and reverse.

The boat will slowly swing around, backing slightly left in reverse even though the rudder should make it back to the right. The reason is that the paddlewheel or torque effect of the prop in reverse is stronger than the steering effect of the rudder. It takes some time but it works—as long as a strong wind or tide doesn't interfere!

Easy Job: Picking Up a Mooring

Moorings are large permanent anchors secured well out from the docks in a harbor. They allow large boats to avoid the hassles of docking, and also increase the usable overnight space in a harbor.

Picking up a mooring is an "easy" job: It's easy to miss it, and it's easy to have a crewperson jerked overboard. So everyone has to pay attention for the few moments this "easy" job takes until the bow line is secured to the mooring.

The mooring is marked by a large buoy, which is attached to the heavy line or chain below. Also usually attached to the buoy is a smaller pick-up float with a ring in the top, making it easy to hook with a boat hook or gaff. To moor, you pick up the small float with a boat hook, then attach the pendant to a bow cleat.

Some moorings don't have the smaller float, just the main float attached to the anchor chain. Use your anchor line to attach to the bottom of the main buoy. (Don't attach your anchor line to the ring on top of the pendant buoy, though—they're not designed for heavy loads.)

One problem that might arise is that the skipper sometimes can't see the float as it comes "under" the bow, particularly in larger boats with lots of freeboard. So a crewperson stands up front and guides him in—hand signals are easier than shouting.

Provided the approach is accurate, the crewperson simply plucks up the mooring float, the boat is put into reverse to bring it to a halt, and then the pendant is brought aboard and cleated off. If you miss the float, just go around again—it's not going anywhere, and probably nobody is watching. Just don't ask the crewperson to lunge at it, because everybody *will* watch a guy falling overboard.

Be careful, though. If you see that the boat won't stop quickly enough to prevent the crewman from being pulled overboard if he hangs on to the mooring line, have him cast it off and try again. This can go from funny to dangerous very quickly because you're traveling forward and the props are close to where the swimmer will fall.

Tidal Tie-Ups

Tides vary from a few inches in south Florida to more than 40 feet in Canada. If you tie your boat up close in an area that has a lot of variation between high and low tide, you may have it swinging from the docks when the tide goes out.

No kidding, I've seen it happen with rowboats and skiffs. They often turn over when the water leaves, dumping out life jackets, paddles, and whatever else is left aboard.

Even worse, tying up too loosely may allow your boat to drift *under* the dock. When the tide comes back, the boat gets a hydraulic crush. The lifting force of water is amazing—it can crack the cowling of an outboard, smash a windshield, even crumple a cabin top.

Obviously, tying up properly is critical for coastal boaters. (I'll discuss more about on how tides affect coastal boating in Chapter 16.)

Dock Lines

You need at least four dock lines twice the length of the boat if you live in an area with maximum tides, while in moderate tide zones like south Florida the four lines should be about the length of the boat. You don't use all this length very often, but you will need it sooner or later if you cruise a lot.

The best dock lines are woven nylon, $^3/_8$-inch or better. The larger the line, the stronger it is and the longer it lasts—and the easier it is on your hands. But line that's too big won't fit the cleats of a smaller boat, and it costs a lot more than smaller stuff.

Securing Your Boat

The best tie is a four-point "suspension"—two lines on the bow, two on the stern. The longer the line run, the less it restricts the rise and fall of the boat, which is why the lines are run to opposite cleats on the transom—that is, the line from the port side of the dock goes to the starboard cleat, and vice versa.

With a long run, it's possible to tighten down the lines securely, holding the boat in the slip so it doesn't touch the pilings at any point, yet still has enough vertical movement to ride the tides.

Secure your boat in a slip so that it stays clear of dock and pilings on both high and low tides.

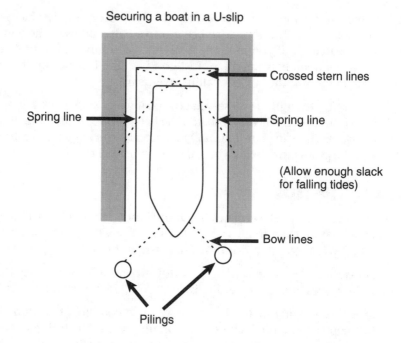

Securing a boat in a U-slip

Crossed stern lines

Spring line

Spring line

(Allow enough slack for falling tides)

Bow lines

Pilings

A single after spring line is often added in U-slips to keep the transom from getting under the dock. For long-term storage, most add a pair of spring lines amidships, running fore or aft, to hold the position longitudinally.

Chafing Gear for Your Lines

If the boat is to be left in the slip long-term (more than a week), and if it's more than 20 feet long, it's a good idea to add chafing gear to the lines anywhere they pass through a metal chock or scrape across a dock edge.

These are simply split lengths of old garden hose, or they can be the ubiquitous duct tape—anything to prevent the friction from weakening the line. (The best tape for this is a thick vinyl that won't give out when exposed to rain and salt.)

Fenders Are Meant to Be Squashed

Fenders in boats are not quite the same thing as fenders in cars. If your teenager squashes the fender of your BMW, you'll be exceedingly unhappy. If he squashes the fenders of the boat, you'll note that he's learning to be a competent skipper.

Boat fenders are meant to be squashed, squeezed, and crushed. They're made of tough but pliable vinyl or other materials that absorb shock, and they're designed to fit between a boat and a dock, pier, or other solid structure, or sometimes between two boats.

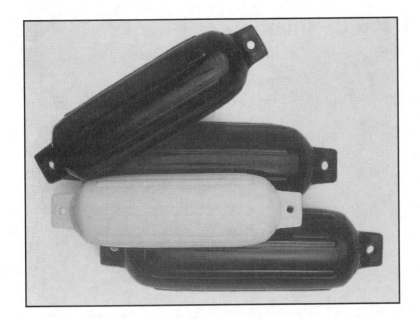

Heavy vinyl fenders inflated with air act as cushions or bumpers to keep the gunnels and sides of your boat from being damaged by docks and other boats. (Photo credit: Polyform Fenders)

Fenders can be anything from a piece of Styrofoam to a boat cushion, but the best fenders are the commercial models, usually inflatable, and made of thick vinyl. Cylindrical fenders are most common, although spheres are also sometimes used. They range in size from a foot to three feet long, with diameters from six inches to a foot or more.

The bigger your boat, the bigger the fenders you need, because a 20-ton yacht can generate enormous crushing force when rocked by a wave. And a boat docked in an open area subject to wave action will require bigger fenders than one docked in a well-protected harbor.

The fenders have to be fitted to the boat, hung over the side where contact with the fixed object is most likely. This may not be where there's a convenient cleat or rail stanchion—if not, run a stout line between two cleats and hang the fender from that.

The usual arrangement is to put one fender in the center of the boat and one on each end, so that however the boat works back and forth on the dock lines, it will be protected.

A dock board is sometimes hung on the docks outside of the fenders if the dock is particularly rough or covered with barnacles. This prevents the sharp edges from puncturing the fenders.

The Least You Need to Know

➤ Always consider wind and current when leaving or approaching a dock.

➤ Inform your crew of your docking plan.

➤ When learning how to maneuver in and out of a slip, remember that practice makes perfect.

➤ Consider tides when tying up your boat for the night.

➤ Fenders are your boat's best friend.

Chapter 7

People Management Aboard

In This Chapter

➤ Who's in charge here? The captain

➤ Help your passengers help themselves

➤ Ten tips for coping with seasickness

➤ Protecting your crew from the elements

➤ Keeping bugs at bay

In the pages that follow, we'll review some of the ways that the skipper can help all aboard stay safe, happy, and healthy. Your boat is much like your home, both in that you want your guests to enjoy themselves, and that you want them to follow some basic rules so that everyone else can stay happy, as well.

As any business leader these days knows, you don't just manage a business, you manage people. It's like that aboard nearly every boat, too—except maybe a one-person kayak (and even there you may have to manage yourself at times, especially when the boat is upside-down and the water is fast and icy and stark terror seems the normal response rather than thinking about the mechanics of the Eskimo roll).

Nobody likes rules in their recreation, but unfortunately there are a few in just about every sport, and boating is no exception. The captain's job is to make them clear to the passengers and crew. That way everybody remains comfortable, happy, and safe while aboard.

Taking Care of Business: The Captain Is the Boss

A boat can't be run by committee. The boss is the man or woman at the wheel—that's the individual who has to know what he's doing and be able to make decisions quickly.

Don't come across as Captain Bligh or you'll soon have all your crew jumping ship. But you can gently assert this authority, and also give new crew members a sense of security, if you give a brief explanation of procedures afloat before you leave the dock.

This talk should cover the following:

➤ Tell everyone where the life jackets are stowed, and how they should be put on. Don't imply that their emergency use is imminent or you may have some folks stepping back ashore right there. But responsible skippering requires that everyone knows where the personal flotation devices (PFDs) are located and how to use them. Non-swimmers and kids should put them on before the boat leaves the dock, and in high-performance boats or in dicey conditions, all aboard should wear their PFDs.

➤ If the boat is under 20 feet long, remind everyone that they must be sitting down when the boat is underway. On larger sailboats, trawlers, cruisers, pontoons, and deck-type boats that run at moderate speeds, some moving around is okay by those agile enough to deal with the ups and downs of life afloat.

➤ Explain the basic operation of VHF radio or your cell phone, particularly if you're the only "salt" aboard. If something happens to you, somebody else will need to know how to call for help. (For details on marine communications gear, see Chapter 14.)

➤ Explain your route of travel for the same reason. If you're in an area where there's a lot of shallow water, or if you'll be out during low tide, explain where the safe routes are.

➤ Select a second-in-command and explain basic boat operation to him or her. Again, if you're disabled, this person will have to keep the boat under control until the boat docks or help arrives.

➤ Tell everyone where the head or marine toilet is and explain how to use it.

➤ Remind all that there will be no smoking during refueling. None, period.

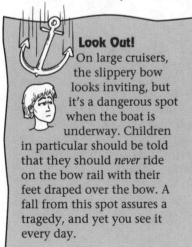

Look Out!
On large cruisers, the slippery bow looks inviting, but it's a dangerous spot when the boat is underway. Children in particular should be told that they should *never* ride on the bow rail with their feet draped over the bow. A fall from this spot assures a tragedy, and yet you see it every day.

Make this all light and informational—the object is to make your crew aware without making them nervous.

Protection From the Sun

I don't like to read health warnings any better than anyone else, but for those new to life afloat, the relationship with the sun is a whole new ball game. That friendly Mr. Sun that gives your cheeks a rosy glow when exposed during a walk in a park will fry your skin into purple blisters if it's not protected during several hours of open-water boating.

The fact that there's no shade and no greenery to soak up the rays at sea doubles or triples the impact of sun on human skin, and failure to protect yourself and your crew guarantees discomfort—and maybe lasting damage that can lead to the first stages of skin cancer. It's not an option to protect yourself; it's *mandatory*. Ask any dermatologist who deals with melanoma and you'll get the same firm advice: Avoid getting a sunburn.

Sunscreen with UVA and UVB protectors is the ticket. Buy the drugstore versions, which are half as costly but just as effective as the name brands, and buy them by the gallon. SP-15 is reportedly the most cost-effective buy. Higher SP numbers cost more, but doctors say they offer no added skin protection.

Don't even consider leaving the docks without everyone aboard swabbing down thoroughly. Insist—many people think they'll go back to shore with a great tan if they don't use sunscreen, when in fact they'll go back with second-degree burns.

The best plan for a family outing is for everyone to apply sunscreen before leaving the house, even before shirts and shorts and shoes are put on. That way you don't miss those touchy spots around the collar and at the leg of the shorts, and the stuff stays on longer if it has a chance to dry before you go out into the heat and humidity.

Boater-ese
Sunscreens are categorized by their *Sun Protection Factor* or *SPF*. An SPF of 2 supposedly allows you to stay in the sun twice as long without burning as you could without any type of sunscreen. Most doctors recommend using a screen with an SPF of 15, and applying it repeatedly during the day to all exposed skin. The best screens block out both types of the sun's radiation, *UVA* and *UVB*, which are the terms designating different wave lengths of the invisible ultraviolet rays.

Boat Bytes
White is the best color for any clothing worn in hot weather—it can make a huge difference in how much heat you feel. Dark, dull-finished material soaks up heat and sends it through to your skin. Keep cool with white.

Sun protection includes a shirt with a collar and sleeves, a long-billed hat, and polarized sunglasses. And don't forget to cover all exposed skin with an SP-15 sunscreen! (Photo credit: Darla Sargeant)

Boat Bytes
A "cap-keeper" is a big help in keeping your cap on aboard boats that run more than 20 mph. It can be as simple as a cord around your chin. One useful model has alligator clips at each end of a cord; clip one to your cap and the other to the back of your shirt collar.

Wear a Hat

If your hair is at all thin, a hat is a must—skin cancers on top of the head are very common, as are those on the tops of the ears.

Baseball caps, a favorite of anglers, don't protect the ears at all. Hats that have a full brim do much better, although it's hard to keep them on. The goofy-looking Florida flats guide hats, with brims fore and aft, are very useful and stay on well. They also protect the back of the neck.

Your Feet Need Protection, Too

Don't forget to protect the tops of your feet if you don't wear socks—the area between your ankle and your toenails is exposed to the direct rays at a near-vertical angle and will burn much quicker than your legs. Boaters often go barefoot or sockless in hot weather, so this area is highly vulnerable.

Wear Sunglasses

You and your crew *must* have sunglasses to go boating, and they should be polarized. Polarized glasses have a film built into them that acts like Venetian blinds, letting in light horizontally but not vertically. This gets rid of much of the blinding glare that's common when sun strikes water, making it much more comfortable afloat. Just as important, the polarizing effect allows the skipper to see through the surface of the water to any hazards that might be below. Anglers love polarized sunglasses because they allow easy sighting of fish and bait several feet below the surface.

The best boating glasses have side panels to keep out glare. They should have ear pieces that fit snugly and stay put even when you tip your head forward.

The best sunglasses for boating use are polarized, which allow you to see through the surface glare to avoid shoals and rocks. They also prevent eyestrain.

However, even with good ear pieces, sunglasses can be blown off your face by the wind blasts of high-speed boating. Don't even consider taking your $100 shades aboard until you equip them with a strap of some sort—a simple piece of surgical tubing of the sort used by anglers to lure barracuda is all that's needed, but there are many good commercial versions, available for $2 to $4, as well.

Coping With Seasickness

Seasickness is no joke if you are the one who is seasick. Although some old salts don't like to admit it, even the most seasoned captain can be touched by Big Ralph at times.

There are ways to ease the discomfort, however. Here's some advice you can give new crew members:

1. Eat and drink moderately the night before a voyage, and try to get your usual amount of sleep. Don't start at a disadvantage. If you wake up with a cold-sweats hangover, you don't have a chance.

2. Eat a light breakfast—cereal and fruit, nothing greasy.

3. Make use of preventatives early. Pills, acupressure wrist bands, or ear stick-on patches work for some people, but it takes several hours for these things to take full effect. If you wait until you start to feel queasy to make use of them, it's too late. It's not a bad idea to start the medications the night before, other remedies a couple of hours before you leave the dock.

4. Stay out of the cabin. There's something about the effect of swinging curtains and sliding cups that makes the stomach unhappy. (Actually, it makes the inner ear unhappy, but you feel it in your stomach.)

5. Stay well aft and off the bridge. Boats pitch worst at the bow, and wave action is accentuated when you get above the main deck.

6. Avoid sitting next to the transom if there's a blow-back of diesel fumes. Sitting near the stern is best because the boat rocks least there.

7. Keep your eyes on the horizon. It looks still compared to those waves that keep rolling…rolling…rolling…

8. Try drinking carbonated soda and eating dry crackers. Avoid smelly, oily foods.

9. Keep in mind that, no matter how bad it may be, it will end the instant you set foot on solid land again. (Shooting a skipper who refuses to take you in is not justifiable homicide, however.)

10. Remember, caution is the better part of valor. There are some days when those prone to seasickness should stay home—conditions are just too rough.

The Right Footwear

Nobody requires regulation Topsiders aboard any more, but it is definitely foolish to go boating in your Florsheim Oxfords. Advise anyone who will be joining you, in advance, that footwear is important. Anything without a rubberized sole is a definite liability aboard because it will sooner or later cause the wearer to fall on his keister. And yes, some non-boating shoes with dark soles do leave little black marks on white decks.

Boat shoes should have soft vinyl or rubber soles so that they'll grip the deck. The most common "boat shoe" seen these days are jogging shoes, although the old salts for the most part wear the standard slit-soled slip-ons made by Topsider, Bass, Dexter, and others. Some boat shoes now look like jogging shoes on the uppers and are just as comfortable, but have the unique "sticky" soles that keep you safe aboard. Prices range from $55 to $100.

Boat Bytes
There's a reason traditional boating shoes are slip-on's: because they slip off just as easily when you fall overboard. Ever try to swim with a pair of Nikes on your feet?

These shoes have exceptionally soft rubber in the soles, and that, along with the razor-cut slits in the flat bottoms, make them sticky as flies' feet. (Personally, I think it's possible flies actually wear tiny little Topsiders so they can walk up walls.)

The leather laces that come on most boat shoes are constantly coming untied, and they also look like the knots you tied in your shoes when you were in second grade. Here's a tip: After your shoes are broken in so that they slip on easily with the tie secured, get rid of the shoestring tie and replace it with a neat, tight square knot. Then cut off the ends about one-half inch from the knot. This makes the shoe look a lot better, and they'll never again come untied.

Dressing for Cold-Weather Boating

The best way to experience cold weather boating is via video as you sit in front of your fireplace sipping hot Earl Grey tea. A 20-knot north wind with temperatures in the 30s takes most of the pleasure out of pleasure boating.

However, for those who like to extend the season a bit, dressing appropriately can make it downright comfortable, even on those chilly November dawns. Warn your crew before they leave home if you suspect it may be a bit nippy on the water. If it's chilly ashore, it will be twice as chilly when you get on the water and are exposed to wind and humidity. And, even though that brisk air may feel fine in shorts and a sweatshirt when you go for your morning jog, it won't feel so good as you sit still in the boat for a few hours.

As with so much in life, underwear is the answer. (The secret of happiness, my father used to say, is to buy your BVDs two sizes too large.) Long underwear, in this case. Polypropylene will wick away the moisture while keeping you warm. Add a pair of warm pants, wool if it's really cold.

Boat Bytes
Suspenders may make you look like an escapee from a Norman Rockwell painting, but their big advantage is that they don't reduce blood flow to your legs and feet like wearing a tight belt does. Go for nautical versions, red and green, if you must be stylish, but try them—you'll be amazed at how much warmer your feet will feel.

Boat Bytes
Just as wearing white colors is best when it's hot, wearing dark colors is best when it's cold. If there's any sun, dull, dark gray, dark green, or black material will soak up lots more heat. You'll be amazed at the difference it can make on a chilly but bright day.

Over the top of your soft inner clothes you need a windbreaker of some sort. A good rain suit (see the following section) is the most common choice.

Gore-Tex gloves are also a must—waterproof, but they let sweat escape so your hands don't get clammy. The type with Thermax or other insulation is best for powerboat operation.

If you're fishing or running a sailboat, where you have to use your fingers frequently, lighter gloves are essential. Neoprene diving gloves are waterproof and give you a good grip, plus fairly good warmth. Standard sailing gloves, which expose your fingertips but protect your fingerpads and palms with canvas and leather, are good in moderate weather but not warm enough when it's frosty. Wool gloves don't hold out water, but they do remain warm when wet—they make a good extra pair to have in your pocket.

Singing in the Rain With Good Rain Gear

Rain may not make you sing, but it won't make you or your crew that unhappy if you have enough good rain gear aboard. Rain gear varies hugely in quality and price, from the $4.99 drugstore poncho that's about as durable as a garbage bag to some serious stuff suited for ocean crossings that costs close to $400 for coat, pants, and hood.

Boat Bytes
Opt for a bright-colored rain suit: In the unlikely event that you or any crewperson ever falls overboard, yellow or bright orange is a lot easier to see in the water than green.

The cheap stuff is worth what you pay for it, which is nothing.

The best rain gear is nylon-coated with neoprene rubber or PVC waterproofer. These suits may last for a decade or more if cared for properly, and they absolutely don't leak. Gore-Tex got a bad name early on when it tended to seep in heavy rain storms. The problems have been cured with later generations, and it's good stuff, although quite expensive. It offers the no-sweat advantage—it lets your sweat evaporate through the fabric but keeps out rain.

The best hoods have a broad, stiff brim that will act like a miniature umbrella to keep rain off your face—a big plus when it's really coming down. The brim can be rolled up for better visibility when you want it more for wind protection than to stop rain. (The hood is a major factor in keeping you warm, because a lot of lost body heat exits through the head.)

Don't forget rain gear for your feet, particularly if you do your boating on cold water. Sperry and others make boots with cushioned insoles and razor-cut soles that are both dry and "sticky" when it comes to walking on a wet deck. And they kick off easily should you ever take an unscheduled trip overboard. Prices range from $30 to $50.

What's Bugging You?

Insects love the water as much as boaters do, and there are some unpleasant specimens out there in considerable numbers. If you run into lots of bugs and your crew is unprepared, they'll want to go home, pronto.

Mosquitoes are the most common problem and the easiest to deal with. They hate DEET, and if you use a spray containing plenty of it, they will leave you alone.

No-see-ums are biting gnats found throughout mangrove country, roughly from Georgia southward along the Atlantic and Gulf coasts. They are, true to their name, almost too small to see, but have jaws as large as alligators. They crawl into your hair, inside your ears and nose, and every place else they can reach.

An easy solution is to cover up, because they're not much for getting inside your clothes and they can't bite through even a thin shirt, as mosquitoes can. But it's often too hot in no-see-um country for a lot of clothing. So opt for Avon's Skin So Soft, a product which the company categorically denies is insect repellent, but which is known to be the only effective no-see-um stopper by all who live in their range. In recent years, another product that stops these gnats has become available, Johnson's Skintastic, and Johnson sells this oil as bug repellent. It smells suspiciously like—guess what?

Black flies take over a little north of where the no-see-ums end. They're the scourge of boaters and anglers from Michigan, Minnesota, and Maine northward, rising in clouds, invading nostrils, ears, and open sleeves and leaving seeping welts anywhere they bite. Again, heavy doses of DEET repellent and covering all exposed areas are the cure.

In general, if you can stay away from shorelines, you'll attract fewer bugs. Seek areas where the wind blows regularly—a narrow creek where the breeze can't stir will be alive with insects on any summer evening, while an airy beach just a mile away may be completely bug-free on the same evening.

There's also something to the idea of keeping the bugs upwind when you can—they find you by scent, sort of like little winged bloodhounds. So, if you have a

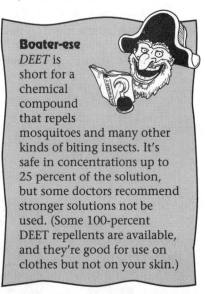

Boater-ese
DEET is short for a chemical compound that repels mosquitoes and many other kinds of biting insects. It's safe in concentrations up to 25 percent of the solution, but some doctors recommend stronger solutions not be used. (Some 100-percent DEET repellents are available, and they're good for use on clothes but not on your skin.)

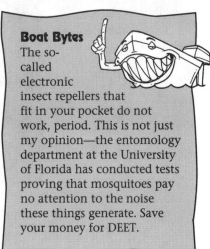

Boat Bytes
The so-called electronic insect repellers that fit in your pocket do not work, period. This is not just my opinion—the entomology department at the University of Florida has conducted tests proving that mosquitoes pay no attention to the noise these things generate. Save your money for DEET.

choice, anchor on the downwind side of a heavily vegetated island. You'll get less wave action, and hopefully fewer bugs.

Of course, if breezes are light, you may need to go well offshore on the upwind side to stop and watch the sunset without lots of insect company.

Cameras and Water Do Not Always Mix

There are a lot of wonderful photographs to be taken around the water, but warn all aboard that a few drops of salt water in an otherwise dry compartment can wreak havoc in your $800 camera. On the other hand, if you're afraid to get out your camera, you won't capture some wonderful memories.

One solution is to leave your expensive camera at home and instead bring a quality, fixed-lens waterproof camera. They produce pro-class photos and it doesn't matter if they get wet. Prices for these cameras are around $150 to $200.

If your camera budget is tight, opt for a one-time-use camera. Waterproof models are available. When you've finished the roll of film, you send in the whole camera to develop the film and the camera never comes back.

Waterproof cameras are much more useful on board than expensive models that have to be kept dry. Keep the camera handy to record the tough moments as well as those that are fun. (Photo credit: Pentax Corp.)

Take plenty of photos of your crew, even when it's pouring down rain or they're covered with mud from pushing off a bar—these are memories they'll appreciate someday.

The Least You Need to Know

➤ Let your crew know the basics before you leave the dock.

➤ Sunburn and seasickness can ruin any day afloat—take proper precautions before you leave the dock.

➤ Equip yourself and your crew for inclement weather.

➤ Insect protection is a must in warm weather.

Chapter 8

Anchors Aweigh! Making Your Boat Stay Put

In This Chapter

➤ Types of anchors and what they do

➤ Offshore anchoring

➤ Anchoring at the beach

➤ How to avoid losing your anchor

➤ How to get your anchor back once you've lost it

Knowing how to handle your boat when underway is only part of successful skippering. You'll also want to know how to make the boat stay in one spot while you enjoy a sundown, try to winch up a snapper dinner, or maybe leave the boat on its own while you take the dinghy to a secluded beach.

The anchor is the key to making your boat stay put without being fastened to anything—except to Mother Earth. In this chapter, we'll look at what makes a good anchor, the gear or "tackle" that attaches the anchor to the boat, and the secrets of making the anchor securely grab the bottom in all sorts of depths and wave conditions.

Anchors by Design

Dead weight is one way of securing a boat—a rock on a vine was probably the first anchor. But dead weight has a major drawback. It's very hard to handle.

Heavy anchors go down easy but come up hard. Gross weight is not what makes an anchor function. The engine block from a '57 Buick will definitely hold your boat in place, but it would be hell to raise back up to the deck.

The trick in anchor design is to get the anchor to grab hold of the bottom and use earth itself as your security. Thus, "patent" anchors were devised to burrow their way into the bottom and use the weight of wet mud and sand to do the job in place of lots of specific gravity.

Anchoring in Style

There are many styles or designs of anchors that work well without excessive weight. The most common include:

➤ Danforth or fluke-style anchor

➤ Plow or CQR anchor

➤ Navy anchor

➤ Mushroom anchor

➤ Grapnel or grappling anchor

We'll take a closer look at each of these in the following sections.

Fluke (Danforth) Anchors

The fluke anchor (or Danforth anchor, as it's more commonly known) is the most widely used recreational boating anchor in the world. It's made of two flat steel or aluminum flukes on a pivoting shaft. The pointed flukes dig into the bottom when pressure is put on the shaft at an angle lower than about 60 degrees. When the angle of pull approaches 90 degrees vertically, the anchor turns over and comes out of the bottom, making it easy to raise.

Fluke anchors also stow flat, making it easy to fit them into a compartment until needed.

There are a wide variety of strength levels in fluke anchors, though, and the strongest cost a whole lot more than the weakest. For example, a standard galvanized-steel Danforth-design fluke anchor in the five-pound class lists for about $25. A high-tensile version of the same anchor from the same company lists for about $65, almost three times more! The high-tensile version is a specially treated steel that won't bend under pressure.

The difference? It's not the label. The high-tensile model is rated for 500 pounds of holding power, the standard model just 300 pounds.

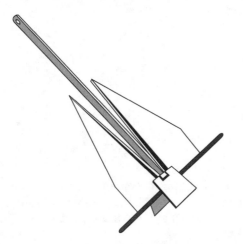

The fluke or Danforth anchor is light in weight, has excellent holding power, and takes up little storage space.

Plow Anchors

Plow anchors, also called CQR anchors, look exactly like a plow. If you haven't been on a John Deere lately, that means they have a sharp, curved spade fluke or blade attached to a long shaft that runs forward rather than up. When pressure is put on the shaft, the plow burrows its way down through weeds, mud, or whatever until it finds solid holding.

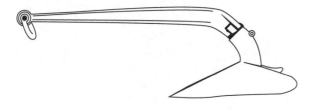

Plow anchors have excellent holding power, plowing deeper under heavy strain. They're a favorite yacht anchor.

Plow anchors are very strong and hold in extreme weather, but unless your boat has a bow pulpit where the anchor can hang when not in use, they are large, bulky, and hard to store. They're also fairly heavy—most models start at 15 pounds. They're best for boats 25 feet and up. Prices range from $130 for a 14-pounder to over $690 for a 60-pounder.

Navy Anchors

Navy-style anchors look like anchors have traditionally looked, (picture the one tattooed on Popeye's arm). They're the anchors that hang on the bow of older sea-going ships, and also, much smaller and in gold, on the necks of tanned, middle-aged guys throughout south Florida.

The navy anchor is strong and dependable, although it's heavier at a given holding power than a Danforth.

Navy anchors rely on both their weight and their hooked flukes to hold the bottom, and tend to start at about the weight of a Jeep and go up a whole lot from there. They're not often used on recreational boats because they're so heavy, but some small ones are used as storm anchors on larger yachts.

Mushroom Anchors

This anchor looks like an upside-down mushroom, hence the name. It depends mostly on weight for holding power, although the cup does dig into the bottom to help a bit. These anchors are suitable only for boats under 15 feet long in protected water.

The mushroom is low in price and adequate for small boats anchored out of strong winds and waves.

Mushrooms are inexpensive, $15 for an eight-pounder, and PVC-coated models protect against rust. They're also good for inflatable boats because they have no sharp edges like fluke anchors.

Grapnel Anchors

Grapnels are useful when the bottom is too rocky for conventional anchors to grab. The prongs or hooks sink into a crevasse and hold on. They don't work at all in mud or sand, but for hard bottom they're great.

The grapnel is a handy extra anchor to put on shore during a lunch stop. It can also help you retrieve the fishing rod Junior dropped overboard, because it's light enough for throwing. Grapnel anchors cost $25 and up.

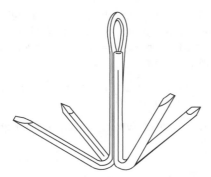

The grapnel or grappling anchor is capable of holding onto rocks where standard anchors drag. It's also useful for retrieving objects lost overboard.

Stronger Is Better

Why is it better to have a stronger anchor, since your boat isn't going to pull all that hard on the line? There are two reasons:

➤ If you ever get caught in a really severe storm, the surges of your boat might well exceed the rated holding power of the weaker anchor as the boat rises and falls on tall waves.

➤ If the anchor gets stuck on a rock and you try to use the motor to pull it free, the cheaper model will quickly turn into a twisted piece of junk that can never again be used as an anchor, while the high-tensile model will bring whatever it's latched onto up to the surface with it.

The following table is an approximate guide to the holding power needed for the working anchor, the standard everyday anchor suggested for various boats, according to the American Boat and Yacht Council. (The "holding power" of an anchor is a measure, in pounds, of the amount of pull it can sustain without breaking free in good bottom.) I've added the approximate weight of a standard fluke anchor providing the suggested holding power.

Boat Length	Working Load	Approximate Weight (in Pounds)
15 feet	250	5
20 feet	360	5
25 feet	490	9
30 feet	700	14
35 feet	900	14
40 feet	1,300	16
50 feet	1,600	23

There are a few high-tech anchors on the market that advertise lower weights with higher holding power, such as the high-tensile aluminum alloy Fortress anchors. In tests conducted by BOAT U.S., these anchors proved their claims—a six-pounder, although rated for 900 pounds, survived a 2,000-pound test load.

Note the weight is less than half that of a conventional fluke anchor of similar holding power—nice when you're the designated anchor-puller.

These are expensive anchors, as you might expect, with the six-pounder going for around $85, but they're lifetime products.

Anchors That Float—Sea Anchors

These aren't really anchors in the conventional sense, in that they don't actually sink to the bottom to hold the boat in one spot. Instead, they're designed to slow the drift of a boat and maintain a heading without power.

Sea anchors are nylon or canvas bags that create drag when trailed from bow or stern. They're used to slow a drift rather than to fix the boat in one place.

Sea anchors, also called "drogues," are made of heavy nylon and fold up to the size of a loaf of bread when not in use. When put in the water, they open like a watery parachute, creating a huge amount of drag. The cost is $30 to $60 for lightweight models, $200 or more for "storm" models.

Why would you want one of these? They're handy for anglers who want to slow down their boat for live-bait trolling. The sea anchor can cut the drifting speed of a boat in half. And, should you ever be caught offshore in bad weather with a sick motor, the sea anchor trailed from your bow can keep the boat pointed into the oncoming seas—it can be a lifesaver.

In extreme conditions, the sea anchor is sometimes trailed from a *bridle* on the stern as a low-powered boat runs through an inlet. A bridle is a harness made from heavy rope, draped from each side of the transom lifting eyes (stout rings through-bolted to the transom) to form a secure, centered attachment for a sea anchor or for a line used to tow other boats. The idea is to keep the stern straight, preventing waves from pushing it into the trough and rolling the boat.

Anchor Tackle

"Ground tackle" is your anchoring stuff, the rope (called "rode" or "line" by old salts) and all the other gear that helps you hold bottom.

Anchors work a lot better if equipped with three to six feet of heavy galvanized chain between shank and line. The chain lies along bottom, keeping the angle of pull on the shank low and helping the anchor to dig in.

Galvanized anchors are steel coated with zinc to make them rustproof. A *shackle* is a C-shaped fastener with a clevis bolt used to secure the eye of the anchor to the anchor rode, usually through a *thimble*—a rounded, hard plastic or galvanized steel insert spliced into an anchor rode to prevent abrasion against the shackle.

A thimble is used to prevent chafing where the anchor chain attaches to the anchor rode or rope.

The chain also acts as a shock absorber as the boat rocks in the waves, keeping pressure off the anchor itself. And if there are sharp rocks or junk on the bottom, the chain helps prevent your anchor line from being cut.

BOAT U.S. suggests the guidelines shown in the following table for chain used on anchors.

Boat Length	Chain Size	Chain Length
10–15 feet	$3/16$ inch	3 feet
16–32 feet	$1/4$ inch	6 feet
33–44 feet	$5/16$ inch	6 feet
45–60 feet	$3/8$ inch	6 feet

Galvanized chain does not rust—much. It does rust a little, leaving unsightly stains wherever it lies. If you're fastidious about this, choose vinyl-coated anchor chain.

Don't get the cheap discount-store kind that's dipped whole, because as soon as these flex a few times the coating will crack and rust will come out. Links that are individually dipped make the chain more expensive, but a lot better.

Galvanized shackles hook the chain to the anchor at one end and the chain to the anchor line at the other. A thimble spliced into the rope prevents abrasion from the shackle. The shackle is secured with a little toggle bolt.

Shackles are used to attach anchor to chain and chain to anchor line. They allow you to remove the line for storage.

Put some waterproof grease on the toggle bolt before you tighten it, or you won't ever be removing it again. And use a "keeper" wire on the bolt, in case it comes loose on its own—a piece of stainless-steel wire is the Bristol fashion, but a couple of plastic tie-wraps work fine, too. ("Bristol" fashion means neat, orderly, and shipshape. The name comes from an English seafaring town.)

Deep Stuff—Anchoring Offshore

The deeper the water, the more difficult it is to make an anchor stay put, and anchoring offshore in deep, rough water to fish or dive can be a test of seaperson-ship. But it's not that difficult if you have the right ground tackle and some know-how.

Proceed uptide or upwind from the spot where you want the boat to hang, a distance at least three times the water depth in calm, non-tidal water, six times if wind or tide is strong, and eight to 12 times if staying overnight or in stormy weather.

This gives your anchor adequate "scope" or length in comparison to the water depth to form a moderate angle of pull and stay buried in the bottom. A minimum scope of 3:1 (with "3" being anchor line length and "1" being water depth) is required to hold in anything other than dead calm.

For example, if you're anchoring in 10 feet, you go uptide of where you want the boat to be at least 30 feet, and then you're going to let out enough line to make that 3:1 ratio.

Actually, if you go forward 30 feet from your selected spot, you'll let out a little more than 31 feet of line to drop back to the same spot.

How do you know when you've let out 20 feet of line, or 50 or 100? The best way is to mark your anchor line. Some put little tags in the weave of the rope, but the easiest way is to mark your line with a waterproof marker. I start at 20 feet with one mark and add more marks for every added 20 feet—thus there are two marks at 40 feet, three at 60, and so on.

Lower the hook—*never throw it*—from the bow and then back away, with the crew paying out line as you go. (Why shouldn't you throw it? Because if your foot or your favorite fishing rod happens to be wrapped in the line when the anchor is tossed, you or the rod will follow. Plus, throwing the anchor scares fish, if you happen to be fishing or diving. It also marks you as a boating dork.)

When you're over your spot, cleat the line, put a little tension on it by remaining in reverse for a moment to dig the anchor in, and you're set.

Bet You Didn't Know

The moment when you lower the anchor is prime time for falling overboard. It's happened to me twice, and I'm supposed to know better. The problem is that you're up front on a sometimes slippery and rocking deck, you're leaning over, and you've got the weight of the anchor tipping you toward the water. One misstep or the rocking of a wave and you take a swim.

It's funny if it ends well, (funnier for those watching than for those falling over, I'd say, based on my experience) but there's a grave danger here—if your hands or feet get tangled in the anchor line, you will follow the anchor to the bottom.

Never stand on an anchor coil for this reason, and if you feel yourself falling, the first thing to do is get rid of the anchor. (Then hold your nose and try to look as graceful as possible as you make a complete fool of yourself.)

Anchoring in a Harbor

When anchoring in a harbor, it's important to allow enough "swing" space so that if the wind changes at 2 a.m., you won't be slamming into neighboring boats. The boat can travel in a circle, the radius of which is about the length of your anchor line, so allow plenty of space.

When Two Anchors Are Better Than One

When anchoring larger boats overnight, particularly in a crowded harbor, you may want to use two anchors at a 45-degree angle from the bow. The extra anchor keeps your boat from swinging widely and banging into other boats, and also gives you added security in a storm.

If space is really tight, you might go to a pair of anchors set at close to 180 degrees, with the boat suspended in the center. This keeps the boat from doing anything but swinging in a circle by the bow as the winds and tide change.

Boat Bytes
Sea Tow is one of several franchised nationwide commercial towing companies. The company has branches nationwide and can be reached via cellular phone as well as marine operators. Check your local phone directory for the number of a towing company and keep it in your wallet—you may need it in a hurry someday.

Putting out a second anchor is easiest to do with a small boat to run out the second anchor after the first is set, but if you don't have a dingy, two crewpeople handling lines from aboard the big boat can manage it.

You drop the first anchor, back away, then motor at an angle to the second anchor-drop and lower that one as crewperson number 1 pays out line. When both anchors are down, you back away, paying out line to give adequate scope and set them as described earlier.

Beaching It

The first thing many families want to do with their boats is to go "beaching"—visiting those enchanting, private beaches far from the crowds. But you can't simply slide a powerboat up on the sand like a canoe.

Well, you *can*, and many do through accident or ignorance, but then they have some unique problems in getting back afloat once again.

The best way of anchoring at a beach is bow to the seas. This presents the tallest part of the boat to the rolling seas, and also brings the swim platform usually found at the transom nearest to the beach.

Look Out!
Never approach a beach with a boat when the waves are much over a foot or so. (You never see people beaching on the open Atlantic or Pacific shores because waves are too tall.) It is doable many days in lakes, bays, and the calmer Gulf of Mexico in summer.

Before you drop the bow anchor, touch the bow in on the sand and let everybody hop out so they don't get their feet wet.

Drop the bow anchor well offshore and back down until the stern is within a few yards of the beach. In calm weather it can be within 10 feet. Remember to allow at least a 3:1 scope on your anchor line.

When the Anchor Goes Ashore

A second anchor from the stern keeps the boat from washing sideways when you anchor near a beach. It also prevents you from having to make a long swim if the wind changes and starts to blow offshore.

Don't put the stern anchor in the water—the wash of even a gentle surf will prevent it from holding. Walk it up on the shore about 30 feet and bury it in the sand. You can sometimes tie the rode to a tree or rock on shore.

This approach not only keeps waves and boat wakes out of the boat, but in tidal areas it ensures that you don't come back to a grounded boat as the water flows out from under it.

Grounding—On Purpose

On flat-calm rivers and lake beaches, when you're not going out of sight of the boat, you can simply ground the boat bow on, which keeps your prop well out in the water and hopefully not grounded. Put an anchor out from the stern so that the boat doesn't wash sideways and ground the prop, and tie a bow line to a tree ashore. On outboards and stern drives, you may want to tilt up the lower unit.

Look Out!
Never ground the boat on a full or falling tide, because the water will soon fall out from under it. This leaves the hull lying on its side like a beached whale— and about as easy to lift.

On a calm shore, it's possible to anchor bow to the beach temporarily. In rougher water or for a long stay, anchor bow to the water, and add a second anchor ashore from the stern. (Photo credit: Grady White Boats)

If You Lose Your Anchor

It happens. Somebody forgets to secure the bitter end of the anchor rode to a cleat and the first thing you know, anchor and line are deep-sixed, or even worse, deep-sixtied. Sometimes an anchor can't be broken loose from bottom. Sometimes the anchor line is cut by coral or wreckage.

Boater-ese
The *bitter end* is the end you hold when making a knot, or the tag end of any piece of line.

You can't just swim down to bottom, grab the anchor, and swim back up with it, not even if you're Mark Spitz. If you lost the whole shebang including the anchor line, one approach is to swim down, grab the loose end of the line—not the one with the anchor—and swim it back to the surface. A safer alternative is to take a light line down with you, tie that to the anchor line, and then hoist line and hook once you get back aboard.

Avoid losing your anchor by putting a foam crab-trap float on the bitter end of your anchor line. Secure it with a stopper knot like the figure-eight shown in the following figure (for more on knots, see Chapter 9). Then, when Cousin Ermal lets the whole thing go over the side, the float will save the day. (It's also handy when you have to cast off in a hurry to chase a tuna!)

The figure-eight knot is a quick and easy "stopper" knot, used to prevent a line from slipping out of a block or float.

Snagged Anchors

A snagged anchor may have to be retrieved by diving, too. But don't push your abilities. If the water is cold or deeper than 10 feet, it's usually better to leave it there and buy another. (A large, expensive yacht anchor can be marked by tying a large buoy to the anchor line, so that scuba divers can come back and retrieve it later.)

Breaking Free

Breaking free from mud is usually a simple matter of motoring uptide or upwind to a point well beyond the anchor, cleating off on an aft cleat, and then applying a little power. This "turns over" the flukes, pulling on them from the wrong direction, and the anchor pops free.

Anchors sometimes stick to whatever it is that made them grab bottom in the first place. This is particularly common over a rock bottom, and it also happens in harbors and commercial areas where cables and other snags cause problems.

The best way to avoid problems is to put a trip line on the base of the anchor, the crown. This is a lighter cord secured with light nylon tie-wraps that will break under stress and cause the trip line to pull from the crown instead of the top (see the following figure). This usually slides the hook free. The trip line is somewhat of a bother to handle, though, and isn't used except on a very snaggy bottom.

Look Out!
Be sure to keep the props well clear of the anchor line as you attempt to turn over the anchor.

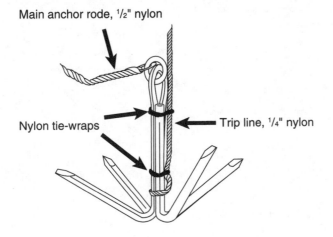

Main anchor rode, ½" nylon

Nylon tie-wraps

Trip line, ¼" nylon

Putting a trip line on the base of the anchor will help free the anchor from a muddy bottom.

If it doesn't, you may need to secure the anchor line to a transom lifting eye (not a cleat, because the cleat may pull out of the deck under heavy load), get well uptide of the spot where you dropped the anchor, and then apply increasing engine power until the hook pops free. The more line you let out, the better your chances of getting the anchor back.

The Least You Need to Know

➤ Anchors should be matched to the boat and the mission.

➤ The gear that attaches the anchor to the boat is as important as the anchor itself.

➤ Scope is as important as anchor design. The minimum scope is 3:1.

➤ Anchoring along a beach requires special precautions.

➤ The best way to avoid losing an anchor is to rig it correctly in advance; but even if you do lose an anchor, it can be retrieved.

Chapter 9

Nautical Knots

In This Chapter

➤ When a rope is not a rope

➤ Learning the ropes—types of line

➤ Caring for your line

➤ The most useful knots you'll need to know

Remember when you were in Boy (or Girl) Scouts and didn't pay attention while the scoutmaster was showing you how to tie the sheepshank? I didn't either. And you know what? I'm glad. I have never missed the ability to tie a sheepshank thus far in my life. I've never met anyone who said they have, either.

However, there are a lot of other knots that boaters use with some regularity. (Okay, there are some situations where you will find the sheepshank very useful, too.) In this chapter, you'll learn what ropes are, what sizes and types work best around a boat, and how to tie the most useful knots.

When a Rope Is Not a Rope—Nautical Cordage

First, let's take a look at what we tie. It's not rope—at least, not in the terminology of the sea. What we call "rope" ashore may be called cordage, line, rode, or sheet to salts, depending on how it's used.

"Cordage" is the term used to cover pretty much all the various ropes used on a boat, whether they're attached to the docks, the anchor, or used to hang out the laundry. In general, "line" is what you use to tie up the boat—dock lines, for example. Although we often think of line as string-sized ashore, it may be $5/8$-inch braid afloat. (This is not to be confused with fishing line, which is in fact called line.)

Boater-ese
Cordage is the general term used to refer to all the ropes, lines, anchor rodes, etc. used aboard a boat. *Line* is what's normally called "rope" ashore—it can be of any size and either twisted or braided. It's usually classified according to diameter, with a $1/4$-line being $1/4$-inch thick. A *rode* is a line attached to an anchor. *Sheets* are lines used to tension sails.

The rope used on the anchor is most often referred to as the "rode," although it's also called the anchor line in practical use. And "sheets" are not what go on your bed afloat, but the ropes used to control tension in the sails of a sailboat. In general, though, anything that would be called a rope ashore is referred to as a "line" on board.

The strength of a rope or line is most affected by the diameter of the finished product, and lines used in boating are designated by their diameter. For example, a $1/4$-inch line is about $1/4$-inch thick. The strength of a line increases by a factor of about 3.5 to 4 for every doubling of diameter. The breaking strength of a typical $1/4$-inch braided nylon line is around 1,500 pounds, while the breaking strength of most $1/2$-inch braided nylon is around 6,000 pounds. (Different rope materials also have different strengths at a given size.)

What Is Rope Made of?

To a landlubber, rope is rope—you go down to the discount store and buy whatever is handy and cheap. To a boater, the material and the way the line is built is important, even critical in some applications. Let's look at some of the most common rope materials.

Nylon—The Universal Soldier

Nylon is the preferred material for most boating uses, including for dock lines and anchor lines. The cost is reasonable—about 20 cents a foot for a $3/8$-inch line, up to 50 cents a foot for a $5/8$-inch line. Nylon is very durable, strong at a given diameter, and can withstand years in the sun.

Nylon also has a certain amount of stretch that acts as a shock-absorber, making it more forgiving as an anchor line or for use in towing another boat.

Polypropylene—Low in Price (But Also Low in Strength)

Polypropylene's only place aboard is to act as a clothesline for drying your swimsuit. It's not strong for its size, it frays easily, and it breaks down rapidly in direct sunlight. It's also a "hard" line, rough on the hands when used as anchor line.

However, it is in fact sometimes sold as very inexpensive anchor line. It's okay for jon boats used in a pond, but just doesn't have the qualities to be suitable for anchoring or tying up large boats.

One legitimate use of poly is as a ski-tow rope. Because it floats, it's much easier to pick up than nylon, which sinks and may foul your prop. It stretches more than nylon, too, so it's easier on the hands and shoulders. The price is the lowest of any man-made fiber, around 12 to 15 cents a foot for $3/8$-inch diameter.

Polyester and Dacron—The Higher-Priced Spreads

Polyester lines, not to be confused with polypropylene, are excellent for many boating uses. They're very strong, flexible, and resist abrasion well. They are expensive, however, with good $3/8$-inch going for over 50 cents a foot.

Dacron is a low-stretch line that is very strong, durable, and easy to handle, but also very expensive—up to 65 cents a foot for $3/8$-inch line. It's often used in sailboat rigging due to low stretch, but sees limited use aboard powerboats.

Sailors also use many more exotic materials, including Spectra-cored ropes encased in polyester weave that go for over $3 a foot in the larger diameters. These lines have no more give than a steel cable and wear practically forever, but their high cost limits their use for the most part to rigging aboard the larger offshore sailboats.

Hemp—The Natural Ropes

Smoke 'em if you must, but don't ever use 'em aboard your boat. Hemp ropes and other natural fibers are not strong to begin with compared to the synthetics, and the fact that they rot easily if they're not kept dry makes them obsolete for boaters, even though they're very inexpensive.

Twisted, Stirred, or Shaken?

"Laid" ropes are manufactured by twisting small strands together. There are usually three cord-sized strands in a typical marine line. Laid ropes are inexpensive, durable, and widely available.

"Braided" rope is woven from hundreds of small strands into a smooth, even finish that's easy on the hands and that runs through fittings without excess friction. They're also more flexible than laid ropes and less subject to kinking or fraying. Braided rope also comes in decorative colors, making it nice for dock lines. However, you can't splice braid as easily as you can laid rope, and it's about twice as costly as laid rope in the usual form.

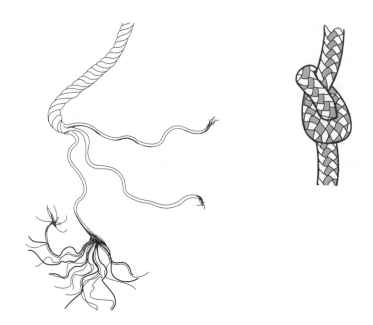

Twisted or laid rope (left) is made up of three strands of smaller material. It's inexpensive, strong, and easy to splice. Braided rope (right) has a smoother surface than twisted rope, making it easier on the hands, and is available in a variety of colors.

Size Counts

Line sizes should match the weight of the load they'll be expected to bear. Thus, you need bigger lines to tie up bigger boats. BOAT U.S., the nation's largest boating organization, suggests the following:

Boat Size	Line Size
20–30 feet	$3/8$-inch
30–40 feet	$5/8$-inch
Over 40 feet	$3/4$-inch

Note that a premium laid rope in the $5/8$-inch diameter has a breaking strength of 12,800 pounds, many times the strength it takes to hold even a 40-footer at the dock under normal conditions.

But you don't buy for the norm—you buy for the hurricane or for the day when a barge wake sends a three-foot swell into the harbor. The larger lines also maintain their strength many more years than smaller lines, so it pays to buy large.

For anchor lines, most experienced boaters use $3/8$-inch for boats up to about 25 feet, $1/2$-inch for boats 25 to 35 feet, $5/8$-inch for boats 35 to 50 feet, and $3/4$-inch for larger yachts.

However, many charterboat skippers rely on $5/8$-inch even for 20-foot boats. It's easier to handle, lasts forever, and doesn't tangle as readily as thinner diameters. On the downside,

$^5/_8$-inch is more than twice as expensive as $^3/_8$-inch for a given length, heavier, and takes more storage space. It also won't fit around the undersized cleats on smaller boats, although it works fine with larger (at least eight-inch) cleats.

Line Care

Nylon requires almost no care, which is what boaters love about it. Even with nylon, though, you'll improve its longevity if you wash off salt and sand with fresh water after each trip. Otherwise, the grit gets inside the weave, causing abrasion and eventually weakening the line.

Dry the line in the sun (this avoids mildew) and then store it in the shade inside your anchor box. Long-term exposure to sun gradually burns out even the best lines.

The Bitter End

When lines are cut, they leave unsightly ends that are subject to fraying. The standard method for treating this problem used to be "whipping"—wrapping or serving the end of the rope with small cord.

These days, there are better ways. If you buy nylon in a marine store, they'll probably cut it with an electric heating iron. The heat melts the nylon and instantly secures all strands. If not, you can do it yourself. A soldering iron will do the job neatly.

No soldering iron? If you're careful, you can use a cigarette lighter or a candle to burn the ends slightly until the nylon becomes liquid. As it cools, roll it between two pieces of 2 × 4 to make a rounded end. This gives a solid end on the line that will never unravel.

There are also commercial "whipping compounds" or rope dips that act as a glue. You dip the ends of the rope in them, let it dry, and it secures the strands. There's also a heat-sealing tape with which you wrap the end, then apply a flame, and the tape shrinks and seals to form a permanent whipping. This is quick, relatively safe, and forms a dependable bond—carry some aboard.

Boat Bytes
Avoid splashing the lines with bleach when you're washing down your boat—it will weaken the fibers. If the lines are soiled with fish offal or oil, put them in a five-gallon bucket, add some dish detergent and warm water (not hot!) and let them soak overnight, agitating now and then.

Look Out!
Be very careful when melting nylon. It is extremely hot, and if it drips on your skin, it will burn you badly! Also, remember that nylon ignites easily—the drips can start a fire. It's a job best done out of doors, and not aboard your boat.

Boat Bytes
When you have to cut a line and don't have other means of securing the ends, plain old duct tape will do the job temporarily. Just take three tight wraps around the line and presto, it's whipped.

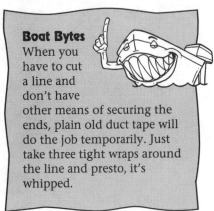

Coiling Lines

Take care of your lines every trip, and they'll take care of you when you need them.

The first rule is to never put a line away without coiling it. There's a little trick to this. You can't simply pick up some line and make a bunch of loops over your hand. It won't lie "fair" or flush, one coil exactly like the next, and this will lead to tangles when you use it.

The trick to getting it flat is to give the line a little half-twist, to the right or clockwise, each time you go over the hand holding the coil. Make the coils about 18 inches in diameter, a comfortable handling size in most lines. To prevent kinks, make the coils in a clockwise direction.

Braided line has less tendency to kink than laid line, and there's no need to impart the twist as you coil it. It will lay in a fairly regular loop or sometimes in a figure eight, but these run out without tangles.

Once you've got it all laid in, secure the coils by taking a turn counterclockwise around them with the bitter end (the end you hold while making a knot, or the tag or cut end of any piece of line). Then pass a short bight or bend through the loop, passing above the turn at the back side of the coils. Bring the bitter end up through this loop, draw it tight, and you've got the coil complete and ready to hang or stow. (Just be sure that anyone who wants to uncoil this line understands that first you pull the loop back over the top and unwrap the turns, or you'll have a mess!)

Proper coiling keeps a line tangle-free and ready for immediate use.

Handling the Anchor Line

Many boats have an anchor hanger in the box, and this should give you a tip about how the tackle goes in—first you put in all the line or rode, then the chain, then the anchor—not vice versa. This is so that everything comes out in the order you want it when you need it.

There's no need to coil the anchor line—just feed it in hand-over-hand and take it out the same way. Don't store other equipment on top of it because this leads to tangles.

On some boats, line is fed through a hawse pipe or fitting through the front deck into a rope compartment or locker.

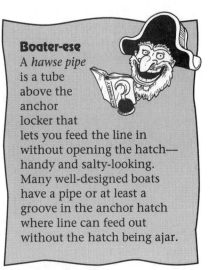

Boater-ese
A *hawse pipe* is a tube above the anchor locker that lets you feed the line in without opening the hatch—handy and salty-looking. Many well-designed boats have a pipe or at least a groove in the anchor hatch where line can feed out without the hatch being ajar.

Cleating Off

Cleats are two-horned monsters that will murder a bare toe, but they are a boater's best friend when the boat must be secured. Instead of tying a knot around the steering wheel or your mother-in-law, you simply make a few turns and a half-hitch over the horns of the cleat and the boat stays put. (A half-hitch is the most basic of knots—see "Getting Hitched" later in this chapter for details on how to tie it.) And, when you want to leave, the turns come off easily, unlike most types of knots.

First, you need rope that fits the cleats. A 5/8-inch line won't work on a four-inch cleat because it won't fit under the horns for more than a single turn. Quarter-inch line is adequate for tying up small boats under 16 feet long, while 3/8-inch line is a good choice for securing boats from 16 to 30 feet long.

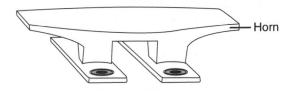
Horn

Cleats make for quick tie-ups. They're usually located at the bow and stern, with spring cleats sometimes added amidships. They're also found on most docks.

To cleat off, take a turn under the away side of the horn, completely around the base, make a figure eight by going over the top center and under each horn, and then finish off with a half hitch around one horn. The figure on the following page shows you how to do it.

127

Note that no knots other than a half-hitch to finish off are required to secure to a cleat.

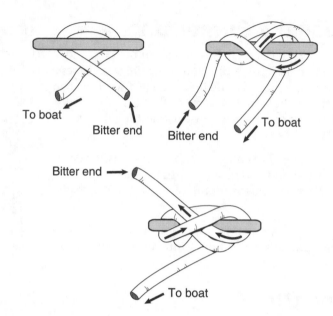

To boat

Bitter end

Bitter end

To boat

Bitter end →

To boat

You haven't really made a secure knot with this arrangement, but the friction of the line against the horn does the job so that there's no pressure against the half-hitch. It won't slip.

Boat Bytes
Always store the same lines in the same boxes. Be compulsive about this—put all the gear you use into the same boxes all the time. That way, in an emergency or hurry-up situation, you can quickly find what you need and it'll be ready to go.

It doesn't take 10 half-hitches to hold your boat. You can add a couple more turns around the base and a final half-hitch if you're leaving it for a long period—it will make you feel better, even if it doesn't hold the boat any better.

Coil any excess rope neatly on the dock as near the edge as possible, so it won't tangle with people's feet.

A neat coil of line next to the cleat is a mark of good seamanship. The easy way to make this coil is to start with the bitter end laid flat on the dock. Turn it clockwise to form a circular loop on the dock. Continue to turn it to pull in all the remaining line, right up to the cleat, forming a series of neat, concentric coils that won't tangle with the feet of passers-by (see the photo on the next page).

The circular coil is a neat way to handle the loose end of a dock line. It lies flat, doesn't tangle, and won't trip passers-by.

Knots You'll Use Most Often

There are dozens of knots that the salts and scoutmasters of the world would have you learn, but between surfing the Internet and figuring out how to program your VCR, you probably don't have time for all that stuff. It's better to learn only a couple knots really well so that you can tie them fast and flawlessly, even under the most challenging of conditions.

Here are four knots that you'll use most often while boating, plus a bonus knot for you anglers:

➤ Bowline

➤ Half-hitch

➤ Two half-hitches

➤ Clove hitch

➤ Uni-knot

I'll discuss each of these knots in the following sections.

The Ubiquitous Bowline

If you were to learn only one knot that could get you through many different situations, it might be the bowline. It's simple and fast to tie and can do a lot of things well. It's pronounced "bo-lin," by the way, as in "Bo knows sports," not "bow-line," even though that would seem to make more sense, nautically speaking.

The bowline is used to create a secure loop that can be dropped over a piling, its most common use. It can also be tied through a mooring ring, and two bowlines can be used to join a pair of lines. A running noose (which functions like a hangman's noose or choker) can be made by passing the free end of the line through the loop.

129

The bowline is easy and quick to tie. The loop makes it easy to secure a line to a piling.

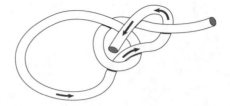

Basically, the classic method for tying the bowline is this, as taught by Scoutmaster Rex Morgan back in Jeromesville, Ohio: Rabbit comes out of hole, rabbit goes around the tree, rabbit goes back in the hole. The "rabbit" is the bitter end, the "hole" is a closed bight or loop, and the "tree" is the standing part of the line.

The only trick is to get the small loop with the free end on top of the standing part of the line. (If you put it beneath the standing part, the tree collapses and kills the rabbit; the knot simply refuses to tie.) Then, rabbit out of hole, around tree, and back into hole. Draw up both ends at once and you've got it.

Confused by the rabbit method? Here's a step-by-step guide for tying a bowline:

1. Make an overhand loop in the line about two feet from the bitter end.
2. Run the bitter end through the loop and around the standing part of the line, making a "working bight"—the larger main loop you'll drop over a piling.
3. Bring the bitter end back through the overhand loop.
4. Adjust the size of the working bight so it fits the piling.
5. Draw the knot tight by pulling on the standing part of the line and the bitter end.

There you have it—a perfect bowline.

Getting Hitched

The half-hitch is made by passing a loop around the standing line, the working part of the rope that runs from your knot to a cleat, piling, etc., usually after passing through a fitting or over a post. The finishing steps of the common shoelace tie is a half-hitch, but with the ends "slipped" or looped so that they can be drawn loose with a tug on the bitter ends.

A single half-hitch won't do much more than support the weight of the line itself, but it's the starting point of several other knots. Add a second half-hitch, making a knot uncleverly called "two half-hitches," and you've got a secure and very quick knot.

Two half-hitches tend to jam under strain, so you don't want to use the knot where you might have to untie it quickly, but it's a good knot for lines that are left in place, such as line that remains attached to the bow eye of a dingy.

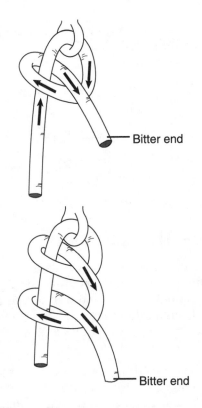

Bitter end

The half-hitch is the simplest of all knots, and is the beginning of many other knots.

Two half-hitches make a stout knot that won't slip and that can be tied by anyone quickly.

Bitter end

You can keep a half-hitch, or any other knot, from jamming by making several round turns around the piling or eye you're tying to before starting the knot. Friction will keep pressure off the knot and prevent it from jamming.

Clove Hitch

The clove hitch is used to tie up to dock pilings when you're not staying long, as for a waterside dinner. It's basically a couple of loops tossed together and is very easy to tie and untie.

Start by making the first loop over the piling so that the standing line passes over the top of the running line. Then, make a second loop around the piling so that the bitter end passes under the running line. Pull on both ends and the hitch snugs down.

You can convert this into a permanent knot for dock lines left in place at your slip by adding two

Look Out!
A clove hitch tied where pressure is not constant on both ends is likely to slip and fall down the piling, and maybe even come untied com- pletely. Tie it so that there's pressure on both ends, or secure it with a half-hitch to make it more dependable.

131

half-hitches over the standing line. Since the clove hitch bears all the strain, the half-hitches won't jam, but they secure everything.

The clove hitch is a good temporary tie-up to a piling, but may slip down the pole if there's no strain on the lines.

One Knot That Fits All—The Uni-Knot

This is a knot originally invented for the slick monofilament used in fishing line, and it won't work with large, rough ropes. It's sometimes useful in light rope, especially if started with a round turn so that it doesn't take extreme loads and thus doesn't jam. Its most important use, though, is for anglers. It's quick and retains almost 100 percent of the line strength.

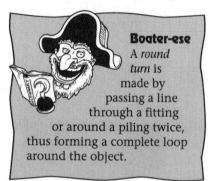

Boater-ese
A *round turn* is made by passing a line through a fitting or around a piling twice, thus forming a complete loop around the object.

The nice thing about the uni is that it's an all-purpose knot, good for tying on a lure, tying a leader to running line, or tying two equal-sized lines together. Learn this one and you won't have to worry about most of the other fishing knots.

Basically, you make a loop so that the end overlaps the running part of the line about six inches, make five turns through the loop, then pull the tag end tight to jam the wraps. Pull on the standing line and the loop closes to form the knot.

To use the uni to tie on a leader, make a loop in the running line overlapping the leader, and a second in the leader overlapping the running line, and then tie the knots. Draw them down, clip off the tag ends close, and you're done.

The Least You Need to Know

➤ Nylon is the most commonly used material for anchor and dock lines.

➤ Line diameters must be matched to load, determined mostly by boat length.

➤ Don't ignore basic line care to keep your lines in good condition and ready when needed.

➤ Learn a few knots well, so that you can tie them in a hurry under stress.

Chapter 10

Paddle Power:
Canoes, Kayaks,
and Rowboats

In This Chapter

➤ Paddling your own canoe

➤ The kayaker's art

➤ Plain and simple: Rowboats

Sometimes, simpler really is better.

In boating, it doesn't get any simpler than a boat that boasts neither motor nor sail. Canoes, kayaks, and rowboats offer a blessed simplicity that requires very little initial investment, almost zero maintenance, no fuel costs, no rigging problems, and no need for a trailer or a slip.

These feather-light, timeless boats hark back to man's first ventures on the water, but right now paddle power is at a modern high in popularity, offering communion with nature as well as a great workout. They produce no air pollution whatsoever, no noise, and last practically forever when built of modern materials—many canoes and rowboats last through several generations of paddlers.

In this chapter, you'll learn how to paddle and steer canoes and kayaks, how to handle a basic rowboat, and a bit about what these boats can and can't do on the water.

I Can—Canoe?

The dugout log was the first canoe. Easy to make (if you don't mind a lot of chopping), incredibly strong, and durable, 400-year-old cypress-log canoes have been dug out of the Florida mud still in near-perfect shape. The problem? They weighed about as much as a tree.

That's why more recent Native Americans turned to wood frames covered with birch bark or animal skins. The strength was still good, the capacity great, but the weight became minimal—a critical factor in a day when there was no such thing as a boat trailer or a fork lift to launch and retrieve your favorite watercraft.

In the 1800s, the first canvas-covered, wood-frame canoes came along. Since around 1950, modern materials—including aluminum, fiberglass, and an assortment of composite plastics—have taken over the market.

Bet You Didn't Know

Old Town Canoe of Old Town, Maine, was among the first mass producers of canoes, with the company building wood and canvas models in 1898 in a hardware store. Old Town began producing fiberglass canoes in 1965 and molded plastics in the early 1970s. Old Town canoes are now sold throughout the U.S. and in 18 other nations.

Modern canoes combine light weight with easy paddling, amazing toughness, longevity, and excellent load capacity.

Canoes come in a great variety of designs, some made for all-around recreational paddling and fishing, others for long-distance voyages while heavily loaded, still others for taking on the twists and turns of white water in boiling mountain rivers.

Modern canoes like this one from Coleman are molded from flexible plastics that bounce off rocks with ease, yet are light enough for easy handling solo. (Photo credit: Coleman Marine)

Weighty Subject

When it comes to portability, some canoes are amazingly easy to shoulder. One-person models such as the Pack Canoe from Old Town weigh just 33 pounds, yet are rated to carry a total of 400 pounds.

Move up to larger, deeper family models in the 17-foot range and capacity goes to over a half-ton, yet the hulls weigh less than 75 pounds. And larger cargo models designed for extended back-country voyages are rated to carry more than many medium-sized powerboats, with some 20-footers rated for as much as 1,700 pounds, yet weighing just over 100 pounds.

Getting a canoe up on your shoulders without injuring your back takes care. Although these boats are not all that heavy, they're awkwardly shaped, making for difficult lifts.

The best tactic for single carries of a small canoe is to lift up the bow, walk back to the center as you hand over hand the gunnels, and then let the boat settle on your shoulders with the amidships thwart or yoke

Boat Bytes
How much boat can you load on top of your car or carry over a portage? It depends on your physical condition, of course, but most male/female teams have no problem with canoes weighing up to 75 pounds. For singles, you won't be happy balancing much over 50 pounds on your shoulders, less if you're small-framed. Of course, for young athletic pairs who don't yet have a personal chiropractor, big, stout boats of 80 to 100 pounds can be handled.

135

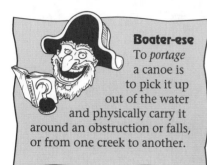

Boater-ese
To *portage* a canoe is to pick it up out of the water and physically carry it around an obstruction or falls, or from one creek to another.

Portaging or carrying a canoe is easy for two adults. Lift with your legs to avoid back strain. (Photo credit: Mad River Canoes)

across the back of your neck and shoulders. Rock the forward end upward a bit so that you can see where you're going, and don't try turning any sharp corners next to trees!

Smaller canoes can simply be boosted up on the thighs, gripped by the thwart, and hoisted to the shoulder. With two carriers, it's usually best to work from the outside with the hull upright; both portagers squat amidships, grip the yoke or gunnels, and stand up together, lifting with the legs rather than the back.

Shaped Up

The most common canoe shape features an upswept bow and stern, with relatively low freeboard amidships. This keeps both meeting and following waves from slopping into the hull, and the sharpened ends of the boat slice through waves cleanly. A flat aft section like that in a rowboat can be caught by a wave or fast-moving river to throw the boat sideways, but the sharpened stern of a canoe avoids this fate.

Canoes come in a variety of designs, with the lowest, smallest, and lightest designed for easier carrying and better performance but less load and less stability.

Boat Bytes
Some canoes are "square-enders," with a flat stern or transom where a small electric motor or gasoline outboard can be mounted. This makes them less suitable for paddling, particularly in fast water, but does greatly increase their range, the distance that can be covered in a given amount of time. Double-ender canoes can be fitted with a side-mount for a small outboard, as well.

Longer, heavier, and deeper canoes can carry huge loads, but they require more paddle power to move and more muscle to lift to the roof of a vehicle or over a downed log. (With canoes, the greater the load, the more stable the hull becomes, up to the point where it sits low enough in the water to "ship" a wave—to allow water to slop over the gunnels.)

The Appeal of the Keel

The *keel line* is an imaginary line down the longitudinal center of a canoe's bottom. The keel-line design greatly affects canoe performance. Canoes that have a flat or straight keel line from bow to stern are designed for the best *tracking*, which is the tendency of a canoe to continue in a straight line without added steering by the paddlers. These canoes also require fewer steering strokes, so they are the preferred version for flat-water canoeists.

Although we speak of the keel line in canoes, many have no obvious keel showing on the outside—the bottom is most often smooth, either flat or rounded. External keels are used on some boats to assist in tracking, but there are more without than with.

Canoes that have "rocker" in the keel, a curve upward at the bow and stern so that the boat actually can be rocked when placed on flat ground, are designed for easier turning, needed for white-water use. These boats don't track well, so they're not favored by casual paddlers who use their canoes for wildlife watching, fishing, or general voyaging on lakes and ponds. Most recreational or family canoes have just a bit of rocker, making turning reasonably easy without sacrificing tracking.

Boater-ese
Most canoes do not have visible keels, but designers speak of the keel line when they refer to some design features such as *rocker*, which is the curve of the keel line from bow to stern. A canoe that has a flat bottom from bow to stern has no rocker and tends to travel in a straight line easily. One with a rockered keel line turns easily, but does not travel in a straight line well.

Is Wider Really Better?

In general, wide or beamy canoes are slow but stable and capable of carrying heavy loads. Narrower canoes are easier to paddle and faster, but less stable and have lower load capacities.

An unusual measure of width is often applied to canoes, the "width at four-inch water-line." This is a measurement of the beam of a canoe measured with the boat in the water and loaded so that the lowest point of the bottom is four inches below the surface. This measurement gives a better idea of how the canoe will perform than the width measured at the gunnels. The measure is usually an inch or two less than the gunnel width for touring and white-water hulls, as little as a half-inch for general-purpose models.

Typical family canoes are 36 to 40 inches wide at the gunnels. Performance or white-water models are usually 34 to 36 inches wide at the gunnels, and solo pack models as narrow as 31 inches.

Hulls that are considerably wider at the gunnels than at the four-inch waterline are said to have flare, which helps knock down spray and also helps right the hull should it tip very far to one side. Most family models are flared.

The sides of some canoes curve inward from waterline to gunnels, which makes it easier to reach into the water with a paddle, particularly for those with short arms. This inward curvature is called *tumblehome*. Canoes with lots of tumblehome can be a bit more tippy than those with lots of *flare*, which is the outward curvature of a boat's sides from waterline to gunnels or topsides, usually most acute near the bow. They also don't knock down spray as well, so they may be a bit wetter for the occupants. Many family canoes have straight sides, which make them reasonably easy to paddle yet less tippy than those with narrower beam at the gunnels.

Tippicanoe? Maintaining Stability in Canoes

Canoes have an unfortunate—but accurate—reputation of being "tippy" compared to other boats. Because they're light in weight and many have a rounded bottom, they tend to roll easily when the center of gravity is elevated, as it is when you stand up in the boat.

And since there's very little weight to counterbalance any tilt of the center of gravity, it's easy to wind up swimming when you board a canoe or when you stand up in one.

Capsizing is not common in recreational canoes used in flat water, but it can happen. It's a good idea to wear PFDs and stow anything that would be damaged by water, such as cameras and wallets, in watertight, air-filled bags, just in case.

Canoes have remarkable load capacity, and actually become more stable with heavier loads positioned low in the hull. This makes them ideal for wilderness camping trips. (Photo credit: Coleman Marine)

Here are some tips for keeping yourself dry and your canoe right side up:

➤ When boarding, keep your weight on your shoreward leg until your leading foot is fixed in the center of the boat's beam.

➤ Board directly into the paddling position. For example, if you'll be paddling from the aft seat, step in where you can sit down in that seat without any added movement.

➤ Grip the center of a thwart to steady the boat as you step in and sit down immediately.

➤ Once you're in the canoe, keep your center of gravity low—avoid standing.

➤ Keep passengers centered relative to the beam.

➤ Add cargo weight for increased stability.

➤ Balance the load fore and aft when possible.

Different Strokes for Different Folks

As any beginning paddler soon learns, there are some tricks to paddling a canoe.

With two paddlers aboard, one in the forward seat and one aft, it's not difficult—one paddles on each side, pulling as near straight back as possible. If the strokes are about equal in power, the boat goes straight. The stern paddler controls direction by dipping his paddle as needed and using it as a rudder, or by using the J-stroke, which we'll look at in a moment.

Paddling solo is more challenging. If you paddle straight ahead on the starboard side from the aft seat, the usual position for a right-handed paddler, the boat persistently turns to port and you go around in a never-ending circle.

The beginner's first response is to keep switching sides with the paddle. It works, but it's slow and wet. Once you become a more experienced paddler, you'll learn a better way: the J-stroke, which alternately pushes then pulls on the stern and hopefully keeps the bow going fairly straight. All while you keep paddling on your "strong" side of the hull.

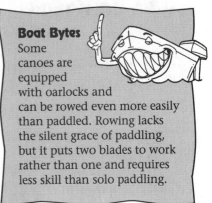

Boat Bytes
What size canoe paddle do you need? A good choice for all-around paddling is one that's about chin height. Choose a paddle with an aluminum shaft and plastic blade for starting out—it's inexpensive and durable.

Boat Bytes
Some canoes are equipped with oarlocks and can be rowed even more easily than paddled. Rowing lacks the silent grace of paddling, but it puts two blades to work rather than one and requires less skill than solo paddling.

Boater-ese
The *J-stroke* is a paddling stroke that roughly follows the outline of the letter J if viewed from directly overhead. It's used most often by the stern paddler to keep a canoe going straight.

Here's how to do it:

1. Start with a conventional stroke from well forward, but as you come back even with your hip, turn the blade by twisting your upper hand (the left, for those paddling on the right) 90 degrees. Now, the blade is running sideways through the water like a rudder.

2. Bring the shaft of the paddle against the side of the canoe, pull in slightly on the handle, and lever the blade out a bit. (If you want to keep things quieter, use your blade hand as the fulcrum to push the blade outward.) This causes the stern of the boat to move to the left, which brings the bow back to the right and in line with your direction of travel.

It's a matter of adjusting the force applied on the "J" part of the stroke to keep the hull traveling straight. It's easy with a bit of practice.

Keen on Kayaks

Kayaks were the invention of the Inuit peoples (formerly called "Eskimos") of the Arctic. They were hunting boats; frames made of wood or bone with animal skins stretched over them. They were light and tough—but not so light and tough as modern composite plastic and Kevlar versions.

Kayaks differ from canoes primarily in that the top is closed over in most, helping to keep water out. Consequently, bow and stern do not have to be upswept as in a canoe, and wind resistance is lessened as a result. Most kayaks are designed for one person only, although a few, such as the Pamlico series from Wilderness Systems, can handle two people.

Kayaks are narrower than canoes, usually designed for only one person, and feature a closed deck rather than an open hull. They're designed to be paddled with a two-bladed paddle. (Photo credit: Wilderness Systems)

Kayaks tend to be narrower in the beam than canoes, and are designed for double-bladed paddles that dip on both sides, rather than the single-blade used on one side as in the canoe. Kayaks have less load capacity than canoes, typically half as much at a given length.

Because the paddler sits low in the water, they tend to be more stable at a given beam width. (Narrow touring kayaks can be tippy, however!)

Typical general-purpose kayaks measure about 28 to 32 inches wide, while touring models are 22 to 24 inches wide. As with canoes, wider models are more stable and carry greater loads, but are slower and harder to paddle.

Serious kayakers also are concerned with volume, the amount of space enclosed by the entire outer hull of the kayak, which affects its buoyancy. A high-volume kayak floats like a ping-pong ball and is the preferred boat for beginners learning white-water tactics as well as for straight-line white-water racers. Low-volume models, which look almost like javelins, are the choice of the most skilled of slalom racers and trick paddlers, but are far too tippy for amateurs.

> **Boater-ese**
> *Volume*, as it's applied to kayaks, refers to the total area enclosed by the outer hull. It's a way of measuring the buoyancy of one kayak design against another.

Open or Shut Case?

Open kayaks allow the paddler to sit in a small compartment or cockpit with legs and feet exposed and provide more readily accessible space for gear.

Closed kayaks have only a "manhole" in the center for the kayaker to fit into. Feet and legs are under the closed-bow deck, and in rough water it's common to attach a "skirt" that fits snugly around the paddler's chest and snaps to the edges of the manhole, sealing out water. The paddler in effect "wears" the boat.

Adjustable foot pads form a place to brace for maneuvering the boat, and a seat with a backrest allows comfortable all-day paddling.

Storage is in separate compartments under the bow and stern decks, plus whatever you can strap down on top. There's not a lot of space below decks for storage because much of it is filled with flotation materials.

Small molded-plastic kayaks, from nine to 12 feet long, are great car-toppers thanks to weights under 50 pounds, and are also favored by wildlife photographers who like to slip silently into weedy marshes where larger boats can't pass. The smaller models are also the choice for white water or for taking on the surf because they turn quickly.

Kayaks that are 12 to 14 feet long are the usual choice for general recreational paddling, fishing, and wildlife watching. Some of the open models have enough space to bring along a child or a dog in the cockpit, and weights of no more than 60 pounds make them easy to handle.

Sea-touring kayaks are 16 to 18 feet long and usually include a rudder so that the paddler can adjust for side winds and currents. Paradoxically, the greater length of these boats actually makes them easier to paddle—as with all displacement boats, the longer the waterline length, the faster they can go.

Kayaks of this size are easy to transport and easy to portage over obstacles. This model has an open deck, allowing for easier storage of fishing gear. (Photo credit: Wilderness Systems)

Kayak Handling

Kayaks are paddled about like free-style swimmers swim—left-right-left-right. This keeps you going straight as long as there's no wind or current to push you sideways, and as long as you put the same force and depth into strokes on each side.

Boat Bytes
It's possible to pull most kayaks sideways (tougher with the longer sea-touring models). You do this by leaning to one side, tilting the paddle overhead to that side, and reaching out with the bottom blade as far as possible to draw the boat in that direction. It's handy for getting close to a dock or getting away from an overhanging bank.

When the boat starts to veer off to one side, you simply paddle a few extra strokes or harder strokes on that side to bring it back to dead ahead.

The kayak paddle can also be used as a rudder to turn or straighten the boat once it's underway. This is done by dipping the paddle deep into the water on the side toward which you want to turn, and then levering it outward slightly. Keep the pressure on as long as you want to continue the turn, then go back to the standard alternating strokes.

If you want to make a sharp turn, it's better to use power strokes—starting all the way forward, sweeping the paddle fully submerged but out as far from the hull as you can reach and bringing it all the way to the hull behind you, followed by a second stroke on the opposite side that reverses the stroke direction, starting aft and sweeping forward. This pushes on one side and pulls on the other, and causes the boat to spin in its own length, much like putting one motor in forward and the other in reverse on a twin-engined powerboat.

The boat can be stopped by simply reversing with the alternating strokes, pushing forward instead of pulling backwards.

Skirting a Spill: Recovery Strokes

In both canoes and kayaks, it's possible to turn the agony of defeat into the joy of victory with recovery strokes designed to pull a tipping boat back from the edge of disaster. The idea is to stop the tipping action by bracing the boat against the paddle blade on the surface of the water.

As the boat tips, you reach far out to the side with the blade held flat to the surface and push down, very hard, to bring the hull back upright. This pushes the blade into the water, so you have to turn it at 90 degrees to bring it back to the surface without counter-acting your push.

In kayaks, you can help the recovery by swiveling your hips to bring the boat back under you.

Boater-ese

A *recovery stroke* is a stroke made to prevent the kayak from overturning, or to right it once it has turned over.

These steps are also part of a remarkable maneuver known as the "Eskimo roll," in which a kayak turned completely upside down pops back upright. Because your legs are enclosed in "manhole"-type kayaks, you don't fall out when the boat rolls over, but you're suspended upside down. If you don't do something quick, you're going to be breathing water!

The Eskimo roll is not a skill learned easily from a book—you'll probably want local hands-on instruction and a helper to stand by while you learn how to handle being upside down under water. With practice, it does get easier.

Row, Row, Row Your Boat

Rowing differs from paddling in that the paddles of a rowboat—the "oars"—are secured in oarlocks. This creates a lever, making it easier to apply the force needed to move the boat. This is why many rowboats can be both wider and heavier than canoes and kayaks. Most rowboats except sculls also have square sterns, so that they can be operated with electrical or gasoline motors as well.

Rowboats used to be planked or plywood, and a few custom builders still lovingly put together such collector's items. But the most common material in rowboats today is aluminum.

Although rowboats are larger and heavier than canoes and kayaks, many aluminum models are light enough to be car-topped. (Photo credit: Lund Boats)

Who Needs a Rowboat?

You do, if you want to take a family of four or five for a trip via muscle power. Canoes and kayaks don't have space for this many people, but rowboats usually have at least three bench seats where a number of passengers can sit in comfort. Be sure to check the capacity plate so that you don't overload, though. It's mounted on the console or transom by the manufacturer and lists the safe load capacity for the boat.

Boater-ese
Rowboats made with a blunt bow and a flat bottom are known as *jon boats*. Rowboats made with a tapered bow and slight vee bottom are known as *utility boats*. Both jon boats and utility boats have flat transoms and can be powered by outboards as well as rowed.

Rowboats are also a favorite of anglers because of their great stability—they allow you to stand up to cast and to survey the water for fish, something that's pretty tricky in most canoes and kayaks.

Rowboats are also better suited for motors than other boats that are regularly moved by muscle power. Most can handle kickers of five to 10 horses, and many can even plane with adequate power, giving a fast ride home when you're done rowing around to sneak up on the fish or photograph the wildlife.

Handling Basics

Most rowing is done facing aft, which gives the back muscles and legs a chance to do the work. Rowing facing forward forces the arms to do the work, and they soon tire.

Beginning rowers often find that they have a problem keeping the boat going straight as they try to look over their shoulder to steer, but experienced rowers learn to watch their wake and keep it straight, ensuring that the boat goes straight ahead. (You still have to look over your shoulder now and then to be sure you're not approaching another boat—or a waterfall!)

There's not much to know about rowing a rowboat—when facing aft, pull on the port oar grip and the boat goes to starboard, pull on the starboard oar grip and it goes to port, push both grips aft and the boat goes backwards. Raising the oars between strokes is the only motion that takes any practice—beginners frequently dip water on the backstroke, ruining their rhythm and sometimes splashing aft passengers.

The tricks of rowing a racing scull, a white-water raft, or other specialty rowing rigs are less self-evident. It takes instruction beyond the scope of this book plus practice to bring out the potential of these rigs. Most dealers who sell them will provide you with books, videotapes, or hands-on instruction.

The Least You Need to Know

➤ Paddle-power designs should be chosen depending on their intended use.

➤ Learn the basic strokes and you'll find paddling a canoe simple.

➤ Kayaks are probably the easiest of all boats to propel, but they don't have the load capacity or passenger space of canoes.

➤ Understanding a few basic strokes makes propelling and steering both canoes and kayaks simple.

➤ Rowboats require more muscle power to move than canoes or kayaks, but offer greater stability and space.

Part 3
Getting From Point A to Point B: Marine Navigation

You don't know the players without a program, and you don't know the waters without a chart! In this part, we'll take a look at where to find charts and how to get the most out of them.

You'll also learn how to apply what you see on the chart to the markers and buoys you see out there on the water ahead, and we'll explore the basics of using compasses and electronics to "find yourself."

And when you feel you're ready for that first long cruise, turn to this section for a chapter on how to go about it.

Chapter 11

Nautical Road Maps: Marine Charts

In This Chapter

➤ Nautical charts: Don't leave shore without them

➤ The colors in charts are not just for decoration

➤ What you don't know about navigation can hurt you

➤ The lowdown on latitude and longitude

➤ Scales are not only for fish—distance measurements

In boating there are no corner filling stations where you can stop and ask for directions (or refuse to, if you're like some people). Either you know where you are or you have problems. Maintaining a good sense of where you are on the water is called *navigating*.

There are several ways to avoid getting lost afloat. The first is simply never to go out of sight of the boat ramp, although this considerably limits your boating opportunities. But if you hope for broader horizons, a bit of navigating may be called for. Navigating starts with a nautical road map called a *chart*—a map of the water that shows depth and navigational details.

In this chapter, you'll learn where to buy nautical charts and how to use them, as well as the basics of latitude and longitude, the imaginary lines that help boaters navigate.

The Art of the Chart

Charts show the shape of the waterway, and just as importantly, the depth. Boaters view depth as aviators view altitude—if you have plenty of either, your craft will not have problems from colliding with the earth. (These collisions tend to be less serious in boating than in flying, fortunately, but they're still to be avoided.)

A navigational chart can cover any area ranging from a single harbor to an entire ocean, but all show the same basic information:

➤ Water depth

➤ Shape of any land masses

➤ Location and description of navigational markers

➤ Latitude and longitude lines

Some privately produced charts offer additional information, including location of launching ramps, good fishing spots, artificial reefs, and so on, but these too include the basic data on depth and geographic locations.

Thus, no wise boater will ever take on anything more than a pond he or she can see across without looking over a chart first. On the chart, the hazards are all marked, the safe passages are clear, the navigation markers and shoreline landmarks all obvious. All you have to do is figure out how to translate what's on the chart to what you see from the wheel and follow the safe water. It sounds easy and it should be.

So why do highly paid professional skippers still run ships aground on occasion? Hard to say, but if they do it, you might do it. Learn the art of the chart and keep it in mind any time you're underway and you'll have few problems.

Charts Are Where You Find 'Em

Charts are produced by the U.S. National Oceanic and Atmospheric Administration—NOAA, which everybody pronounces "Noah." The government produces the charts because nobody else can afford the time, money, or manpower to survey the world's oceans. But they are plagiarized, legally, by everybody who can think of a profitable use for them, including me—I've written two books of fishing maps.

You can get the official charts from NOAA at Distribution Division, N/ACC3, Riverdale, MD 20743-1199, (301) 436-6990. Local stores listed under "maps" in your telephone directory also carry charts in coastal areas, as do marinas and outdoor stores.

Charts used to be dirt cheap, but then the government figured out that they were operating at a loss, so they started charging more. They're about $14 each at present.

The Profit Motive—Commercial Charts

When NOAA raised prices, they opened the door for privately produced commercial charts, allowing competitive pricing. Now there are private charts based on the NOAA charts that are actually better than the originals because they include two charts on one piece of paper—one on the front, one on the back.

Some add lots of specialized information especially for recreational boaters and anglers. And some of the private versions are printed on waterproof paper and include neat stuff like the location of a good fishing reef, which the government charts don't.

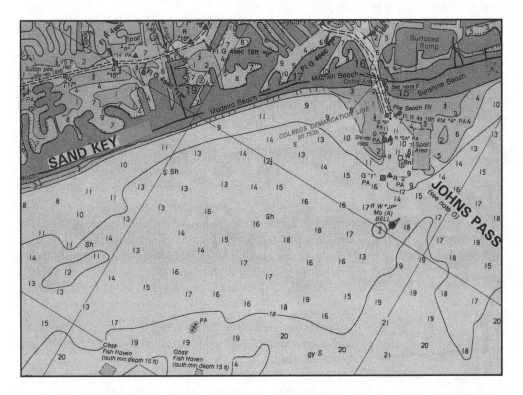

This chart section from International Sailing Supply indicates boat ramps and other data of use to recreational boaters, usually not found on government charts. (Photo credit: International Sailing Supply)

International Sailing Supply, 320 Cross Street, Punta Gorda, FL 33950, (941) 639-7626 is a great source, and their charts are printed on a paper so tough that you can hardly tear it if you try. (Do not say this to a six-year-old stoned on Slurpees, or he will prove you wrong.) The charts are $18.95 to $21.95 for two-siders. The company also offers collections of charts on CD-ROM, very handy for those who carry lap-top computers aboard. The price is around $100 per region.

By the Book

If you go boating in a lot of different areas, you might invest in a *Chart Kit*, an 18 × 24-inch spiral-bound book from Better Boating Association, Box 407, Needham, MA 02192, (800) 225-8317. These books offer up to 80 pages of large-scale charts and are super-useful for planning cruises and fishing trips outside your home waters.

They also indicate local boat ramps, compass courses between popular destinations, and mileages. You'll pay $60 to $100 for one of these books, but they're a real bargain if you use a lot of different charts, and the chart books are a more convenient size to use and stow than the loose government charts.

One book covers Florida's east coast and the Keys, one Florida's west coast and the rest of the U.S. portion of the Gulf of Mexico, one the entire Bahamas, and so on.

Whether you buy government or private charts, it's wise to invest in the official "Chart #1" from NOAA, because it's the key to all the markings and symbols on all other charts. It's an education in itself, opening the wealth of information the chart series provides—get it and use it.

It Was Deep Enough Yesterday

The charts show the depth at "mean low water" (MLW), which is the average low tide at the indicated spot.

Note that the average low tide is not necessarily as shallow as it gets in that particular spot. Maximum "spring" tides may subtract several feet of water from the depth, as can strong winds blowing seaward. And areas that might be too shallow for your draft on low water might be fine on high tide. Use the chart in conjunction with the tide tables to be safe. (Many marinas and bait shops offer free weekly tide cards for their local waters.)

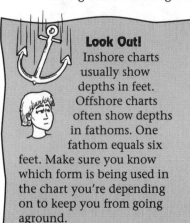

Look Out!
Inshore charts usually show depths in feet. Offshore charts often show depths in fathoms. One fathom equals six feet. Make sure you know which form is being used in the chart you're depending on to keep you from going aground.

By the way, depth-indication or "hydrography," as the chartmakers call it, is not necessarily updated regularly in areas where commercial ocean traffic never travels. Thus, some of the shallow areas that are very attractive to boaters and anglers may display depths that were last ground-truthed—by sending in a boat with a depth finder or sounding lead—50 years ago.

So always take chart depths with a grain of salt, so to speak. This is particularly true around all inlets, where depths can change due to storm waves and currents from day to day, let alone year to year.

The Color of Water

Charts are printed in color, not to make them pretty as wall-hangings in your beach house (although many wind up that way) but to convey navigational information. Here's what the colors mean:

➤ *White:* Water deeper than three fathoms (18 feet), safe for navigating most any recreational boat.

➤ *Light blue:* Water deeper than one fathom but not more than three fathoms. Still safe for anything but large yachts or keeled sailboats.

➤ *Medium blue:* Water one fathom or less, potentially dangerous for larger recreational boats.

➤ *Light greenish-tan:* Shoals that sometimes uncover at low tide—good for fishing, bad for boating.

➤ *Light tan:* Sandbars and oyster bars that go dry at low tide—very dangerous spots if you're not an oyster or a crab. (Also used in Florida for low-lying coastal land currently inhabited by lots of people, but that will be inhabited by fish after the next major hurricane.)

➤ *Medium tan:* High, dry land, terra firma, where your boat will be if you don't keep a sharp watch on the chart and the horizon.

➤ *Magenta:* Navigational information—danger zones and markers. Red navigational markers are designated in magenta on the chart.

➤ *Dark green:* Green navigational markers.

Buoy, oh Buoy

Navigational aids and buoys are numbered on the charts, just as they are out there in reality. The channel marker numbering system begins at 1 at the most seaward marker of each channel and goes up as you head toward the harbor. In long channels, the numbers may exceed three figures by the time you get to port. Odd numbers always go on the port side, even numbers on the starboard side, as you head inland.

By comparing the buoy numbers with those on the chart, you can tell exactly where you are in the channel without the help of any electronic navigation device. They're like the street names on a landside map.

Navigation by Degree

Along the edges of the chart are marked the *latitude* lines (on the left and right) and *longitude* lines (on the top and bottom). The intersections of these lines make it possible to give a number coordinate for every point on the earth on both land and sea, and thus anyone in any nation can understand the system.

There's also a scale of miles along the top and/or bottom of the chart, but the scale is in nautical miles, which are slightly different from the statute miles (5,280 feet) measured by your car's odometer.

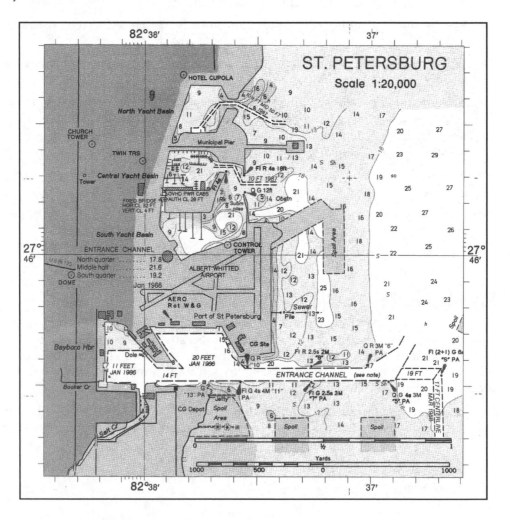

This large-scale harbor chart shows details that would be omitted on a small-scale coastal chart. Note the mileage scale at the bottom and the latitude/longitude indications along the edges.

Bet You Didn't Know

Why can't a nautical mile be the same thing as a good old U.S. land mile? Because the world's oceans touch nations around the globe, and many of them have different measures for their land miles. The nautical mile is an agreed-upon international distance recognized by everyone for marine navigation worldwide. Here are some numbers you might want to know:

➤ The earth is divided into 360 degrees of longitude, with the lines running north to south.

➤ The earth is divided into two halves, east longitude and west longitude.

➤ The earth is divided into degrees of latitude, with the lines running around the globe east and west.

➤ Each degree is subdivided into 60 minutes.

➤ Each minute is subdivided into 60 seconds.

➤ A nautical mile is one minute of latitude.

➤ A nautical mile is 6,080 feet.

➤ A nautical mile is 1.15 U.S. statute miles.

➤ A statute mile is about 0.87 nautical mile.

So when an old salt tells you his boat will go 40 knots, he will take affront if you tell him your boat is faster because it runs 45 mph. Forty knots × 1.15 is 46 statute mph, therefore his boat is faster.

Longitude Lines Are Long-Ways

Didn't pay attention when your teacher went over latitude and longitude in ninth-grade science, did you? Okay, me neither—I was checking out Andrea Horowitz's mini-skirt, which is why I had to learn navigation later. Here are the basics, one more time.

Longitude lines (meridians of longitude, the experts say) are imaginary lines running from the north pole to the south pole. The zero longitude line (the "Prime Meridian") arbitrarily runs through Greenwich, England. (Guess who made up the system?) From there, meridians or imaginary lines from pole to pole mark off the degrees east or west of the line.

The International Date Line

Yes, it's true that the "International Date Line" is a great name for a pickup bar in Switzerland. However, that's not what we're talking about here.

The numbers on longitude lines go up to 180 degrees in each direction. They meet at the International Date Line, which runs through the mid-Pacific.

Traveling west, every 15 degrees of longitude lengthens the day by one hour, while traveling east the same amount shortens the day by one hour, which is why there are different time zones world wide. Where the zones meet, east of the line is designated as one day earlier than west of the zone. The name for this line is—yep—the International Date Line.

Avoiding Platitudes About Latitudes

Latitude lines begin with zero at the equator and rise as they proceed toward the poles. Those north of the equator are designated north latitude, those south as south latitude.

Latitude lines are spaced 60 nautical miles apart. And one nautical mile is $1/60$ of the distance between latitude lines, designated as a "minute" of latitude.

"X" Marks the Spot

The crossing of latitude and longitude lines provide a precise means of navigation. Particularly now that satellites linked to electronic reading devices can instantly measure the location of any spot on the globe, the latitude/longitude system makes for very precise navigation even in open ocean.

The latitude/longitude numbers correspond to the numbers you see on an electronic machine called a Global Positioning System (GPS), so they show your exact position on the chart.

A Fading Acronym—LORAN

LORAN is the acronym for the Long Range Navigation system in U.S. waters, based on a network of radio towers that send out directional signals over coastal areas.

LORAN lines, which are slightly curved, are also shown on many charts, although LORAN is gradually being phased out by GPS. By reading coordinates from two towers, the LORAN machines provide exacting navigation, usually to within 100 yards. For more on this system, see Chapter 13.

The Compass Rose

The compass rose is a direction-indicator printed at several locations on most charts. It's used in laying out compass courses. The "rose" is a circle about the diameter of a grapefruit printed on the chart, aligned with true north toward the top. It's printed in a reddish maroon ink, thus the "rose" designation.

The circle is divided into 360 degrees. There's a second circle within the outer circle, also divided into degrees. This inner circle is an indication of magnetic north, which moves around as much as a sitting president's politics, left one day, right the next.

Look closely and you'll note that the inner circle doesn't show exactly the same "North" as the outer circle. Does this mean map-makers are afraid to make a decision? No. But it does indicate something even more unsettling, which is that the magnetic poles of the earth are in motion! Don't call Arthur C. Clarke on this one. It's been going on for a very long time and nobody is concerned.

By use of parallel rules, you can measure the direction of a course you want to follow from this rose. Line up the course, then walk the rulers to the nearest rose and run one through its center to get the course.

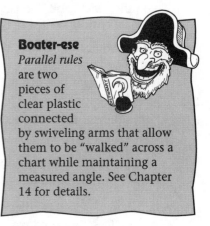

Boater-ese
Parallel rules are two pieces of clear plastic connected by swiveling arms that allow them to be "walked" across a chart while maintaining a measured angle. See Chapter 14 for details.

If you're not going far, say you're in a shallow-draft boat and you're heading toward a large, visible landfall such as a lighthouse, the common method is to look at the compass rose, estimate the direction as, say north-northeast, and head in that direction.

For longer voyages in deep draft vessels or when you need to find a small object such as a navigational buoy, it's standard operating procedure to use the parallel rules and the compass rose to compute an exact course.

Variables of Variation

The outer circle of numbers on the compass rose indicates true north, the inner circle magnetic north—the North your compass points to. They're not exactly the same in many parts of the globe, because the magnetic centers of the earth are not exactly the geographic centers—another of God's little tricks to keep us occupied. The difference between magnetic and geographic north is called *variation*.

The difference can be significant in some areas, and particularly for longer voyages it must be included in calculations or you could wind up many miles from your intended destination.

As another example of nature's sense of humor, the variation does not remain constant. It changes a few minutes (sixtieths of a degree) or so each year. It takes a long time for this minor change to be significant, but you don't want to try an open ocean crossing with hundred-year-old charts.

The concern with variation is gradually disappearing due to GPS navigation. But if you're in the middle of that 2,000 mile run to Tahiti and your electronics go out, you'd better know something about variation.

What You Don't Know Can Hurt You— Bottom Conditions

One of the objects of safe skippering is to stay out of areas where the bottom is too close to the top, and charts tell you how to do that with their depth indication.

But there are times when you must enter shallow areas, as when you want to have lunch on the beach, and knowing whether the bottom along the beach is soft sand or hard rock can be critical to the safety of the lower units of both your boat and your passengers.

You also need to know the bottom conditions when you look for a spot to anchor. Soft mud and grass make for tough anchoring, as does smooth rock. Hard sand is the preferred anchorage—it's soft enough for the anchor to dig in yet firm enough to hold against heavy strain once it does.

How do you find out what's down there, short of donning a mask and fins? Again, you look on the chart:

➤ "Grs" indicates a grassy area where fishing may be good.

➤ "Hrd" indicates a sand bottom that's good for anchoring.

➤ "Rky" is rocky, maybe good for bottom fishing, not good for anchoring.

➤ "Oys" is a good place to find hors d'ouevres, but a bad place to run your boat— it marks an oyster bar.

➤ "Sft Md" means soft mud—no place to go wading, and not a good place to try anchoring either, because the anchor won't hold.

➤ "Obstr" means obstruction—a broken-off channel marker, rock, or other danger— steer clear!

➤ "Shoaling" means that currents and waves create unpredictable movement of the bar, and passage is not recommended.

Scale Models

There are scales on fish, scales in bathrooms, and scales of justice, but the scales that concern boaters most are the scales on charts—the ratio of size on the chart to size in reality.

Some small-scale charts show hundreds of miles of coastline, and are only suitable for offshore voyagers. The scale on these charts is commonly one inch = 550,000 inches. That is to say, one inch on the chart equals about 8.7 statute miles.

Inshore charts offer a larger scale, with one inch = 94,000 inches common; an inch on the chart is equal to a bit over 1.5 miles. These charts are much more useful for weekend boaters, showing greatly expanded views of the coastline and offering the details needed for navigation.

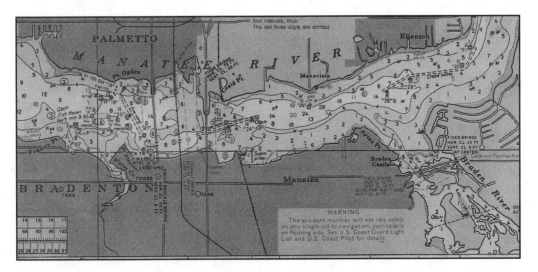

This inshore chart shows a navigable river running many miles inland from Tampa Bay on Florida's west coast. Note the marker numbers and shapes along the channel.

Harbor charts sometimes go as large as one inch = 35,000 inches; an inch on the chart equals only about a half-mile on the water. This will show every little creek and sandbar, so it's the one most useful for inshore boaters and anglers.

Measuring Chart Distances

There are mileage scales printed along the bottom of most charts, making it possible to easily measure distance with a set of dividers. Dividers don't actually divide anything, like a calculator. A divider is a two-legged device with sharp points on the legs that is designed to let you transfer a measurement from the chart to the mileage scale along the edges or at the bottom of the chart.

The Least You Need to Know

➤ Charts are watergoing road maps.

➤ Charts contain depth information based on color and numbers as well as shape of land masses and shoals.

➤ Markers shown on charts help to locate your position afloat.

➤ Choosing the right scale for your type of boating makes a chart much more useful.

Chapter 12

Rules of the Marine Road

> ## In This Chapter
>
> ➤ Buoys are the street signs of the sea
>
> ➤ Pleased to meet you (but not head-on)
>
> ➤ Horning in—using sound to signal other boats
>
> ➤ Passing etiquette
>
> ➤ Boating after dark

Part of the appeal of boating is that there's a certain freedom you don't feel ashore—fewer people, less traffic, fewer rules. But there are some basic regulations known as the "rules of the road" designed to keep everyone safe, and these are "musts" in your boating education.

You have to learn exactly what these rules mean and react to them properly *every time*, just as you have to react to a stop sign ashore every time, or you can get into serious trouble.

In this chapter, you'll learn what the buoys and markers you see on the water mean, the driving rules that apply when you meet or pass other boats, a bit about sound signals afloat, and some tips for operating safely after sundown.

Where the Buoys Are—Aids to Navigation

Nautical markers or buoys are the street signs of the sea. They tell you where the safe course lies, directing you around the rocks, shoals, wrecks, and snags that can otherwise spoil your boating life.

In U.S. waters, markers are usually big, stout, permanent fixtures placed by the Coast Guard, although some can be as simple as a stick with a can on top, put there by your Uncle Bill who hit a rock on that spot a few years back. Only the Coast Guard and state marine agencies are authorized to put up markers, but many private citizens do it anyway.

Boater-ese

Markers are generally fixed pilings or tripod towers set into the bottom, and are most commonly used inshore in waters less than four fathoms (24 feet) deep. They're also called "day markers," although many are equipped with lights for night navigation. *Buoys* are floating navigational aids, and may be used in waters of any depth.

The government markers are dependable, the private ones are suspect. Do you go to the right of the stick, or the left? Only a busted prop will tell.

When I was a guide in a little Gulf Coast town called Homosassa, some of the locals who didn't like the weekend yuppie invasions put out markers directing boaters onto oyster reefs and rock piles! (I always suspected the guy who owned the prop shop had something to do with it, too.)

The government markers have a system or language that offers lots of information to those who understand it. Unfortunately, it's quite a bit different from the rules for driving ashore. Red and green do not mean stop and go at sea. Remember these two basic rules:

➤ As you return from the sea, red markers go on your right and green markers go on your left.

➤ As you proceed inland, red markers on your right will have even numbers and the green markers on your left will have odd numbers.

This is called the *lateral buoyage system* because the marks lie along the side of the safe channel, and it's easiest to remember when you start out by memorizing Red/Right/Returning/Even (RRRE, for you retired military folks), and Green/Port/Odd/Entering, (GPOE). Or you can remember it like this: RRR2, GP1E. That is, the red ones start with the numeral 2, the green ones with the numeral 1.

After dark, some of the red markers display red lights, and some of the green ones display green lights. But not all day markers have lights, and there's no particular rhyme or reason to which do and which don't. Usually, markers in heavily traveled routes such as the Intracoastal Waterway (ICW) will all be lighted, but those to local harbors may have only the outside marker lighted, and maybe one or two others at danger points along the route. Always proceed slowly and have the next marker in view via moon-glow or spotlight before passing into a channel without lighted marks.

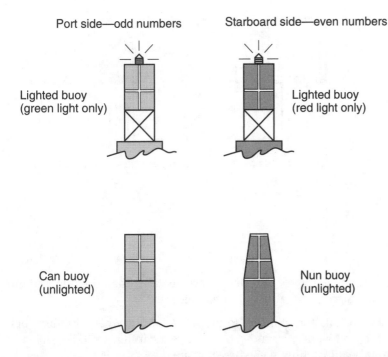

Port side—odd numbers

Starboard side—even numbers

Lighted buoy
(green light only)

Lighted buoy
(red light only)

Can buoy
(unlighted)

Nun buoy
(unlighted)

The lateral buoyage system places red, even-numbered, nun-shaped buoys to the right or starboard side of a ship entering a channel and green, odd-numbered can-shaped buoys to the left or port of an entering vessel.

Bet You Didn't Know

The Intracoastal Waterway (ICW) runs from Boston, Massachusetts, to Brownsville, Texas, along the length of the Atlantic and Gulf coasts. It provides a clearly marked channel with adequate depth to float 100-foot barges as well as the largest private boats. The waterway often runs inside the barrier islands that are found along most coastlines, providing an all-weather passage as well as thousands of inviting places to visit.

Shaping a Course

The shape of the markers is also informative. The red buoys are frequently conical on their upper sections, while the green buoys are cylindrical. And on marker posts, the GPOE symbols are square, the RRRE symbols triangular (see the figure on the following page). On a foggy day, you can often pick out the shape before the color, so this is a useful thing to know.

Some boaters call buoys with conical tops *nun buoys*, because the outline does look a bit like a nun's hat from a distance. The cylindrical buoys are sometimes called *can buoys*, again for their shape. It's expected that you will know if someone tells you to watch for the can buoy that you are looking for a green or black buoy with an odd number.

Day markers, displayed on pilings, feature green, square-shaped, odd-numbered markers to port; and red, triangular, even-numbered markers to starboard of a boat heading landward.

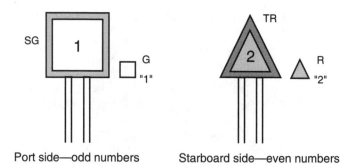

Port side—odd numbers

Starboard side—even numbers

Sound Decisions

Offshore buoys with lights, bells, gongs, or whistles are usually taller than the nun and can buoys, and their shape is not significant, although their color is.

Why should buoys come with bells and whistles, so to speak? Because when visibility goes to zero, as it sometimes does in fog, rain, or snow, the strange moaning "OOOOAAA" of a whistle buoy can save your boat by telling you where you are.

Look Out!
Slow down when you're operating at night, or in fog or rain. At these times, the markers themselves can become hazards to navigation, and you may collide with them if you don't slow down and keep a sharp eye out. Slowing down also cuts engine noise, allowing you to hear the warning sounds from the bell, whistle, and gong buoys.

Heading Out to Sea

The color/number/shape system reverses when you head downstream, or from land toward the open sea. Now, the red, even-numbered markers are kept on the left or port side, while the green or black, odd-numbered markers are kept on the right or starboard side.

With this lesson firmly grasped, you can confidently enter any harbor anywhere in the U.S. and in most other nations throughout the Western Hemisphere. (Unfortunately, there's a different system in the Eastern Hemisphere, where the colors and routes are almost exactly opposite!)

The same system applies in the Great Lakes and in any rivers which lead to the sea, which nearly all large ones do.

Special Situations

Okay, but what about a channel that heads north and south, when you know that the ocean is to the east? There, a designated landward is used; that is, the government agency placing the markers decides which ways will be considered landward and seaward.

For the Intracoastal Waterway, one of the most used recreational boat routes in the world, the designated landward course is south along the Atlantic shore, north and then west along the Gulf of Mexico. ICW markers usually have a yellow horizontal band added to the conventional color to indicate that they are not part of the main harbor marking system.

On the Pacific coast, traveling northward is considered heading toward land. The steep and often rocky shore here offers no protected waterway or inside passage until you get to Puget Sound, however.

Note that the coastal marker system, proceeding clockwise around the U.S. coast, keeps the red markers always on the landward side, making it easier to remember.

Inland Buoyage

The states have agreed among themselves on a system called the Uniform State Waterway Marking System (USWMS). It follows the lateral system discussed earlier, except that it substitutes black for green in the GPOE system, and also in that buoy shape has no meaning—all are cans.

Also in the USWMS system, informational markers indicating rocks, idle zones, swimming areas, or directions to distant lakes or rivers are displayed on white cans or signs with orange borders and symbols and black lettering.

Other Navigational Aids

Lighthouses are not likely to be overlooked by anybody—the blinding sweep of their lights can be seen for many miles and can act as an auxiliary compass point anywhere you're within range. You can see the tower by day for miles, too.

Range markers are two markers set one behind the other so that when they are viewed from the safe channel, they appear in perfect alignment, one directly above the other. The rear marker is taller than the front one. If one marker is off to one side, you're not in the center of the channel the towers are indicating. (See the figure on the following page.) They're sometimes lighted, and for night operation you try to put one light atop the other with your course.

Look Out!
Range markers are effective only when you're in a specific portion of a channel. Many are built in shallow water, so if you get too close, you could leave the channel marked with the familiar lateral red and green marks and run aground.

Range markers line up perfectly when your boat is in the safe channel, but appear to be out of alignment when you are off course.

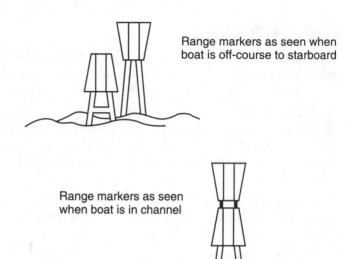

Range markers as seen when boat is off-course to starboard

Range markers as seen when boat is in channel

Radio towers and smokestacks also work well as long-distance markers. A tall stack can be seen from 20 miles away by day, and the red- or white-strobe aircraft warning lights on tall structures are visible at long distances after sundown.

By knowing where these fixed structures are in relation to your intended course, you can roughly fix your position even if you have no compass or electronics. (A group of tall buildings can also work this way—many a Bahamas crossing has come to a happy end when anglers sight the towers of Miami Beach or Palm Beach beckoning them home!)

Pleased to Meet You—Meeting Situations

When two boats meet head to head, the preferred method to avoid collision is to pass port to port (left side to left side) by both boats altering course to starboard, or to the right of the driver.

There are obvious situations in which you can't do this; if there's a marker or rock pile in the way of a starboard turn, for example. In that case, usually the best thing to do is to pull back to dead slow and sound your horn with five short blasts, signaling danger.

There are two things to remember in this situation:

1. You are supposed to use horn signals to tell the other boat what you are going to do.

2. Very few people do!

The vast majority of recreational boaters simply don't use their horns as signals, except in the same way they use them as signals ashore—to indicate displeasure. However, to be legally correct, you should know the sound signals and use them any time there's danger that an approaching boater may not understand your intentions.

Many skippers use VHF radio (which I'll cover in Chapter 14) to inform other boats of their intentions. This is really a better approach than sound signals because you can convey more information. However, some small boats don't have VHF, and the situation may not allow you enough time to make a connection by radio, so it's important to know and use sound signals.

The correct ways to signal with your horn on inland and coastal waters are as follows:

➤ *One short blast:* I am turning to starboard and will leave you to my port side.

➤ *Two short blasts:* I am turning to port and will leave you to my starboard side.

➤ *Three short blasts:* I am reversing engines.

➤ *One long blast:* I am getting underway (used when leaving a dock).

➤ *One long blast followed by one short blast:* Please open the drawbridge.

➤ *Five short blasts:* Danger—get out of the way, or don't do what your signal says you intend to do.

The other vessel (or the bridge tender) should repeat with his horn what he heard to confirm. If the other vessel does not repeat your signal, he either didn't hear it or doesn't understand horn signaling. If he does not repeat your signal but issues five short blasts, he is telling you that your intended action is dangerous. In either case, it's prudent to slow to idle and review the situation before proceeding.

Just remember, if you do use horn signals when approaching a small boat, there's about a 95 percent chance the other skipper won't have any idea what these signals mean, so keep a very close eye on the situation and maneuver to avoid the other boat. Or better yet, make contact on your VHF radio and find out his or her intentions.

Making a Pass

You can pass a slower boat moving in the same direction as you are on either side. The horn signals are the same as listed earlier, and they can be just as important in the passing situation as in a head-on meeting because the skipper being passed is unlikely to know you're there until you're right beside him. He or she may make a sharp turn right into your path if you don't signal or make VHF contact.

By marine law, you are not supposed to pass another vessel until he acknowledges your horn signal or responds via VHF. However, in actual practice among small outboard boats in inland waters, this rule is universally ignored. But be aware of it and do your part correctly—if the overtaken skipper doesn't know the rules and doesn't respond to your signals, you'll have to pass with extra caution, being aware that you are responsible for keeping clear should he make an unexpected maneuver.

Once you signal and the skipper turns to look at you, go ahead and make the pass smartly, before other traffic comes along or you enter a narrow area where passing will be difficult.

So what if you're the vessel being passed? If you agree passing is safe, return the passing vessel's signal or VHF message and maintain your course and speed. (Accelerating like some drivers do when somebody tries to pass them on the interstate is a no-no!)

Who Has the Right of Way?

The "right of way" applies in a crossing situation on the water even more emphatically than it does on shore. A boat approaching from your right is supposed to hold its course and speed and pass in front of you; it has the right of way (unless you are in a sailboat under sail; see the following section). Your job is to slow down or alter your course so as not to get in the way. A boat approaching from your left is supposed to slow down and/or alter course to let you pass in front of it.

Yes, but how far to the right does this right extend?

The rule reads that a boat "112.5 degrees or less off the starboard bow" has the right of way. So if a boat approaches from 112.6 degrees, you're within the law to assert your rights—but put on your crash helmet first! (Of course, if there's any question as to who has the right of way, it's always wiser to defer to the other boat and allow it to pass in front of you.)

Look Out!
Ship crews do not always maintain a lookout. They often run on autopilot when they're off-shore, and if you get in the way, they may run you down without ever knowing you're there. Give them a wide berth. Even in bays and rivers, the pilot can't stop a ship for as many as three miles, so don't tempt fate by cutting close in front of them—it's like crossing a railroad track on a dare. Even if your motor has never stopped before, it may choose to stop then.

Other Situations—Sailboats and Ships

Sailboats under sail and boats powered by oars or paddles usually have the right of way over powerboats. Even though they're coming from the left or port, don't cut close in front of them—they have a hard time changing course abruptly, while it's easy for powerboats to do so. It's also common courtesy to slow down when passing small sailboats and rowboats to avoid rocking them with your wake.

The same is true for ships—even though you absolutely have the right of way, never argue with 1,000-foot oil tanker. (Remember, the ship can't stay afloat outside of marked channels inside shallow bays, and also can't stop for several miles. Stay well clear.)

One signal ship crews do use is the five short blasts that signify danger. Remember that one—it usually means, "Get the heck out of the way if you want to keep breathing."

When passing a ship, recreational boaters must stay well clear (at least 100 yards) and observe sound warnings. (Photo credit: Frank Sargeant)

Other Ship Cautions

Ships are fascinating to watch, but they can be extremely dangerous to recreational boaters who get too close. Here are some basic rules to keep you safe if you boat where the big boys pass nearby:

➤ Never pull a water-skier across the path of a ship—if he falls, you may not be able to get him out of the way in time.

➤ Never tow a broken-down boat across the path of a ship—if the line breaks, the towed rig will be in deep doodoo.

➤ Keep your eyes open for passing ships, even if they're a long way off. Remember that ships put out tremendous waves from both bow and stern. If you're close as they pass at speed, these waves may roll right over your gunnels. Even if you're several miles away, the huge swells a ship produces may send a fast boat airborne. If your passengers don't expect it, they may go up when the boat goes down, and vice versa, with painful results. And when the swells roll onto a shoal or bar, they become breakers that can turn over a canoe or jon boat.

Night Moves—Signals After Sundown

Most recreational boaters don't intend to operate after dark, but sooner or later wind up staying out late and having to do so. Boating at night is pleasant and safe, provided you keep your eyes open and understand the rules.

We've already touched on the use of red and green lights on navigation markers. Some marker lights blink out a little code so that they can be positively identified at a distance. Their code is indicated on the navigation charts for the area, so that if, for example, you are entering a harbor and see a green light give three short flashes, you can be sure that's the outside marker or marker number 1, and not green marker number 3, which is identified by three long flashes, and which may be separated from open water by a dangerous sandbar.

Boats also have lights for night operation so that they can be seen by the skippers of approaching boats. In small boats it's common for the forward running light to be a single light on the bow, with a red lens on the port or left side and a green lens on the starboard or right side. On larger boats, there are usually two separate lights, red on the port bow quarter, green on the starboard bow quarter. These lights can only be seen by boats from dead ahead to 112.5 degrees on either side.

The aft light on most open powerboats less than 12 meters (about 40 feet) long is a white light visible from 360 degrees. The most common aft light on cabin vessels and larger recreational boats is a white light visible from 135 degrees astern only.

Boats longer than 12 meters must also carry a masthead light forward of the stern light, and it must be at least 2.5 meters (8.2 feet) above the gunnels. The masthead light is visible only in an arc of 225 degrees ahead of the boat.

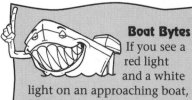

Boat Bytes
If you see a red light and a white light on an approaching boat, it's going to pass port side to. Green plus white, it's going to starboard. Red and green at once, it's headed right at you—change course! (On boats without a masthead light or a 360-degree stern light you will see only the red; you'll see the green bow lights as it approaches head on.)

Sailboats also display the bow and stern lights described above when underway, and alternatively may display masthead lights that include both the red/green lights visible only from ahead and the white light visible only from astern. Sailboats can also put a red light above a green light on their mast.

All small boats at anchor display a single 360-degree white light. This may be the stern light in outboard boats or a masthead light in cabin boats and sailboats. (The "mast" on a powerboat with a cabin is a short staff, usually no more than a yard long, that supports the light.)

A few words to the wise when boating after dark: Red light doesn't wipe out night vision like white light, so it's wise to have instruments lighted dimly in red. And if you must use a white spotlight to find an unlighted marker, avoid looking at the beam—have the light-handler stand well ahead of the skipper if possible.

Be sure you never shine a spotlight directly at the skipper of another vessel underway. You'll temporarily blind him, and there's actually a rule against doing so, making you liable should he run aground or into another boat shortly after.

The Least You Need to Know

➤ Navigational markers convey information by their color, shape, number, sounds, and lights.

➤ Horn signals are useful in keeping clear of other boats.

➤ The "right of way" gives boats approaching from starboard the right to pass ahead of you.

➤ Sailboats, boats powered by oars or paddles, and ships always have the right of way.

➤ Boating at night can be safe and pleasant, provided you take the proper precautions.

Chapter 13

Tools and Tricks of Navigation

sextant   compass   Polaris

In This Chapter

➤ The marine compass has a magnetic personality

➤ Compass calculus—variation and deviation

➤ Doing it the easy way with electronic navigation

➤ GPS, chart plotters, depth finders, and other amazing gadgets

When you graduate to traveling far enough in your boat that you can no longer see the dock or the launching ramp, you may want to start learning the arts of navigation afloat.

Although there's a certain mystery to plotting a course through untracked water far from land, there's also a delight to it, and knowing where you are at all times will quickly build your confidence as a competent boater.

Modern electronic navigation systems are absolutely wonderful, the ultimate navigation tool that can convert anyone into an open-sea navigator. But there will be times with these systems when the batteries go dead, a wire comes loose, or a fuse blows. Whatever can go wrong will go wrong sooner or later on a boat.

In this chapter, you'll learn how to navigate by compass and how to make the adjustments necessary to make this ancient navigational tool accurate anywhere you boat. We'll also take a look at modern electronics and touch on their basic use, and I'll offer some suggestions on which might be the best value for the type of boating you do.

The Unfailing Compass

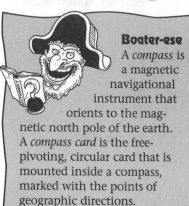

Boater-ese
A *compass* is a magnetic navigational instrument that orients to the magnetic north pole of the earth. A *compass card* is the free-pivoting, circular card that is mounted inside a compass, marked with the points of geographic directions.

Basically, a compass is a magnet suspended on a nearly frictionless pivot point. The compass always finds magnetic north, and with that single bit of information you can usually get home, or at least find land, even at night or in a heavy fog.

The compass is always there, right in front of you, always "on," and never breaks. So compass basics are also part of the navigator's educational kit.

Note that the compass card or magnet itself doesn't move—the compass, attached to the boat, pivots around it. In fact, the boat itself pivots, while that nearly weightless card steadfastly maintains position—it's magic when you visualize what's truly happening.

The compass card is a disk marked every five degrees into a 360-degree circle, and compass courses are designated by degrees on that circle. If you run due east, you are on a course of 090 degrees; due south, 180; west, 270; and north, 000.

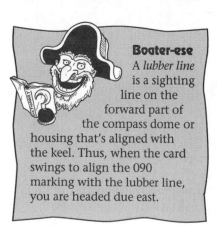

Boater-ese
A *lubber line* is a sighting line on the forward part of the compass dome or housing that's aligned with the keel. Thus, when the card swings to align the 090 marking with the lubber line, you are headed due east.

Compass courses are designated by three digits when written on charts, to help emphasize that they are courses and not angles. A course of 1 degree east of north is written "001."

The compass is secured on the console as nearly dead center with the steering wheel as possible and aligned parallel with the boat's keel. A lubber line—a dark line that's aligned with the centerline or keel of the boat to make steering easier—is marked on the compass dome.

Compasses vary in price from as little as $30 to over $1,000. Larger compasses make it easier to read precise courses than smaller models.

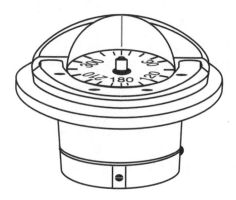

In compasses, bigger is better. The larger the compass card, the easier it is to read and the more accurately you can follow a course. Larger compasses cost more, but are worth the investment in boats run regularly out of sight of land.

Variable Variation

Boat Bytes
A bit of old mariner's advice is also worth remembering: If you're on Florida's side of the Gulf of Mexico or on the Pacific Coast and you start to head home at sundown but the sun is in your eyes, turn around. Nature's clues are never wrong—stay attuned to them.

Compasses point to magnetic north, but meridians on a chart are laid out relative to geographic north. The difference between the two is known as *variation*. Variation is a compass error resulting from the fact that magnetic north and geographic north are not identical directions on most parts of the earth.

For short voyages and in some locations, variation is insignificant. For longer journeys and in other spots, particularly in more northern latitudes, it can be very significant.

Variation approaches 20 degrees along the coasts of Maine and Washington, and 10 degrees along the California shore. On a long coastal voyage, that much alteration in the course could put you hundreds of miles off course, run you aground, or get you lost for days.

The error introduced by variation is westerly on the East Coast and easterly on the West Coast. Thus, easterly errors are added to the true course you wish to follow as laid out on a chart, and westerly errors are subtracted.

For example, if you want to follow a course of 45 degrees true—that is, relative to the geographic north pole—along the coast of Maine, you would have to add about 16 degrees, the variation in that area, to the magnetic course shown. It looks like an Algebra II equation, but it's simple addition or subtraction:

$$45T + 16W = 61M$$

In this simple equation, *T* stands for the true course (one accurately measured in relation to the geographic north pole, with corrections made for variation and deviation of the compass), *W* stands for the variation or compass deflection to the west from true north caused by the location of magnetic north, and *M* stands for the magnetic course, or the compass course you would steer to adjust for or "compensate" for the variation.

So, to travel 45 degrees true in that area, you'd steer 61 degrees on the compass.

Devious Deviation

Boat Bytes
Hand-held "fluxgate" or digital compasses operate on built-in batteries and can be moved from boat to boat. They also act as a hand-bearing compass, allowing you to check your navigation by getting the bearing of landmarks ashore and markers at sea. They cost about $150.

Boat Bytes
Some binoculars have built-in bearing compasses. They help you spot markers and give you a magnetic bearing to them, plus act as a compass back-up. Be sure to choose a waterproof set for boating use. Prices are $200 and up.

As if this were not enough to remember, there's also a second possible compass error called *deviation*. Deviation is compass deflection from magnetic north caused by ferrous (iron or steel) materials or electrical currents aboard your boat.

It doesn't change with location, but it does change with the heading of your boat. Ideally, you want to make deviation as small as possible by keeping all materials that can affect magnets well away from the compass. Wiring should also be kept clear, since it can create a magnetic field in some cases.

Deviation is determined by "swinging ship," taking bearings on a known course line to a distant marker as the boat is rotated in place, and writing down any deflection at a number of headings.

It's not something normally done by weekend boaters, but you should at least be aware that this is where deviation tables come from. If your compass deviates more than a few degrees, it's best to have it compensated or adjusted by a pro at a good marina.

However, most marine compasses can be compensated for moderate deviation errors by adjustment screws that move tiny internal magnets nearer or farther from the card.

"Can Dead Men Vote Twice?"

The entire equation for canceling out compass errors for variation and deviation can be remembered via the nautical question "Can Dead Men Vote Twice?": *CDMVT*.

➤ *C* stands for the compass course.

➤ *D* stands for the deviation.

➤ *M* stands for the magnetic course.

➤ *V* stands for the variation.

➤ *T* stands for the true course.

So, if you have a true course written on a chart and want to know what compass course to steer, you add or subtract the variation, which gives you the magnetic course, and then add or subtract the deviation, which gives you the compass course:

C + D = M + V = T

In this case, the rule is to add easterly errors and subtract westerly errors. If you know the compass course to a landmark ahead and want to know the true bearing, you work the equation the other way: Add or subtract the deviation to get magnetic course, and then add or subtract the variation to get true course, useful in plotting your exact position on a chart:

$$T + V = M + D = C$$

In this equation, you subtract easterly errors and add westerly errors.

Electronic Navigation

Now that you've seen this much about compass navigation, you probably want to forget all about it.

Fortunately, you can. Modern electronic navigation gear takes care of all the calculations for you and puts you exactly where you want to be every time...as long as it doesn't break.

Although electronic navigation is as good as it gets, it's always wise to have a backup if your primary set goes down, and a compass in case all else fails.

LORAN Waves Good-Bye

Long Range Navigation Systems (LORAN) are on their way out, but they're still the darlings of thousands of offshore anglers.

The reason is that all these folks have their bottom fishing spots located with LORAN numbers, and LORAN has proven itself strong in the "repeatability" department—that is, it returns your boat to almost the same exact position time after time for a given set of numbers, unlike Global Positioning Systems or GPS, which tends to wander a bit from day to day.

However, LORAN towers are being phased out by the government, and as the LORAN boxes die, most won't be repaired but rather replaced by the less-expensive GPS units.

GPS—The Ultimate Navigator

GPS is the wave of the future, and the future is now. They can locate any point on the globe to within a few meters. The units pick up satellite signals to work their magic, and unlike LORAN, they do not have to be in range of a shore-based transmitter to work.

Global Positioning Systems can be dash-mounted units, like this one, or portable units. The dash-mounted models rely on a separate antenna about the size of a hockey puck, which can be mounted anywhere with a clear view of the sky. (Photo credit: Furuno Corporation)

Global Positioning Systems also work on the tiniest lakes hundreds of miles from the nearest coastal navigation systems, which is why they were standard issue for Gulf War forces navigating the featureless deserts of the Middle East.

Boat Bytes

Do you really need electronic navigation gear? If you do your boating on inland lakes and rivers, you'll probably never miss it, although it could be a help in finding your favorite offshore fishing spots at times. On the other hand, if you operate on the Great Lakes or the coasts, out of sight of land, electronic positioning equipment is a must. It's by far the most reliable and easiest way of keeping track of where you are.

GPS receivers rely on a fleet of U.S. military satellites circling the globe to provide precise navigation anywhere on earth.

The system is remarkable for its accuracy—the military versions can send a missile down a chimney at ranges of several hundred miles. The civilian versions can be just as accurate, but are only designed to offer 100-meter accuracy out of the box. More common is 100-foot accuracy. Add a "differential receiver" designed to read fine-tuning broadcasts from land-based senders, and the accuracy gets down to the 8- to 20-meter range.

Global Positioning Systems are becoming more affordable each year, and are now available in console models for around $200. Unlike radios, portable or handheld GPS units are just as useful as fixed units, and just as accurate. They burn batteries rapidly, but converters allow you to hook them to the boat batteries. Some cost as little as $100, or less than a tenth of what the first units to hit the civilian market went for!

Do-It-All Chart Plotters

The ultimate inshore navigational tool is a chart plotter with a built-in GPS. On the screen, you zoom in on a navigational chart of the area you're cruising, usually via postage-stamp–sized chart cards that insert into the machine.

The GPS then positions your boat on the chart, and you can see your progress as it tracks your course. Even the buoys and other navigational aids are shown, and you can track your boat on-screen as it zooms past Marker 1 and heads for home.

Recent models like the Northstar Point & Shoot allow you to simply place a cursor on a distant location, click a couple of buttons, and the machine plots a latitude/longitude course to that location.

You can insert as many *waypoints*, locations along the way where you might want to check your navigation or simply stop for a picnic, as you like. You can even get a graphic tide chart of the area as part of the display. (Call (508) 897-0770 for details on the system.)

Simpler, hand-held chart plotter/GPS units have fewer bells and whistles, but some of them, like the Lowrance/Eagle line, also offer charts on-screen. Battery life can be a problem for some, but all offer 12-volt battery hook-ups.

Handheld GPS units are compact, lightweight, and accurate, and can be carried from boat to boat. Charting models like this one can even be used on shore to navigate your car! (Photo credit: Lowrance Electronics)

Both GPS and LORAN look a bit intimidating due to all the buttons, on-screen menus, and numbers, particularly if you're not into computers. But, in fact, anyone can learn to operate either unit within about 30 minutes. (Most companies offer videos for those who need a bit of extra help.)

Boat Bytes
On a "cold start" of a new GPS or one that has been moved to a new location many miles from its home port, it can take 10 to 15 minutes for the machine to lock on to the satellites passing overhead and locate itself again. The display will blink to warn you not to try navigating until the system locks in.

Basically you just turn them on, let them lock on to the nearest satellites, and then punch in latitude/longitude numbers to tell the machine where you want to go.

If you already have waypoints saved in the machine, you can simply hit the "Go To" button and punch the number of the waypoint you want to seek.

The unit then guides you there, suggesting you steer right or left if you wander off course due to inattention or the effect of the wind or currents. When you approach your destination, it sounds an alarm so you don't overshoot. And throughout the run, it gives constant updates on your exact speed, course made good, distance to go, time to go, and course to the destination.

Given the remarkably low price of the hand-held models these days, there's no reason for any recreational boat not to have one tucked in the glove box.

Navigating in Depth—Depth Finders

Depth finders are commonly called "fish finders" by anglers, and they do work well for locating fish and bait. But they're also very important navigational tools for all boaters.

Depth finders give you underwater "eyes" to evade shallows and avoid running aground by following deeper, safer channels. In low visibility, it's possible to find your way home following the depth contours as listed on a large-scale nautical chart.

Boat Bytes
Digital depth finders show the depth in numbers only via an in-dash display smaller than a hockey puck. They're moderately priced, starting at about $120, and take up no space on the dash. If you're not a serious angler, a digital may be all the depth finder you need.

These are sonar systems, sending out a pulse of sound, measuring the time it takes the echo to return and the intensity of the echo, and converting these signals to visual data.

Most used to provide the readout on a paper scroll. They were called "chart" machines, and the nice thing about them was you could cut out the sections of paper that had interesting fishing spots recorded on them, write the data on the side, and store them for future reference. However, paper-chart sonars had lots of moving parts, dirt, and resultant maintenance problems. The paper machines are all gone now.

Most common at present are liquid crystal display (LCD) screen displays, which draw a mono-color chart of the bottom on what looks like the screen of a portable computer.

The bottom appears as a moving gray-black line near the bottom of the page. On the sides, the digital depth appears. You can zoom in for a closer look. Fish and bait appear between bottom and top of the screen, which represent the bottom of the lake or bay and the surface of the water.

Prices begin at less than $100, and most of these units are so waterproof that they will actually function underwater.

Boat Bytes
"Forward-looking" or scanning depth finders are particularly useful for navigation because they can see what's ahead of the boat and off to the sides, making it easier to follow a winding, unmarked channel or avoid an unmarked obstruction. They're also sometimes more useful than conventional sonar for locating fish.

In Living Color

You can also view the depths in color. Cathode Ray Tubes (CRTs) are not space guns, but color depth finders. They function much like a small television set and are about as big—the box on these machines is three to six times larger than a typical LCD. They're also a lot more expensive than LCDs, with prices starting around $750.

CRTs look intimidating, with lots of buttons and dials, but using the basic functions is a one-touch operation. The nice thing about them is that they show different colors for bottom, bait, and gamefish, making it easy to sort things out at a glance, even when traveling fast.

Color depth finders are superior to LCDs because the colors make it much easier to pick out exactly what you're seeing below and the screens are much brighter, but their high cost usually limits their use to big boats and/or very serious bottom fishermen or wreck divers.

A Handy Extra—Radio Direction Finders

Radio Direction Finders (RDFs) are a useful extra tool for those who spend a lot of time offshore and frequently make long coastal cruises where a backup to the GPS is a great comfort.

RDFs are basically moveable radio antennas that provide readouts indicating the direction from which the strongest and weakest signal on a given station comes. Using this information and a marine chart that lists the location of the broadcasting station, boaters can determine lines of position (LOPs). Do it for two or more stations and you have the location of your boat where the LOPs cross.

Radar Shows It All

Radar is rarely used on smaller recreational boats due to its high cost ($1,500 to $3,000), but on larger boats used regularly offshore and in inclement weather, it's a basic part of the navigational tool kit. Radar is similar to sonar but it operates above the surface, and sends out radio waves rather than sound pulses to measure distance.

Radar can draw the shape of a coastline, show the presence of other boats ahead, and measure both distance and bearing to anything appearing on the screen. It's a great asset, particularly at night or in low visibility.

The Least You Need to Know

➤ The compass is the most basic but most dependable of navigational tools.

➤ Compass courses should be corrected for variation and deviation in many areas for longer voyages.

➤ Electronic navigation systems offer a wide variety of features and prices. Review the way you'll actually use your system aboard and select those that provide the most bang for your buck.

Chapter 14

Nautical Radio Gear and Procedures and Your First Longer Cruise

If you've read the rest of Part 3, you're almost ready to try a limited offshore cruise, a longer cruise on inland waters, or maybe a trip from one river port to another.

In this chapter, you'll learn about the marine communications systems important on offshore trips, how to plan the longer voyage, how to take care of the important details on the morning of your trip, and a bit about the art and science of dead reckoning or figuring your position without the use of electronics.

Marine Communications

There are a few more items you'll want in your cockpit before you watch that thin blue horizon that marks land disappear behind you for the first time—or even before you cruise down your local river.

The most important electronic device to carry aboard is some sort of communications device. It's a handy way to find where the fish are biting or which beach the sundown rendezvous is planned for. It's also useful when you want to talk with the harbormaster in a new port to learn which slip he wants you in, and even to call the waterfront restaurant and reserve a corner table.

And if things ever go really bad—sinking boat, life-threatening injury, heart attack—you need dependable contact with the world ashore, pronto.

Boat Bytes
One disadvantage of cell phones? You have to pay every time you hit the "Send" button. Other forms of marine communications are free once you have the basic gear.

Reach Out and Touch Somebody

For lakes and inshore areas, you can't beat a cellular phone. It's immediate, easy to use, dependable, and something that most families already own. Just be sure to put the phone in a waterproof container, and keep the battery charged—a connector to the 12-volt system is a great plus.

Anglers like the cell phone because it doesn't broadcast information on where the fish are biting—they can share secret spots with their pals and not find a fleet bearing down on them.

VHF—Everyman's Radio

VHF stands for Very High Frequency, the most useful of marine radio communications gear.

VHF works where cell phones won't many miles at sea, to allow you to reach out and touch nearby boats or passing ships even if you don't have their telephone number. And you can call as often as you like, at no charge whatsoever!

Boat Bytes
The factors that most affect VHF transmission are the "gain" or amplifying ability and the height of the antenna. A 6-dB gain model or higher is needed for good range. And an antenna atop a flying bridge or on a sailboat mast can reach out miles farther than one on a center console.

Most people monitor a single channel, channel 16, so any time you need to make contact, you can simply broadcast a hailing call and all nearby boats will hear it. The Coast Guard and many marinas also monitor channel 16, so that's where you go if you ever need to broadcast the dreaded MAYDAY call. (Channel 9 is also used as a hailing channel, but it's not monitored by the Coast Guard.)

Although you're welcome to use channel 16 for hailing other boats, you'll get your ears burned if you try to make chit-chat on this channel. It's reserved for initial contact and the Coast Guard—when you get hold of someone you want to talk to, the standard procedure is to change to one of the "working" channels designated for recreational traffic, 68 through 72. (See "The Lingo of VHF" later in this chapter.)

VHF radios cost $160 to $500, and the system requires an antenna about six to eight feet long for good performance, another $100 or more.

Even with a good antenna properly mounted, the range is limited to about 25 miles max. But along the coasts of the U.S., it's rare to be more than 25 miles from another VHF-equipped boat these days, so you can usually reach someone when you need to.

This well-equipped console includes two VHF radios (right), one flush-mounted into the dash. Particularly for offshore operation, a backup is wise. (Photo credit: Frank Sargeant)

VHF radios are small—about half the size of a fax machine—and fit easily inside even the smaller consoles on open boats. They're built to withstand the rigors of life afloat. Some are completely sealed and will operate totally submerged. (Unfortunately, *you* won't—so call for help early if you have problems.)

In the Palm of Your Hand

Handheld VHFs are not a whole lot bigger than a cell phone. They have built-in batteries and can be carried with you from boat to boat. They're great in small boats that have no permanent radio system. They're not significantly cheaper than 25-watt units, with prices ranging from $150 to near $500.

However, they put out only five watts, versus the 25 watts of a fixed system, and the antennas are only

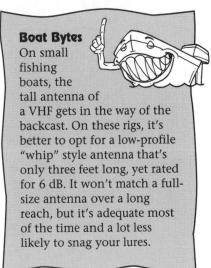

Boat Bytes
On small fishing boats, the tall antenna of a VHF gets in the way of the backcast. On these rigs, it's better to opt for a low-profile "whip" style antenna that's only three feet long, yet rated for 6 dB. It won't match a full-size antenna over a long reach, but it's adequate most of the time and a lot less likely to snag your lures.

Boat Bytes
Want to keep your handheld running all day long? Buy an optional 12-volt accessory hookup with a cigarette-lighter plug, so you can tap into your boat's power system. As long as the main battery is charged, your VHF will be ready to go.

Boat Bytes
You don't have to keep your radio turned on at all times, but if you do have it on, you're supposed to monitor channel 16 at all times. If you try repeatedly to call another boat and get no response, his or her radio is probably off.

about six inches long, so the range is limited to about five miles. Also, they can't be left on continuously because their batteries soon run down, so they're not the best "first" radio for your boat. However, most have rechargeable batteries—just plug them into a charger attached to an AC outlet, and they're back to full power overnight.

The Lingo of VHF

There's a routine format for speaking on the VHF, because you can't both talk at once as on a telephone. You can only transmit when you key your microphone (push the button on the side of the part you hold in your hand), and you can't hear any incoming message while your mike is keyed. So radio conversations are a sort of dance, a timed pattern of communications that keeps everybody from getting stepped on.

Standard operating procedure is to try to get the attention of the target of your call with your first words, so a typical conversation with your buddy aboard the nearby "Done Rovin'" may go like this:

> "Done Rovin', Done Rovin', Done Rovin', this is the Busted Flush, come back."

You repeat the name of the boat you're trying to reach three times to make sure they hear you. The "come back" is the sign you're done speaking for the moment and will listen for the reply. (Some people say "over.") If you get no response after 30 seconds or so, repeat the hailing call. If the other boat hears you, the reply is likely to be:

> "Busted Flush, this is the Done Rovin', come back."

Now you know you're connected, so it's time to get off the hailing channel to a working channel where you won't interfere with other people trying to reach each other:

> "Charlie, let's go to 72, come back."

> "Roger, going to 72, over."

You both now switch your channel selectors to 72 and get on with your conversation. At the end of the communication, it's normal to identify your boat name again and indicate you're finished by saying "out." In everyday use, most boating pals say something like "catch you at the docks"—there's no real need for formal radio language in recreational boating.

Weather Stations, Too

VHF has the added advantage of including several weather channels, which give immediate and continuous access to National Weather Service radio forecasts (see Chapter 15 for details). You simply press the "WX" button to get the continuous reports. The radio can also hook you up with a marine operator so that you can reach the landlines of the telephone system to call home as needed.

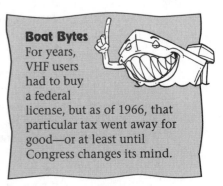

Boat Bytes
For years, VHF users had to buy a federal license, but as of 1966, that particular tax went away for good—or at least until Congress changes its mind.

Breaker One-Nine...Not!

Forget CB radio for use at sea. There's too much clutter on the airwaves, the range is too limited, and most CBs are built to operate inside an air-conditioned vehicle instead of in the salty confines of a center console. Besides, no other boaters have them and they're not monitored—so keep the CB in your pickup truck, 10-4?

One exception might be for use in inland boats, where you're very likely to be able to reach someone driving down a nearby highway on channel 9 if you need assistance. But a cell phone is probably a better option here.

SSB for Maximum Range

Single sideband radio or SSB has far greater range than VHF, in part due to an output of up to 150 watts, six times the maximum VHF output. They're usually hooked to monster antennas more than 20 feet long as well, so the reach is awesome.

Unfortunately, so is the price—a set, with antenna, goes for $1,500 and up. The cost is prohibitive for weekenders, but those who move up to Caribbean crossings and the like may want to make the investment.

A Typical Cruise—Do Your Homework First

Once you understand the basics of charts, markers, navigational tools, and marine communications, you're ready for your first long cruise. Long is relative—we're not talking weeks or even days here. Navigating to anywhere you can't see from the boat ramp is a good first effort.

Step one is to get the appropriate chart before your trip and study your route, from the put-in point to the destination and back.

Look for areas that might cause problems—doglegs or S-curves in a channel, unmarked oyster bars close to your route, inlets that might be rough if wind and tide oppose each other.

If you're in a coastal area, you should check the newspapers or a tide chart for the times of high and low tide on the day of your cruise—you'll need to know them if you cross shallow areas.

If you'll be making a run beyond the marked channels, you'll want to pencil in your courses, using the parallel rules to make them neat and to get the compass courses from the compass rose (see Chapter 11). Indicate the distance in miles by measuring with the two-legged dividers and transferring that measurement to the distance scale on the chart. Write both course and distance along each leg of the trip. Always use a soft pencil to mark your courses on a chart, so that you can erase them when they're no longer needed. Permanent markings may be used for fixed locations, such as the latitude/longitude numbers of a fishing reef, but if you mark your courses in ink, the chart will soon have so many tracks on it that it will become illegible.

You'll usually have several waypoints along the way, fixed objects such as offshore buoys where you can check your route. Or you may have to lay out your course in legs to avoid shallows or other obstructions.

Boat Bytes
You don't have to go through the chart study after you've traveled an area a few times—you'll quickly become familiar with the local navigational aids and landmarks, know the compass routes by heart, and have the secret grouper holes and diving reefs programmed into your GPS. It's only on the first visits that the chart work is critical.

Straight-line courses allow you to stay aware of exactly where you are, so an extended route along a coastline sometimes looks like a connect-the-dots puzzle when it's completed on a chart.

If you're more casual about your route, you may someday look around and discover you don't realize whether that distant marker is the one for your destination or for another harbor 10 miles up the coast—it's amazingly easy to lose track when you're out of sight of land, and sometimes even when you're near shore in unfamiliar waters.

If you get serious about navigation (and you'd better before you make any long voyages), you can pre-program these waypoints into your GPS or LORAN during the week before the cruise. Then, when you're ready to leave the docks, you simply turn on the machine and go for it.

Cruising Day

On the day of the planned cruise, the skipper should get up early and check the weather, both from The Weather Channel on television and on the WX station on the boat's VHF. If the weather is iffy, it might be best to let everybody sleep in and wait until another day.

It's good to drop off a "float plan" (see Chapter 18) with someone ashore, so that people will come looking if you don't return as planned. Run a quick check of all gear. Make sure the boat is gassed up, the sandwiches made, the coolers full of ice and drinks, the PFDs aboard, and the charts and navigational tools handy, and head for the dock.

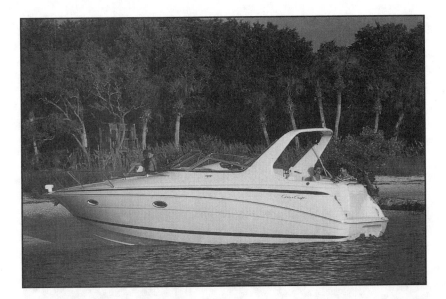

Finding a protected and private beach you can access safely may take a bit of chart study and a careful watch on the depth finder, but it's time well spent. (Photo credit: Chris Craft Boats)

At the ramp or dock, check the chart, note the shape and direction of the channel, and look out across the water to locate the markers that correspond to the route as shown on the chart.

Follow the markers to open water (red ones go on the left or port as you head out to sea, remember) and from marker 1 you punch in your first GPS waypoint toward your destination, or take a compass course in that direction. You're on your way!

Most cruises are straightforward and without problems if you've done your homework. You'll want to keep an eye out for landmarks as you travel—points of land, radio towers, and tall buildings—noting them on the chart as you pass so that you confirm what your GPS is telling you.

It's also prudent to turn on your depth finder the minute you leave the dock and leave it on until you return. Keep an eye on it—any time there's a steady upward trend, you may want to slow down and check what's ahead according to the chart and your position.

Boat Bytes
To steer a compass course, don't look at the compass. At least, don't look at it continuously. Get the boat headed in the right direction and the compass stabilized, and then look into the distance ahead of the boat and pick out a landmark, or a cloud in open ocean, and steer for that. If you try to steer by watching the compass, you'll create a crazed "snake-wake" as you chase the oscillations of the compass card with the waves.

The Color of Water

In many areas, a seasoned skipper can measure water depth simply by looking at its color. To be sure, in the muddy waters of the Mississippi River, not even a catfish can navigate by eye, but in the clear waters of the upper Great Lakes and in most coastal areas, navigation by water color is a useful and accurate art, and one you'll no doubt want to employ on any cruise you take.

Water captures most colors of sunlight but reflects blue, so the deeper the water, the bluer it looks. Extremely clear water like that in Lake Superior offers only shades of blue, while water with a bit of sand in it, like that along much of the coast of Florida, may look pale green in depths to 40 feet.

In most areas, the lighter the shade of water, the shallower it is. Thus, pale blue, pale green, or whitish water may be anywhere from a couple feet to only inches deep.

In general, dark-green water is deeper than light-green water, and water shading toward white is water too shallow for your boat. A pair of polarized sunglasses is a great help in noting color changes. (Photo credit: Frank Sargeant)

Moderate blues and greens are anywhere from four to 40 feet deep, and deep blues and greens are deeper than 40 feet. The green water fades to blue as you move farther offshore and escape the stirred-up sand.

The deepest ocean waters are an indigo to violet shade that is spectacularly beautiful on a sunny, calm day. (The colors on the back of a marlin or a sailfish mimic this magical color.)

There is also a catalog of colors in inshore waters. Here are the most common:

➤ Dark-green spots surrounded by light-green spots: Patches of grass or rock on sand bottom.

➤ Broad, dark-green to gray areas in water that you know is fairly shallow: Sea grass, often prime fishing waters.

➤ Brownish spots: Oyster bars or rocks dangerously near the surface.

➤ Dark blue or emerald through an otherwise pale-green flat: A deep channel, good for boating (also good for finding spiny lobster to grill for dinner).

Understanding water colors will serve you well, even when you're just buzzing out to wet a line before sundown. And in many areas with extensive shallows, such as the Florida Keys and the Bahamas, it's essential for safe navigation.

In general, that's about all there is to it. Ninety-nine trips out of 100, you'll have a completely enjoyable trip without the slightest glitch, particularly after you get the first trip or two behind you. However, there's always that 100th trip...so it's best to do your homework before setting out.

Murphy Rules

It is true that, occasionally, whatever can go wrong will go wrong. In fact, on my boat, it's true that sometimes things that *can't* possibly go wrong go wrong. You have to expect a few problems now and then.

Suppose you're motoring happily along toward your third waypoint, a sea buoy over the horizon off the coast of Maine, when suddenly the GPS goes blank.

Now what?

If it's a long run and your target is small and in danger of being missed, stop the boat and break out the chart; otherwise, you may wind up out on St. Georges Bank eating raw cod.

You can figure about how far along the leg you were when the electronics went kaput using an ancient art known as "dead reckoning."

Dead Reckoning Is Alive and Well

Dead reckoning is the art of estimating position by calculating course, speed, and time, without the aid of electronics.

It's not as accurate or as simple as turning on the GPS chart-plotter, to be sure, but it's a backup for when everything breaks, and it will usually get you within sight of the marker or the harbor you're looking for.

On a long cruise, particularly when you're traveling at night, it's standard procedure to track your course on the chart via dead reckoning to make sure your electronics have not gone bonkers. And, if you don't have a GPS or a LORAN, you can use dead reckoning to calculate about how long it will take you to get from point A to point B.

The basics are the relationships of distance (D), time (T), and speed (S) you learned in elementary school:

Distance = Speed × Time

Speed = Distance ÷ Time

Time = Distance ÷ Speed

So, for example, if you are traveling 30 mph for two hours, you can easily calculate distance covered thus:

D = 2 × 30 = 60 miles

To calculate using minutes, the equations look like this:

D = S(T) ÷ 60

S = 60D ÷ T

T = 60D ÷ S

Maybe you're going from your marina to another at the other end of a big lake and you want to know if you'll arrive in time for lunch. The distance is 40 miles and your boat does 15 mph.

T = 60 (40) ÷ 15 = 160 minutes = 2 hours, 40 minutes

It takes a bit of doodling to keep track of your location with a pencil rather than electronic memory bytes, but after a few trips it becomes second nature, and one more interesting skill you can use as skipper.

Vectoring In

If there were no winds or currents, boats could simply head straight for their destination, like a car traveling down a road, and wind up where the skipper wanted to go.

But boats are greatly affected by both winds and currents, and the slower the boat, the greater the effects.

If you never venture offshore, the offset of wind and current is less important, but not completely irrelevant. When you're heading for a distant shoreline in a low-speed boat such as a pontoon rig, and facing heavy side winds, you may have to steer far above or below your target to travel directly toward it.

The same is true with strong river currents—set the boat at an angle into the current, pointing upstream of your intended landing point, to get to the spot you want to reach. Those trying to get boats back on trailers at river ramps soon learn this tactic.

There's a bit of science to figuring the appropriate vectors for long ocean crossings. The process is more than the beginning boater might want to wade through, but for those who go on to the blue horizons, the current edition of *Chapman's Piloting* (Hearst Marine Books, 1996) has an excellent chapter on how it's done.

Boat Bytes

In crossing the Florida Current between the Bahamas and Florida (commonly but inaccurately known as the Gulf Stream), it's common for slower boats to be offset by many miles due to the northward push of the ocean current measuring 2.5 to 4 knots. Sailboats and trawlers out of Miami's Government Cut must steer southeast to arrive at Bimini, which is almost due east. The difference for a 5-knot boat can be over 30 degrees!

The Least You Need to Know

➤ Every prudent skipper carries some type of communications device, allowing access to emergency services ashore.

➤ It's wise to plan any extended voyage well in advance, and to study the route both before you leave and while you're underway.

➤ Keep track of your position when you cruise, both electronically and via the art of dead reckoning. Someday, you'll be glad you did.

Part 4
Nature's Triple Play: Wind, Weather, and Tides

Boaters soon learn that the weather is both their best friend and their worst enemy. This part tells you what to expect, based both on listening to the professionals and on listening to nature's clues (sometimes they're more reliable!).

And if you're a coastal boater, you'll definitely want to give some attention to Chapter 16 on tides. Their ups and downs and ins and outs are both fascinating and challenging, and affect everything from safe navigation to properly tying a boat to a dock.

Chapter 15

Weather You Like It or Not

In This Chapter

➤ Becoming your own weather-person

➤ Winds and waves and how they affect you as a boater

➤ Interpreting clouds

➤ Handling squalls, lightning, and other dangerous conditions

You quickly learn to become adept at reading the weather when you spend much time afloat, particularly after the first few times you get caught out in a howling thunderstorm when the TV forecaster promised a calm, sunny day.

Conditions change rapidly on the water, and those white, puffy clouds that look so welcoming when you leave the dock can quickly build into towering black thunderstorms while you decide to take a nap to the gentle slap of the waves against the hull.

This doesn't mean you have to learn millibars and isobars and the names of all the types of clouds (another item to which we all should have paid better attention in 9th grade science), but there is a lot of practical weather lore that will help you avoid sticky situations wherever you boat.

In this chapter, you'll learn how to become your own weather forecaster. I'll also tell you how winds affect waves so that you'll know when your favorite waters are likely to be too rough for enjoyable boating. And we'll cover how to deal with dangerous elements such as lightning.

Forecasts—Don't Leave Home Without Them

The favorite source of weather information for most boaters at home has become television's The Weather Channel. It runs 24 hours a day and offers not only the national weather picture repeatedly, preparing you for major, wide-scale changes, but also the local weather, including radar, every eight minutes.

The radar view is particularly useful—any bad weather likely to be in your area within a few hours will appear on the screen. If you've got cable or satellite TV, you won't want to miss checking the data. (Regular news programs' weather forecasts are just as useful, but often aren't on when you need them.)

Boat Bytes
For those with Internet access, check out the weather information on newspaper sites, such as for the *Tampa Tribune* at **http://www.tampatrib.com**. This information is updated regularly and often includes live-action radar.

Newspaper weather information gives a broad view of what might be headed your way, but the information is likely to be at least 24 hours old by the time it gets printed and delivered.

The Weather Service also maintains offices in many coastal areas with telephone-available recorded weather information, updated regularly. Check your local directories for the number.

Once you're at the boat, NOAA Radio offers continuous weather broadcasts that can be picked up on any VHF radio, and these are keyed to the mariner, which The Weather Channel forecast is not. You get data on sea conditions both inshore and off, currents, and so on—all for your localized area of the coast. Press WX-1, WX-2, or WX-3 on your VHF to hear the continuous broadcasts, which are updated several times a day.

The Highs and Lows of Air Pressure

Air pressure as measured by a barometer is a useful indicator of likely weather in your immediate area. A barometer going south in a big hurry indicates a major blow, maybe even a hurricane, as a major low-pressure system approaches. However, it's also true that a rising barometer can foretell strong winds, even though there's unlikely to be rain and lightning attached.

Here's how it works: Unequal heating of the earth between the poles and the equator causes north-south air flows, which are twisted into east-west flows by the rotation of the planet. As they're twisted, they form whirling masses of air that contain pressures that are either higher or lower than the average weight of calm air—weather highs and lows.

Some barometers have "rain" marked on the readings below 29.00 inches, "fair" marked on those above 30.50. But in fact, both rising and falling barometers can mean wind or bad weather. Rapid change is the determining factor, because an abrupt change from high pressure to low pressure or vice versa is sure to create a rapid air flow and lots of wave action with it.

A Feel for Nasty Weather

Although there's a lot of weather lore that just ain't so, there's also a body of "weather sense" among those who make their living on the water that you should not ignore. When a grizzled fishing guide or commercial fisherman looks at the morning sky and advises you to stay at the docks despite a rosy forecast on the morning news, listen to the locals. You, your crew, and your boat will thank you.

The idea that lightning never strikes twice in one place, for example, has repeatedly been proven incorrect. And although the "fish may bite least when the wind's in the east," an east wind does not always foretell a coming storm. The winds blow toward lows approaching from the west, true enough, but whirling storms can also blow from the east after a low passes.

Some skippers can "feel" rain in the air. How? It's a combination of extreme humidity, low hanging clouds, and usually, a soft but persistent wind out of the southwest, the source of most rain in the U.S.

Wind out of the east? In many areas, the skippers will avoid starting a long cruise because they know an east wind is often being sucked toward a low pressure area to the west.

Some can even look at the way the leaves are blowing on a tree and tell you when rain is coming. How do they do it? Prevailing or fair-weather winds cause leaves to grow in one direction. The reversal of winds that comes as a low approaches flips the leaves over and exposes their light-colored undersides, which the savvy mariner views as a warning sign.

> **Boat Bytes**
> Another sure rain forecaster is sound carrying farther and clearer than normal. When low clouds full of rain approach, they trap sound and bounce it back to earth, and the reverberations travel well. If you hear a train whistle blowing miles away, expect rain coming from that direction.

Weather Proverbs

One of the first proverbs we learn is this one:

> Red sky at morning, sailors take warning;
> red sky at night, sailors delight.

Surprisingly, meteorologists agree with mariners on this one. A red sky at dawn results from the sun lighting up the edges of storm clouds moving in from the west, while a red sky at night means the sun has popped clear of the progressing clouds and fair weather is approaching (although it may be windy for a day or two after the front).

Boat Bytes
Although a red sky at night may be a sailor's delight, "orange or yellow can hurt a fellow." Clouds that turn these colors at sundown indicate that humidity is moving in, rain is likely, and storms are possible.

Here's another mariner's favorite:

> Mackerel scales and mares' tails make tall ships carry low sails.

Mackerel scales are altocumulus clouds that form a scale-like pattern overhead, while mares' tails are cirrus clouds with the tails swept upward. Both are harbingers of wind and rain, although the weather usually takes 24 hours or more to arrive.

"Mackerel scale" clouds often mean rain tomorrow, although they show only when the day is sunny. (Photo credit: Frank Sargeant)

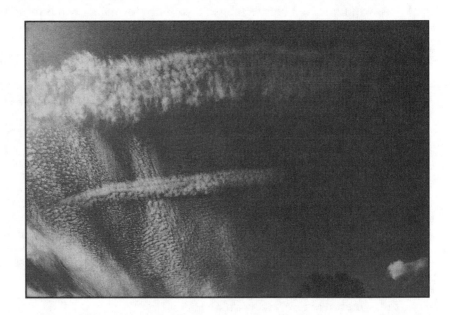

When the sun wears a halo, a luminescent ring that scientists say is ice crystals forming in the atmosphere, it's a good sign that there's a front coming in soon. "Sun dogs" or mock suns, bright spots in the sky displaying the spectrum of colors, show the same conditions, and also are most common when bad weather is on the way.

A rainbow is the mythic promise of an end to flooding, but in reality it depends on when and where you see the phenomenon. A rainbow in the west in the morning may mean rain on the way. In the east in the afternoon, it's usually a sign that the rain has passed.

Wind Speeds

In general, winds are an enemy to the powerboater and friend to the sailor—to a point. Most powerboat-drivers would just as soon see the water dead calm every time they leave the dock, offering a smooth surface where they can let their horses run at full speed without pounding the crew to Jello.

However, for a powerboater, winds up to 10 knots are generally not a concern. Ten to 15 knots makes things uncomfortable, and over 15 knots, only the tough head out.

Sailors hate dead calm with a passion, love 10 to 15 knots, and the young and reckless may take on 20 knots or more in a catamaran. It's wet, wild, and risky, but you go fast.

"Small Craft Advisories" (SCAs) are posted on weather stations and at some large marinas when winds exceed 18 knots. The signal is a triangular red flag, or at night a red light over a white light. They're an indication that anything less than a ship should stay in port.

> **Boat Bytes**
> Although the most common weather pattern in the U.S. is west to east, there are times when rain and storms come from the east. It's common in Florida in summer as storms drift off the Atlantic, and in New England in winter, as particularly vicious storms sweeping in from the southwest rotate as they hit the sea and strike back toward the mainland, producing the dreaded "nor'easter."

Fetching Considerations

The wind is only half of the equation in determining when it's going to be too rough for you and your boat. The other is the fetch, or the distance the wind will blow over unobstructed water. A long fetch can create big waves even on an inland lake with 15 knot winds, while a short fetch will prevent much stronger winds from making the water too rough for comfort.

In the central west coast of Florida where I live, it's common for anglers to go king-mackerel fishing along the beaches in 25-knot winds, as long as the blow comes out of the east or off the land, which it often does after fall fronts pass through. They find flat water in close, and it stays fishable out to several miles. The same wind coming from the west in this area would produce very dangerous water along the beach, because it would have a fetch completely across the Gulf of Mexico.

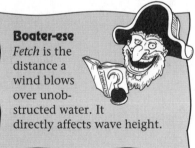

> **Boater-ese**
> *Fetch* is the distance a wind blows over unobstructed water. It directly affects wave height.

The Beaufort Scale

The Beaufort Scale, devised in the 1800s by a British admiral of the same name, is best known as an indicator of gales and hurricanes. But everybody knows you don't want to leave the harbor—or even be around the docks—when winds reach these levels.

The lower levels of the Beaufort Scale are more generally useful to recreational boaters, not because they rate the winds on a 1–12 scale (with "Force 1" being the lowest wind speed and "Force 12" the highest), but because they give the usual sea conditions at a given wind speed. This enables a skipper of moderate experience to have some idea what he or she will face at various wind speeds. The Beaufort Scale is based on open sea conditions with a broad fetch. It's shown in the following table.

Beaufort Wind Scale

Beaufort Number	Wind Speed (in Knots)	Description	Effect on Water
0	Less than 1	Calm	Mirror-calm surface
1	1–3	Light air	Scale-like ripples
2	4–6	Light breeze	Wavelets, no breaking
3	7–10	Gentle breeze	Crests begin to break
4	11–16	Moderate breeze	Waves $1^{1}/_{2}$–4 feet, numerous whitecaps
5	17–21	Fresh breeze	Waves 4–8 feet, some spray
6	22–27	Strong wind	Waves 8–13 feet, whitecaps everywhere
7	28–33	Near gale	Waves 13–20 feet, white foam, wave streaks
8	34–40	Gale	Waves increase in length, foam blown off sea, sea streaks white
9	41–47	Strong gale	Waves over 20 feet, limited visibility
10	48–55	Storm	Waves 20–30 feet, sea heavily streaked
11	56–63	Violent storm	Waves to 45 feet, sea nearly white
12	64–71	Hurricane or extremely violent storm	Waves over 45 feet, sea completely white, visibility near zero

By the time SCAs would be posted, you'd be looking at four- to eight-foot waves in areas with a long fetch. That's a whole lot more wave action than most leisurely weekenders want to deal with, even though it's not necessarily dangerous in a larger yacht.

In reality, most boaters don't want anything to do with steady seas over three feet in boats that are 20 feet long or less, and as you note from the scale, winds of just over 10 knots might bring these in exposed areas.

A Personal Experience

I've only had the opportunity to experience Force 12 winds once on the water, and that was in the completely enclosed harbor at Hopetown in the Bahamas—not a hurricane, but an amazingly violent summer thunderstorm that blew at what locals said was near 100 mph for about 10 minutes before subsiding.

It was an impressive sight, even inside the harbor where there was not enough fetch to create any wave action. The water went white as snow, and about half the anchors and moorings in the harbor let go.

Dozens of yachts and sailboats were soon caroming off each other in a race toward the downwind side of the harbor. Skippers were pushing off, starting their engines, fighting with their lines—it was general chaos, but the saving grace was that it was so brief. There was no damage except for a few bent railings, but it was an exciting interlude. (That's what we called it afterward, exciting. When we were in the middle of it, we were all scared to death.)

Land and Sea Breezes

Land and water heat up at different rates. This causes a pressure differential between the two, and breezes result if no stronger weather system interferes.

During the daytime, the land heats up faster and the air rises and loses density. As a result, the denser, cooler air from the sea blows inland.

In various areas, the time when this breeze starts to blow is very predictable. In my area of the Gulf Coast, it nearly always starts between noon and 1 p.m. in otherwise calm weather. For that reason, a lot of fishermen like to get out in the morning and come in at lunch when it starts to get bumpy, while sailors may have to wait until some time after noon to get reasonable winds.

At night, the land cools rapidly while the sea temperature remains nearly constant, so a breeze from land to sea may result. Again, this most often begins several hours after sundown, when the difference becomes most significant.

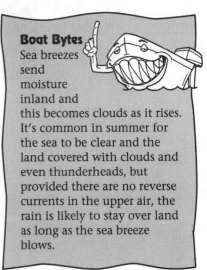

Boat Bytes
Sea breezes send moisture inland and this becomes clouds as it rises. It's common in summer for the sea to be clear and the land covered with clouds and even thunderheads, but provided there are no reverse currents in the upper air, the rain is likely to stay over land as long as the sea breeze blows.

Thunderheads

In some 30 years of bouncing around the waterfronts, I've yet to hear a skipper take a look at the sky and say something like, "Looks like some nasty cumulonimbus clouds forming up this morning—we're going to get some weather." What he or she does say is, "Uh-oh, thunderheads."

A *thunderhead* is an anvil-shaped cloud (technically, it's called a cumulonimbus) that foretells a serious thunderstorm. The direction the anvil points tells you where the storm is going—if it's headed for you, you should be headed for shelter. Seen at a distance, thunderheads appear to be white and fluffy and may appear in an otherwise blue sky. As they draw near, they tend to spread out and turn the sky gray, then nearly black. They can develop quickly and move rapidly—a thunderhead on the horizon can reach you within an hour with the right winds.

The towering, anvil-shaped cloud is a thunderhead. If the anvil points in your direction, expect a lightning storm in short order. (Photo credit: Frank Sargeant)

Squall Lines

Look Out!
Any time you see a black line of clouds approaching on the horizon, it's time to head for home at flank speed. If you're far at sea in a slow boat, the only alternative is to batten down the hatches, put on the PFDs, rain gear, and life lines, and prepare for some excitement.

A low, black bank of clouds stretching from horizon to horizon is a *squall line*, one of the nastiest of the nasties that boaters have to deal with from time to time. Squall lines can travel at a mile a minute, and bring winds from near zero to gale force in nothing flat. They're frequently found on the edge of advancing weather fronts, but these are well forecast and easy to avoid.

Harder to foretell are the smaller but no less dangerous localized squall lines that form along the bottom of fast-moving thunderstorms. These storms run across the sea as fast as most powerboats, and passing through one can be a mind-altering experience, particularly if you're trying to get through a crowded and very angry inlet along with a bunch of other boaters who stayed outside too long.

The best place to be as a squall line approaches is tied up to the dock. The bottom edge of a series of thunderstorms always brings violent weather. (Photo credit: Frank Sargeant)

Lightning

Lightning is more dangerous than wind and waves for the inland and coastal boater, because the wind and waves can readily be avoided by timing your crossings of open water. Lightning, however, can arc across miles of open sky to deliver a knockout punch to you and your boat while the sun still shines brightly overhead—it can leap many miles from a distant thunderhead to strike.

I live in what is allegedly the lightning capital of the world, the Tampa Bay area, where we have dozens of thunderstorms drifting over the peninsula daily in summer and it's an unusual day when at least a distant rumble of thunder is not heard.

In fact, it's a regular occurrence to experience the build-up of electrical charges on boat and gear here, enough so that fishing lines and rods hum and crackle, hair stands straight up, and metal objects deliver an electric shock. I've had it happen dozens of times, despite the fact that I take care not to be out when the lightning starts to fly.

The old rule about determining how far off lightning is striking by counting the seconds and then dividing by five does indeed give you the approximate mileage to the last strike, but unless it's more than five miles off, you are not necessarily safe. With 30 million volts to play with, nature can reach out and touch you at remarkable distances.

There will be times when you get caught out in lightening, however. There's no point trying to run for

Look Out!
Any time lightening gets remotely close to you—within even five miles—head for the marina!

cover once the bolts start to fly—chances are the storm will be over before you can get there. Here's what to do to ride out the storm:

➤ *If you're in a powerboat or sailboat that has a cabin,* go below and keep your hands off grounded metal objects, particularly the steering wheel.

➤ *If you're in an open powerboat or sailboat,* try to make the boat's profile as low as possible by dropping radio antennas, fishing rods, and anything else projecting above the gunnels. Stay as low as possible yourself, try to avoid touching anything that might conduct electricity, and say a prayer or two if you're so inclined.

Sailboats get struck by lightning with some frequency, but their masts are grounded and conduct the charge into the water instantly, usually without injuring passengers. (The fact that a mast is grounded doesn't mean it won't be damaged by a direct strike, however.)

Water Spouts

A *water spout* is a waterborne tornado that comes out of the bottom of a strong thunderstorm. Spouts don't possess the power or size of a tornado ashore, but they are still strong enough to damage a recreational boat in a direct hit. The spouts vary from 20 feet to several hundred feet wide, and they come spiraling down from the bottom of low-hanging cumulonimbus clouds.

Spouts are a scary sight, but they move slowly and can be outrun in a powerboat. (They're usually accompanied by wild thunderstorms and strong surface winds, though, and these can be more of a problem than the waterspouts.) It's not uncommon for offshore sailors to have several in sight at once on a stormy summer afternoon off Florida—most seasoned skippers in seaworthy boats keep their distance but don't necessarily run for cover.

The bottom line is that weather can present some dangers afloat, and that discretion is the better part of valor. Any time conditions are iffy and you have any doubt about your abilities or those of your boat to handle the likely conditions, it's better to stay at the docks and play cards.

The Least You Need to Know

➤ Learn to use weather forecasts as they apply to your local area. Find an around-the-clock source you like and trust.

➤ Nature's clues on approaching weather are always on the mark—learn to read them.

➤ Don't try to out-tough dangerous weather—when the going gets tough, always head for the dock.

Mastering the Tides

Tides are marvelous. They can make rivers run backwards 100 miles from the sea. They have the power to lift 500-ton ships off sandbars...and to push them right up through reinforced concrete bridges!

Like time itself, they wait for no man...or woman.

Tides can also be miserable. I don't think I'm that paranoid, but it seems like the tides are always against me. Especially when I'm in a canoe or sailboat.

Traveling on the right tide can make you look like a hero, but leaving the docks on the wrong flow can make trouble for the most skilled skipper. So every boater who cruises coastal waters needs to know how they work.

The daily coming and going of the ocean's visits to land is controlled by the gravitational pull of the sun and the moon, centrifugal force, and the rotation of the earth, as most of us learned in high school science. Okay, so maybe we didn't really learn *exactly* how it works, but you don't need to know all this scientific stuff to go boating. What you *do* need to know is how the tides create currents and raise and lower the depth of the water, and when they do so. That's what you'll learn in this chapter. (If you're in inland boater, you may want to skip this chapter; lakes and rivers have no tides.)

How the Moon Influences the Tides

The moon is the strongest factor affecting tides via gravitational pull. Although the moon is tiny compared to the sun, it's a lot closer to earth. As a result, tides are very obviously influenced by the moon phases.

Gravity causes the water of the oceans to bulge slightly toward the attracting bodies. The results we see are very long (thousands of miles between peak and trough), low ocean waves. They're not evident at sea, but when they hit land the motion of the waves causes the water to rise and fall, and also creates tidal currents as the water flows over shallows and through narrow passages. Anyone who spends any time around the coast knows this much. The flow varies dramatically based on the shape of the land it meets.

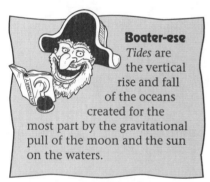

Boater-ese
Tides are the vertical rise and fall of the oceans created for the most part by the gravitational pull of the moon and the sun on the waters.

The strongest tides are on new and full moons when the sun and moon are aligned, while the weakest tides are at the moon quarter-periods, when the moon is at a 90-degree angle to the line of pull of the sun. Because of the progression of the moon phases, today's high tide at noon will become a low tide at about noon seven days from now, and a high tide very close to noon once again 14 days from now.

The moon rotates around the earth not every 24 hours, but every 24 hours and 50 minutes. Thus the tidal periods are 50 minutes later each of our earth-days.

Tide Ranges

Tidal ranges can be as little as a foot from high to low water. On the other end of the scale, in some areas the range exceeds 50 feet—the Bay of Fundy on the coasts of Maine and New Brunswick is the most famous tidal spot in the world, with a maximum range of 53 feet, the result of tidal waves oscillating with each other inside the confines of the bay and one tide stacking atop another.

The result, when these monster tides go out, are big, sucking whirlpools, logs skimming along like racing canoes, and a flow that looks like a fast river—mariners beware!

In other areas, the tide movements are so gradual and so minimal that they go unnoticed by most boaters. But even minimal tides can have a big effect on boating. In shallow areas, a tidal drop of six inches can sometimes bare hundreds of acres of bottom, and a few inches of depth sometimes makes all the difference in whether or not the draft of a boat will be excessive for entering some waters.

Playing the Tides

Tides affect both the depth of the water and the current in coastal areas, and both factors are important in operating many types of boats.

Tide heights listed in tide tables are given as plus or minus heights from the *zero line*, which is the average low tide at that spot year-round, over the previous 19 years. A tide indicated as –1.0 is expected to be one foot lower than the mean low, and one listed as +4.0 will be four feet higher than the mean low.

The greater the variations from zero—that is, the taller the wave—the stronger the tide flow. Because the earth has a slight wobble in its rotation around the sun that repeats on 19-year cycles, the tides today won't be exactly the same until 19 years from now. But for "government purposes," it can be said that tides repeat on yearly cycles in terms of height and current—that is, the December full moon high tide at the mouth of the Chesapeake Bay this year will have about the same height and volume on the December full moon next year, although the full moon will fall on a different date.

So what does this mean to you?

Let's look at an example. If you attempt to cross a bar with a controlling depth of 3.0 feet and there's a –0.5 tide and you have a three-foot draft, you are going to be doing the sandbar boogie for a while. On the other hand, if you try to cross the same bar on high water of a +5.0 tide—or even a +0.5—you will have no problem whatsoever. Knowing both the time and the magnitude of the tide can be critical to coastal boaters in many instances.

For sailors, the tide can be a major factor in both speed and course. Because sailboats travel at relatively slow speeds, proceeding with a strong tide can as much as double their speed, and traveling against it can cut speed in half.

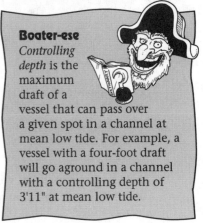

Boat Bytes
Note that mean low water is not mean sea level or just plain sea level, often referred to when measuring altitudes ashore. Sea level is very near the average between mean low and mean high tide levels—it's not a number used regularly by boaters.

Boater-ese
Controlling depth is the maximum draft of a vessel that can pass over a given spot in a channel at mean low tide. For example, a vessel with a four-foot draft will go aground in a channel with a controlling depth of 3'11" at mean low tide.

Large sailboats like this Pearson 36-footer may require five feet or greater depth to keep their keel from touching bottom. Knowledge of tide heights is critical for inshore navigation in deep-draft boats. (Photo credit: Pearson Yachts)

Boater-ese
Course made good is the actual course the boat takes, as it is affected by wind and currents, as opposed to the course steered via the compass, GPS, or LORAN.

Running at an angle across a tide can also greatly change the course made good—the tide becomes a vectoring force that can push you far off course over a period of hours. (For a closer look at how this works, see Chapter 14 on navigation.)

So where do you get this information?

Tide Tables

The tide tables, plotted by the National Ocean Service, provide forecasts of tide height and current data for locations around the world.

The tables come in book form and are available at many boating-gear stores as well as chart and map stores. The book you want will probably be either *Tide Tables, East Coast of North & South America* or *Tide Tables, West Coast of North & South America*. They sell for about $13 each from BOAT U.S. and many other sources. Similar volumes, such as *Tide Current Tables*, are available for the Atlantic Coast of North America and the Pacific Coast of North America, for about $11 each.

The tide tables make it evident that tides arrive at different shore locations at dramatically different times. Note that all times are given in "standard time," as opposed to "daylight savings time," and that they are adjusted for time zone (Eastern, Central, Mountain, or Pacific).

The high tide at the Chesapeake Bay Bridge will be many hours before the high at Annapolis, 100 miles up the bay. In fact, a distance of just a few miles can make several hours' difference in when a tide arrives and leaves.

In general, north/south differences are less than east/west differences along the Atlantic and Pacific coasts of the U.S. For example, there's only about an hour's difference between arrival of high tide at Anna Maria, on Florida's west coast, and Anclote Key, 40 miles northward along the coast. But the time difference from Anna Maria to the Little Manatee River, just 20 miles east/northeast inside Tampa Bay, is over 90 minutes. Constrictions of the bay cause the flow to lag as it moves inside, while the tidal waves in the open Gulf move more rapidly. And if there are any constricting passages, narrow channels, or shallow flats, these slow the tidal wave and retard the times even more. That's why it's possible within a shallow estuary to have rising water at the mouth and falling water up inside the tidal creeks at the same time. The movements are not part of the same tidal period.

The tide tables don't give exact tides for every port on earth, but they do provide conversion tables for a huge number of locations, so you can make time adjustments for nearby ports.

Boat Bytes

For boaters who always stay in their home bay, the full-sized tide tables offer more information than you may want. Most bait shops and marinas offer handy tide charts for free that list local tides, and these are much easier to use than leafing through the tables and converting the data to your home port.

Boat Bytes

For those with computers, TideMaster tide charts are super for planning your trips on prime tides as far as a year into the future. For details, contact Zephyr Services, 1900 Murray Avenue, Pittsburgh, PA 15217, (412) 422-6600.

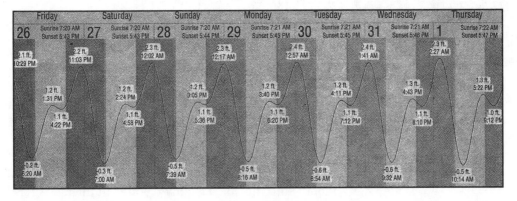

Tides can be expressed in charts as well as in numeric tables. This chart, from the Tampa Tribune, *uses a graph to show highs and lows for a week.*

Using the Tide Tables

The tables list tidal locations in geographical order from north to south and east to west; thus Miami, Florida, comes ahead of Brownsville, Texas. There's an index to look up the station nearest your location.

The table for a given spot lists dates; time of the tides in military time, with 0100 standing for 1 a.m., 1200 standing for noon, and 1800 for 6 p.m.; and the height of the maximum and minimum tides for the day.

Tide Heights and Navigation

If your boat has a draft of three feet, the lowest part of it, probably the skeg, will touch bottom in water that's 2'11" deep. If the mean low tide at a given spot is 3.0 feet and you cross on an average low tide, you won't touch bottom. If you cross on a –0.2 low tide, things will scrape and bump and possibly bend.

But there's more. If there are waves rocking your boat up and down, the water on the shoal will go from deeper to shallower with every cycle of peak to trough. On the bottom of the trough, you may strike bottom, even though you could cross the bar in calm seas. You have to use your judgment and perhaps wait for the tide to flow back in before you cross that particular spot. You refer to the tide tables to see when the water will be rising, and "guesstimate" about when you can cross by looking at the time of high tide and the sea conditions.

Boat Bytes
It's always best to punch around in the backwaters on a rising tide, and to head back for deeper water shortly before the tide peaks and starts to run back out. That way, if you go aground inside, the rising water gives you a good chance to get off and escape; while if you ground on falling water, you're stuck until the next incoming tide.

By the same token, perhaps there's only a foot of water over a bar at a creek mouth at mean low tide, and that's two feet less than you need to get in. But wait until the peak of a +3.0 tide, and there's no problem. That is, there's no problem unless you want to leave that creek at low tide. You're locked in until the next high tide, so keep that in mind any time you go exploring in the shallows.

The tide tables also list nearby locations with time corrections for the nearest main reporting station. They list the latitude and longitude of the location so that you can confirm with your GPS, and the difference in time from the nearest station. The difference may be anywhere from a few minutes to several hours, and is not the same for high and low tides. You subtract minus differences and add positive differences.

For example, suppose you want to figure out the tide for a fishing spot that's 15 miles up your favorite bay from the mouth, and the tides are only reported in the tables for the mouth. Say the report indicates a noon high at the bay mouth, and a +2.0 hours time difference for your fishing location. You would figure it this way:

12:00 + 2 = 2:00 p.m., the time of high tide at your spot

There are very slight variations in tide height at various locations on a given tidal period. In most of the southeastern U.S., this difference is insignificant, but in the northeast it can be considerable. The tide tables list this variation as well, and it should be considered if you're making an iffy passage across a bar.

Bridge Clearance

Do you ever need to know the tide heights if you're not crossing a shallow bar? Maybe.

It could be that problems arise above the water. A low bridge can block passage for fly-bridge cruisers and sailboats on high tide, yet let them pass with space to spare on low. Sometimes even runabouts can be blocked by low-hanging roadways.

You obviously need to know your boat's bridge clearance if you navigate anywhere that passage beneath one of these structures is common. The bridge clearance (BC) refers to the height from the waterline (where the surface meets the hull) to the highest point of any structure on the boat, including the mast, tuna tower, or outriggers. (If your radio antennas and riggers fold down, you don't have to measure them in the equation.)

Bridge clearance is listed on marine charts, with the height above mean high water given. So, if you want to pass under a bridge that has 20-foot listed clearance with your sportfisherman boasting a BC of 19'6", you aren't going to be able to get through at the peak of a spring tide that's a foot taller than normal high tide (more on spring tides later in this chapter). On the other hand, you can get through a bridge with a 19-foot listed clearance on the bottom of a –1.0 low.

Boater-ese

Bridge clearance is the distance from a boat's waterline to the highest point on the topsides. It limits the height of a bridge under which a boat can pass.

Bet You Didn't Know

In most areas there's a normal progression through four tides, but some days have only three tides. How can this be?

As the 50-minute-per-day regression takes place, the p.m. tide gradually advances past midnight, thus leaving one 24-hour period without four tides, even though the tidal movements maintain their steady procession.

Tides in the Estuaries

Tides follow wider, deeper channels first. That's why tide flows show up at major coastal passes long before they arrive at docks and boat ramps several miles inland.

In a bayou fed by several tidal creeks, you may see that the inflow begins on the main arm and is already flowing strong there while it's dead or even going out on the smaller feeders.

The tide comes into an estuary in a plume that you can see on the surface when the water is calm. It has a rounded leading edge, and it stays separate for a time from the residual water left in the backwaters on the previous low. Differences in salinity or temperature probably account for the edge.

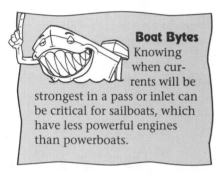

Boat Bytes
Knowing when currents will be strongest in a pass or inlet can be critical for sailboats, which have less powerful engines than powerboats.

The life in the estuaries responds to this pulse—you'll see fish start to jump and gulls start to swirl on tide movements. For anglers, it's often a good time to wet a line.

There are times, too, when the current tables can actually predict sea conditions to some extent—if a strong flow is coming out of a big pass and a wind is blowing in, you can be sure that there will be steep, nasty waves in the passage.

In a powerboat, you may want to stay at anchor until the flow reverses and begins to go with the wind, even though you'll then be working against the current, because the water will be much smoother. In a motorized sailboat or low-powered diesel trawler, you might have no choice but to take advantage of the push of the current to get you outside on the outflow.

Spring Tides

Spring tides are the tides around new and full moons each month when highs are highest and the lows are lowest. Spring tides come in summer, fall, and winter as well as spring. Confusing, isn't it? Around the new and full moon periods in most areas there is one major high and one major low daily, and the magnitude is much greater than at other times of the month. These are designated spring tides.

Neap Tides

Neap (pronounced "nip") *tides* are the tides around the quarter-moon periods each month when tidal variation is minimal. During the "quarter" periods of the moon, in many areas there are two nearly equal highs and two lows each 24-hour period. Less water is moving on each tide, and both highs and lows vary less from mean low water. Remember that the tides repeat themselves on two-week cycles, following the waxing and waning of the moon. And the tides also pretty much repeat themselves each year on a given moon cycle, so if there's a 4.90 high tide in your home port on this year's December full moon, it will be about the same next December. (Remember that the full moon won't come on exactly the same date, though, if you're planning a trip far in advance.)

Tide Sense

Watch natural tidal indicators to get a feel for the movement. The way a stick or a buoy carves the surface can tell you volumes about the flow, and will be much more accurate for your particular location than any forecast printed in a book. Take what the water gives you—many days, you'll find that the published tide tables and nature don't agree.

Learn to read the real-time clues. In general, current speeds are controlled by the difference between the highs and lows, and the time from the high to the low—lots of water moving over a short period of time—means strong currents.

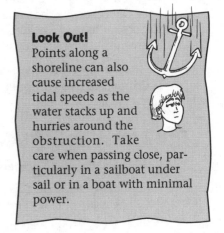

Look Out!
Points along a shoreline can also cause increased tidal speeds as the water stacks up and hurries around the obstruction. Take care when passing close, particularly in a sailboat under sail or in a boat with minimal power.

However, it also pays to understand how the geography of an estuary affects current speeds. Anywhere that lots of water has to fit through a narrow gap between islands or bars there will be a strong flow, even on moderate tidal periods. Some of these areas are obvious, as in the main pass coming out of a large bay. If the pass is narrow, the flow is going to boil through it. In fact, the currents in those areas have created the channels. A big, deep channel equals lots of current, so be wary on new and full moons.

Seasonal Variations

Summer tides are generous, winter tides are stingy. Remember that when you think about running your boat across a shallow flat on a December full-moon low. In summer, the only tides that go below mean low or zero are the spring tides on the few days around the new and full moon. But in winter, it's not uncommon for a week on either side of the moons to be at or below zero at extreme low.

For example, on the full moon in May of 1996, the lowest tide was –0.27 at St. Petersburg Pier in Tampa Bay. On the December full moon at the same spot, the lowest tide was –0.50, less than 0.3 lower. That doesn't sound like a lot, but it's enough to make hundreds of acres go bare in the gentle topography of Florida's west coast. It's also enough to ruin your lower unit if you're not careful where you drive.

The highs are higher in spring and summer, as well—the max on the June 1996 full moon was +2.91 at St. Pete, while the high on the December full was just +2.20, more than .7 foot lower.

Wind Tides

The predicted tides are based on the pull of the moon, sun, and earth, but they can't take into account the effect of winds. In winter on the west coast of Florida, it's very common to get 20- to 30-knot winds out of the northeast after a front, and these can move another six inches to a foot of water out on the extreme lows. Conversely, these same winds pile water into the inlets on the east coast. And in summer, strong winds out of the southwest are not uncommon along the Gulf Coast. These tend to make the already tall summer tides even higher. On the Atlantic Coast of southern Florida, the trade winds that blow from the east make the high tides taller in summer.

Winds can even create tides in fresh water. In winter, strong north winds over several days pile six inches to a foot of water up on the south shore of Florida's 25-mile-wide Lake Okeechobee. The same effect occurs on many big lakes, but most of them don't happen to have the height-above-sea-level measuring devices they have at Okeechobee, so the result is less obvious.

To learn more about tides, currents, and intensive coastal navigation, a good book to get is *Coastal Navigation, Step by Step* by Capt. Warren Norville (International Marine Publishing, 1975).

The Least You Need to Know

➤ In coastal areas, boaters must be familiar with tide cycles for safe navigation.

➤ The tide tables or private copies of the information contained in them give the necessary data for cruising throughout U.S. waters.

➤ Tides not only control water depth, but also currents.

➤ Sustained winds can have major local effects on tide movements.

Part 5
Staying Safe Afloat

If you've read this far, you know most of the basics of spending a day afloat. But don't ignore these very important chapters on keeping yourself and your crew safe.

You'll want to make sure your boat's equipment suits the federal requirements for safety gear before you leave the docks that first time.

It's also wise to remember that the best defense is a good offense, particularly when it comes to avoiding problems afloat—see Chapter 18 for some important cautions.

Real emergencies afloat are rare, but the smart skipper is prepared in advance to deal with whatever comes along, and this part also offers some advice on situations that might someday happen on your boat.

Chapter 17

Gearing Up for Safety

In This Chapter

➤ Determining your boat's class

➤ Choosing a personal flotation device (PFD)

➤ Distinguishing between extinguishers

➤ A look at other safety gear that's good to have

Before you leave the docks for the first time, you have to equip your boat with a set of federally required gear that experience has proven to be essential for basic safety afloat, whether you're boating in a 10-foot jon boat or a 60-foot yacht.

This may not be the most fascinating topic, but it's stuff you have to understand well enough to gear up, so persevere.

In this chapter, you'll learn the types of life preservers, the most basic piece of gear aboard any boat, as well as a bit about all the other equipment that may someday come in handy in an emergency. (Okay, maybe you'll be lucky and never have an emergency, but you'll need all the stuff in this chapter anyway when the Marine Patrol comes calling—they'll send you back to the docks and maybe give you a citation if you fail to have the required gear aboard.)

A Touch of Class

Before tackling the gear, it's necessary to understand how boats are classified by size, because the different classes require different gear. There are four classes of boats based on length, each requiring slightly different levels of safety gear:

➤ *Class A.* This class covers the smallest boats, under 16 feet long. More than half the recreational boats in the U.S. are in this class.

Boat Bytes
The tax man cometh, to boats even as he does to dwellings ashore. Tax bills are based on the class system. While it costs only about $10 to register class A boats under 16 feet in most states, it can cost over $100 per year to register a class 3 yacht. Of course, if you can afford the yacht, you can afford the C-note, and that happens to be exactly the thinking of legislators who pass tax bills.

➤ *Class 1.* (Why isn't this called class B? Just to separate the salts from the landlubbers, I guess.) This class includes boats from 16 feet to less than to 26 feet long. Over 90 percent of the boats in U.S. waters are this size or smaller.

➤ *Class 2.* This class includes boats from 26 to 40 feet, the size that starts to make your banker sit up and take notice.

➤ *Class 3.* This class includes boats from 40 to 65 feet, the realm of the privileged few.

The Coast Guard has not created a class 4 yet, but probably will add your BG class (Bill Gates) sometime soon. (Boats larger than 65 feet fall outside the designated "small boat" category and have their own sets of requirements.)

Why make them classes, instead of just designating them by length? Because the larger the boat, the more likely it is to be taken far offshore; therefore, the more likely it is to need more extensive safety equipment.

The ABCs of PFDs

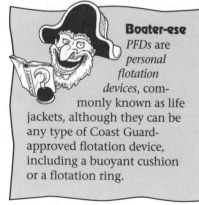

Boater-ese
PFDs are *personal flotation devices,* commonly known as life jackets, although they can be any type of Coast Guard-approved flotation device, including a buoyant cushion or a flotation ring.

The Coast Guard calls life jackets "personal flotation devices" because it's longer. Then they shorten it to PFDs because it's shorter. Those of you have been in the military instinctively understand.

Whatever you call them, these devices are intended to keep you afloat. You *must* have one aboard for each crew member. If the Marine Patrol catches you without enough PFDs aboard for your crew, you're heading back to the dock—it's a mistake no officer will ignore.

If you have kids aboard, you must have life jackets sized to fit them. In many states, children under six must wear the jackets while onboard; in some states, all children under 12 must wear life jackets at all times.

Types of PFDs

PFDs are classified into five types.

Type I is the top-quality offshore jacket with lots of buoyancy or lifting force (22 pounds or more, by law), and it's fitted in a jacket that will stay in place even in rough seas. This type will turn an unconscious wearer face up, a must for high-performance boats and big-water kayakers and canoeists. These jackets are bulky and most are made with blaze-orange shells. They're a bit more expensive than the weekend-type jacket (about $30), but worth it.

Type II is the "horse-collar" or near-shore life jacket, with 15.5 pounds of buoyancy. It does not have to turn an unconscious wearer face up, and it will not necessarily stay on in rough water. But it's inexpensive (under $10). These are the bright-orange jackets you see sold in every discount store. Are they adequate? Maybe, if the only time you ever need one is on a quiet pond where shore is only a few yards away. For the most part, boaters using bigger waters should stay clear of type II jackets—a type I or type III jacket (discussed next) is a better choice.

Type III is currently the most popular type of life jacket because it's the most comfortable (see the photo on the following page). It's made of foam rather than kapok or other bulky material so it flexes with the body, and is finished in attractive colors and materials, often with plenty of pockets to store gear. Type III jackets carry 15.5 pounds of flotation and stay on well due to zippers and straps. They provide good thermal insulation in cold weather and are easy to store because they fold flat. With prices staring at $15, type III jackets are affordable, too.

The disadvantages of type III jackets: In rough water, they float low and you may have a hard time breathing as waves splash in your face. They also do not turn unconscious users right side up.

Type IV is not a jacket at all, but either a throwable cushion with straps or a foam life ring. At least one is required aboard all boats over 16 feet long. The idea is to throw this to someone who falls overboard without a regular life jacket, giving him something to cling to until you get the boat to him. The throwables are not intended to do much more than that.

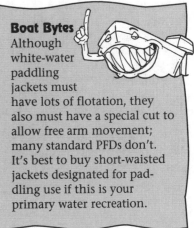

Boat Bytes
Although white-water paddling jackets must have lots of flotation, they also must have a special cut to allow free arm movement; many standard PFDs don't. It's best to buy short-waisted jackets designated for paddling use if this is your primary water recreation.

Look Out!
If you have small children aboard, you *must* have vests sized for them. They slip right through an adult-sized vest in the water. In fact, in many states, kids under 12 *must* wear their vests at all times when the boat is underway.

Boat Bytes
There are also life vests for dogs (the small ones also fit most cats), recommended if you take your pet offshore with you. Dogs have a way of going overboard when you least expect them to, and the jacket helps them stay on top of the water and makes them easier to see. Inshore, don't worry about it—just about any dog can swim to any land within visible range. (In the Florida Keys a few years back, a Lab went eight miles after falling off a boat beyond the barrier reefs.)

Who throws you the type IV cushion if you are boating solo? Nobody, but you're still required to have it on board. Most wind up as seats, although that's not a good idea over the long term since it squashes the flotation.

Type V are survival suits or other special equipment. Survival suits are the best of all life preservers, but they're so heavy and hot that they're only worn in rain or in cold-climate boating. They're both rainproof and packed with thermal insulation—you can survive for hours in cold water or for days in moderate temperatures in one of these suits. They're also very expensive, costing several hundred dollars each.

Which types of PFDs do you need on your boat by law? This is an easy one:

➤ Class A boats: one of any type of PFD for each person

➤ Class 1, 2, and 3 boats: one wearable preserver per person (not a type IV cushion), plus a single type IV throwable

Type III PFDs are soft foam vests that are comfortable to wear. They provide insulation on cold mornings, too. (Photo credit: Stearns Mfg.)

Wearing PFDs

Does anybody actually *wear* these life-saving devices?

Surprisingly, many don't.

There's no law that adults have to wear PFDs aboard, so most don't. Look in any boating magazine and you'll be hard pressed to find a single boater wearing a PFD—unless there's a story about why you should wear PFDs! The fact is that almost nobody wears them, except Coast Guard and Marine Patrol officers on duty. This, despite the fact that nearly every boating advice book tells you that you should wear a PFD any time you're afloat, and despite the fact that boating-related drownings would be cut to a fraction if everyone wore them.

People may not wear PFDs because they're bulky, hot, and unstylish, because the crew is in a hurry to get started, and because they don't want to give the appearance of being boating dorks. They are always worn in boat races and in most bass-fishing tournaments where high-performance boats are involved, but that's only because the rules require that they be worn in these events.

Bet You Didn't Know

New additions to approved type V devices are inflatable jackets, belts, and suspenders. These are likely to take over the market once prices come down, because they're the only life jacket that people will actually wear in most boating weather. They're completely unobtrusive—you never know they're there until you need them, and then you pull a cord and they inflate. (Not all inflatable PFDs are approved by the Coast Guard. Look for the tag before you buy.) Like any contrivance, the CO_2 cartridge can fail. There are manual tubes you can use to blow up the inflatables if that becomes necessary.

When the chips are down, you had better have the jackets close at hand. Mine go on everybody when there's a tough inlet to run or when a squall line stands between us and the harbor, and any time we have non-swimmers aboard, they wear them dock-to-dock.

When PFDs are not being worn, they have to be in a location that's quick to get to, that everyone aboard knows about, and that will allow them to float free if the boat capsizes. If they're buried in the cabin under the bunks, they won't do you much good in an emergency.

Storing PFDs

PFDs are mold magnets. Put them in a damp boat locker for two days and you'll see a major colony sprouting. The only way to avoid this is to dry the PFDs in the sun after each trip. It's not a bad idea to hit mold spots with Lysol or a similar antiseptic spray before you lay them out to dry. Then stow them inside your garage, or even better, inside your air-conditioned house.

The big problem with stowing PFDs outside the boat is that it's easy to forget them when you load up to head for the ramp. One good trick is to clip the boat ignition key to one of the jackets. You may forget the jackets, but you won't forget the boat key. (Usually, that is. I did it once, and had to make a 20-mile drive to retrieve both while the rather abusive crew waited at the ramp. I pointed out to them that we couldn't go out until we had the jackets, anyway, so leaving the key with the jackets is still a good idea.)

If you choose to store PFDs in your boat, place a mildew-preventer such as Star-Brite mildew control bags in the storage compartment. The downside is that this stuff smells so bad that it may run off your passengers, too.

Fire Extinguishers

Federal law also requires a fire extinguisher aboard any boat over 26 feet, and aboard those 26 feet and less where flammable gases can be entrapped below decks. In general, you are required to carry an extinguisher if:

➤ You have inboard or inboard/outboard engines.

➤ You have closed compartments where fuel is stored. (This includes portable fuel tanks.)

➤ You have permanently installed fuel tanks.

➤ Your boat has a double bottom not sealed to the hull with foam.

➤ Your boat has enclosed living spaces.

➤ The boat has closed compartments where flammables are stored.

Boat Bytes
Fire extinguishers must be checked regularly to make sure they're maintaining a full charge. Some are recommended for recharge every six months, some every 12 months. Most have a gauge on top indicating the charge level—check it often, but be aware that it may not be accurate. Weighing the extinguisher is the best way to check it for a full charge.

In short, pretty much *any* powerboat beyond a jon boat is required to carry an extinguisher. Sailboats with gas or diesel power must also have them.

Like everything else required by federal regulations, there are classes of fire extinguishers. No need for us to labor through them all—the type of extinguisher that recreational boaters need is the B-I, which can be foam, CO_2, dry chemicals, or inflammable gas, all designed to put out fuel and oil fires.

Boats to 26 feet need one B-I, those 26 to 40 feet need two B-Is, and those over 40 feet need three B-Is. In the larger two classes, you can substitute a single larger B-II type, which contains the same fire-quenching substances but more of them.

Fire extinguishers should be stored where you can get to them quickly, just like PFDs. Upright clamp brackets that mount on the lower part of the console just to one side of the wheel are probably best. An extinguisher mounted here is always within reach of the skipper.

A nice extra on powerboats with enclosed engine compartments is an automatic fire system. It includes a heat-sensitive spray nozzle, like those used in fire-protection systems in hotels, and a fire extinguisher. If temperature gets too high in the engine compartment, the seal on the nozzle lets go and the contents shoot out to put out the fire.

Look Out!
Never store your extinguisher in an aft compartment, where fuel and batteries are often found. Any fire is likely to start there, and you won't be able to get to your extinguisher for the flames.

Vents and Electrical Fans

All boats with inboard and inboard/outboard engines are required to have vents and electrical fans to suck flammable gases out of the engine area. Any boat you buy is likely to have the required vent system in place, but check to make sure the fans still function and that the hoses still reach to the lowest part of the bilge, the area where the fumes are most likely to gather.

Sound Signals

Boats to 39.4 feet must have some sort of sound signal aboard—an electric horn is fine, as is an air horn with a compressed air can attached. Boats over 39.4 feet must have a signal that can be heard at a half-mile, and must also have a ship's bell.

Arresting Flame Development

All inboard and inboard/outboards have a backfire flame arrester atop the air intake. You can't tell it from an air cleaner by looking at the outside, but there's a series of fine metal or other nonflammable grids inside to block any ignited gases that "backfire" from inside the firing chamber from escaping back up into the engine compartment. This will be in place when you buy the boat, but don't get the idea of improving performance by removing it; this makes your boat both illegal and dangerous.

Boat Bytes
If you ever need to use your visual distress signals, make sure you don't waste them. If there are no boats or aircraft in sight, there may not be anyone near enough to help. There's a temptation to fire the flares immediately when you start taking on water, according to those who have been there, on the hope of immediate rescue. But you'll be more certain to survive if you save the distress signals for when you're sure a potential rescuer is within range.

Visual Distress Signals

Powerboats over 16 feet long are required to carry visual distress signals to let other vessels nearby know when immediate help is needed. Of course, you hope your radio will do the job on this, but the visual signals are your backup.

The most basic signal is an orange flag with a black square and disc. Orange smoke signals are also acceptable, as are red flares. The hand-held type is the simplest and least expensive, but those that can be fired into the air are more visible.

A problem with the smoke and flare type signals is that they may not function if they get wet. And all expire 42 months after the manufacturing date stamped on the device. After that time, they no longer legally fulfill the requirement. However, they are much more visible than a flag at a distance.

It's a good idea to keep your expired flares; they'll usually function even after the expiration date and provide a backup to your updated flares. (Just be sure to boldly mark the expired ones so you'll know which is which.)

Numbers and Licenses

All states require boats to have a number and a current year license. These are available at offices of the state tax collectors. The number is permanent with a given boat, but the license must be renewed every 12 months. The number is displayed on both sides of the bow in block letters at least three inches tall; the license, on the port side adjacent to the number.

Good to Have—Common-Sense Gear

There are a few items not necessarily required that common sense dictates you'll have aboard anyway. An anchor and line is a safety device in the sense that it can keep you from drifting out to sea or into shipping lanes if your motor dies.

An electric bilge pump, manual pump, or even a bailing bucket should be part of the gear on every boat. A bucket is a good idea even if you have an electric pump—they're notorious for jamming up at the worst possible moments.

It's a good idea to carry a second means of propulsion for smaller boats, up through class 1, and many states require it. This can be oars, a push pole, a little kicker motor, or an electric troller—something that will get you home, slowly but surely, should the day come when the motor won't run.

Safety to the Max—Other Gear

A peace-of-mind extra is a waterproof strobe light that pins to your PFD. The strobe can be seen for a couple of miles at night and can make all the difference if you ever go into the water. They can also help the tow boat locate you if you break down after dark. At $25 to $45, strobe lights are worth the price.

Emergency Position Indicating Radio Beacons (EPIRBs) are the best insurance for rescue offshore. When activated, they send out an emergency signal that can reach 300 miles both across the water and into the air, which means it's very likely the signal will be picked up by passing airliners, if not by other boats or ships.

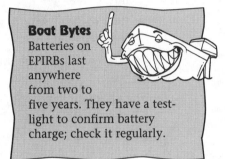

Boat Bytes
Batteries on EPIRBs last anywhere from two to five years. They have a test-light to confirm battery charge; check it regularly.

EPIRBs are self-contained and are designed to be mounted on an open area of the boat where they can float to the surface if the craft sinks. Seawater activates most models; you don't have to turn them on. The cost is around $300 to $1,200.

Man the Lifeboats

The first reaction of boaters viewing the latest movie version of *Titanic* is to start shopping for life rafts. Having one aboard, particularly when land is many miles over the horizon, is a great comfort.

However, buying a raft is a major investment. Prices range from around $2,000 to $4,000 for self-inflating models with a canopy to protect against rain and sun but without a motor. They're built with the same quality as the toughest of full-sized inflatable boats, thus the high prices. Most come equipped with survival kits that include a supply of fresh water, a knife, lights, flares, fishing gear, and more.

Most boaters don't invest in a raft because the likelihood of a boat sinking out from under them is remote. To those it has happened to, however, the raft is worth any price. (What most commonly happens to those who sink without a raft is that they wind up getting to know the inside of a giant ice chest very, very well.)

For the casual boater, a raft is overkill, but for those who regularly make long cruises beyond soundings, they're a wise investment.

The Least You Need to Know

➤ The most basic gear on any boat is a PFD for every passenger—don't leave the docks without them.

➤ Fire afloat is rare, but a good extinguisher, regularly recharged, is insurance you must have.

➤ Gear to create sound, vent your engine compartment, and signal distress is also required in every state.

➤ Boats in U.S. waters must be numbered and licensed, with the license renewed yearly.

➤ Other gear that's good to have (but that's not legally required) includes an electric bilge pump, oars or a spare motor, and a waterproof strobe light.

Chapter 18

The Best Defense Is Common Sense

In This Chapter

➤ Filing a float plan

➤ Storm warnings—making your boat secure

➤ Staying safe while swimming, diving, and water skiing

➤ Slow is good

➤ The importance of keeping a clear head while operating a boat

The best way to deal with problems afloat (or ashore, for that matter) is to avoid getting into them in the first place. Of course, that's easier said than done, and looking in that rearview mirror often makes things much clearer than they were through the windshield. But a bit of caution judiciously applied can prevent most difficult situations before they get started.

In this chapter, I'll give you some added tips for keeping your crew and your boat safe, including the use of float plans to let those ashore know where you've gone and securing your boat against storms. We'll also review the dangers of high-speed boating and alcohol afloat.

Tell Someone Where You're Going

A *float plan* is a simple written communication that tells those ashore where you're going and when you expect to return. If you don't come back on time, they know where to start looking.

The float plan should include the following items:

Boat Bytes
If you leave a float plan with a pal, be absolutely sure to check in when you return. If you forget, causing your protector to launch a series of desperate but unneeded calls to authorities, it's unlikely your designee will ever again pay any attention to your float plans. One way to remember is to tape a reminder to your boat's ignition key.

➤ The skipper's name and home phone—this lets potential rescuers call your house to make sure you didn't slip home without telling anyone.

➤ A description of your boat, including registration numbers, length, and color.

➤ The itinerary of your trip—where you are going (including latitude/longitude for offshore locations), where you are putting in, and the approximate time you expect to return.

➤ Emergency numbers to call in case you don't return on time. The Coast Guard, sheriff's office, and Marine Patrol should be included.

You simply give this information to a friend, relative, or cooperative marina operator, and then check in with the person once you're back ashore.

Storm Warnings

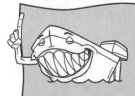

Boat Bytes
The best storm stowage for small boats is inside a garage. If you don't have access to a garage and have a lightweight boat (such as a canoe or jon boat), turn it right side up and fill it with water; the added weight will keep the boat from being blown away. (Add a few tie-downs, staked deeply into the ground, just in case.)

Storms cause millions of dollars in damages to recreational boats each year. Most of it could be avoided if the skippers took precautions well in advance of the storms.

One of the more inventive approaches I've ever seen for avoiding storm damage was that of a sailor in Brownsville, Texas, where I'd gone to report on the aftermath of a hurricane. When the skipper became certain the town was going to take a direct hit, he simply took all his electronics and personal gear off his 30-foot sailboat, tied it with extra long and strong dock lines, and pulled the plug, sinking his own boat before the storm could. Nothing was left above the water but the mast.

The result was no hull damage to his boat whatsoever, although he had to have the wiring redone and the motor rebuilt. But meanwhile, dozens of boats floating normally on either side of him were pounded into kindling by the storm.

This is not to recommend "pre-sinking" as a wise solution to the approach of a storm, unless you enjoy living with the smell of harbor mud and dead crabs long after the fact. But it does show that a bit of thought applied early can avoid major problems.

If a major storm such as a hurricane is forecast well in advance, the best move is to get your boat out of the water and away from the waterfront. The force of many sea storms abates dramatically just a few miles inland, and if you move your boat out of the strike zone, it's unlikely to suffer problems.

For trailered boats stored outside, remove all gear and add extra tie-downs at the bow and stern but pull the drain-plug. High-sided boats can hold so much rain water they may break the trailer springs. Block the trailer wheels as well—you don't want the rig taking a drive by itself.

Boats too large for trailering have to be left in the water, and the trick is to find a "hurricane hole" where they will be protected from winds and seas. Deep coastal rivers are favorites for this, providing narrow waterways, often with steep banks to keep out the winds.

Even in these areas, it's necessary to make the boat extra secure by putting out two or even three anchors and tying off on large trees ashore.

In moderate storms, including minimal hurricanes, many boaters take their chances with leaving their boats at a marina. As long as the storm doesn't make a direct hit, most of these boats survive. But it does take special preparation to see that they do.

Dock lines have to be lengthened significantly to allow for tides that may be three to five times the normal height. Spring lines have to be positioned so that the boat is cradled in place over its slip even though rising water elevates it above the tops of the pilings. (One of the major damages to boats is being holed by these pilings as the hull rocks in the waves.)

> **Boat Bytes**
> It's a good idea to scout out hurricane holes well in advance of the June-October hurricane season—there won't be time once a storm homes in on your section of the coast. And remember, it's likely that other boaters will be headed for the same hole when a storm bears down on you, so plan to get there early.

> **Look Out!**
> Don't forget "storm surge" as a factor in selecting a hurricane hole. A harbor protected by a jetty that's five feet above the normal high tide may go underwater in storm tides, allowing open ocean waves to roll right into your "safe" spot!

Take all your electronics, bedding, and personal belongings off the boat. The driving force of the wind will push water into every crevice, soaking anything that remains. And it's not uncommon for looters to visit the marinas just after a storm, so beat them to the punch by storing your gear safely at home.

Leave Your Boat Behind

One thing that shouldn't be done is to stay with your boat in the hopes of saving it in a major storm. No boat is worth your life, and that's what you put on the line when you decide to stay after the evacuation order comes.

When the roads are flooded and the power lines down, there will be no one to help you and no way out; make your boat as secure as possible, give it a farewell kiss, and then head inland when the hurricane flags fly.

Swimming and Diving

Most boaters use their rigs for swimming at one time or another. Diving, both snorkeling and scuba, is also among the major reasons for being a boat owner.

But hopping overboard does pose some potential problems. The first story I wrote for *Reader's Digest* some 25 years ago was on a young woman and her husband who left their boat to snorkel in the clear waters off Homosassa, Florida, one summer morning and wound up in a struggle for survival that didn't end, for her, until some 24 hours later.

Their mistake? They left no one aboard to pick them up. In the strong currents flowing that day, they soon found themselves so far from the boat that getting back was a struggle. The husband made a decision to leave his wife in hopes that he could get to the boat and rescue her, but when he finally made it to the boat the sun was down and he couldn't find her. She spent a long night treading water, breathing through her snorkel, and hoping no sharks found her. The story had a happy ending the next day when the two were reunited, but it could just as well have been a tragedy.

Snorkeling for scallops is fun, but who's left in the boat to pick up this swimmer if he gets tired? This boat also lacks the legally required "diver down" flag to warn other boaters there's a diver in the water. (Photo credit: Frank Sargeant)

The moral of the story, obviously, is that divers and swimmers must never leave the boat un-captained in waters where the current can make return difficult.

In fact, one of the best ways to explore a reef, search for scallops, or simply snorkel over a grass flat is to let the boat drift right along with the swimmers on the tide movements. When anyone gets tired, the boat is only a few strokes away. An alternative is to swim up-current when exploring from an anchored boat. That way, when you get tired, you simply stop swimming and ride the current back to the boat.

Water Skiing

Water skiing is a major attraction to boating for kids and active adults, but it can also involve some dangers. The best way to avoid problems is to assign one person as the designated "watcher" who faces aft and keeps an eye on the skier at all times, while the skipper keeps his or her mind fully on operating the boat. (A "watcher" is required by law in some states.)

The major danger in operating a boat near skiers is that the prop will be rotating at fairly close proximity to them after a fall or when they want to be picked up. The best policy is to steer a circular course approaching the skier and then shut off the motor, rather than putting it in idle, as you let the boat slip sideways near enough for them to board.

Let the skier swim the last few yards to the boat, rather than trying to motor close to him or her.

Skiers must wear PFDs, of course, and should also learn the basic hand signals for communication with the boat. They are:

Look Out!
The motor should never be running when anyone is on or near the boarding ladder at the stern. Have your designated "watcher" remind you of this fact any time you forget.

➤ *Thumbs up:* Increase speed.

➤ *Thumbs down:* Slow down.

➤ *Hand up:* Stop.

➤ *Chopping motion at the neck:* Shut off the motor.

Skiers should also be aware that they are hard to see when they're down in the water—raising a ski over the head will make them more visible to oncoming traffic.

Water skiing is a great sport for the whole family, but a few simple safety precautions are in order. The skier must wear a PFD and should know basic hand signals to communicate with the driver. (Photo credit: Suzuki Marine)

Loading—and Overloading

One of the most common causes of accidents in small boats is overloading. Although it may be fun to see how many teenagers will fit into a 10-foot jon boat, if that boat is moved anywhere away from the docks loaded with more than the capacity plate recommends, it's probably going to swamp. (The capacity plate, you'll recall, is mounted on the console or transom by the manufacturer. It lists safe load capacity in all boats, as well as maximum legal horse-power for outboard boats.)

Look Out!
Large amounts of rain water or water from leaks accumulating in a deep bilge can sink a boat that appears to be without problems at the dock. The boat may go on plane almost normally, but run in a bow-high position due to the water aft. When the hull drops off plane, the stern squats, sending all the water on the boat rushing toward the transom. The added weight concentrated aft can cause the stern to go under.

Even fairly large boats can be overloaded easily. One of the more common mistakes is with bow-riders, which may have sitting room for four or five large adults in front of the walk-through windshield.

There's sitting room, but the bow doesn't have the buoyancy to support 700 or a thousand pounds up front. If the boat meets a wave of any height—a tugboat wake, for example—water will pour over the bow and it will swamp. That same load distributed aft might cause no problems, because the wider beam and decreased vee toward the rear of most boats can support more weight.

Excess weight doesn't have to come in the form of live bodies, remember. A 40-gallon live well filled with water at eight pounds per gallon can considerably decrease the seaworthiness of a flats boat that already has minimal freeboard. If you're loaded to the max with passengers, the added weight of the water can make the boat sit dangerously low.

Rain water can collect in the bilge of some boats and create a weight problem as well. Always pump out the bilges first when preparing for a day on the water—the boat will float higher, run faster, and burn less fuel.

Speed Thrills—But Also Kills

One bit of advice given to me by an old skipper when I first became a coastal boater has served me well many times: "Go slow and you get in trouble slow," was the way he put it. This is particularly true with larger boats, where mistakes often have to be avoided early if they are to be avoided at all.

If you see a patch of lighter-colored water ahead and you wonder whether it might be a shoal, don't keep on motoring forward at flank speed to let your lower unit answer the question! Slow down to idle, send a crewman forward with a sounding pole (a pole long enough to probe for safe depth), and check it out. If the water is too shallow, back away while you still can.

The same sort of caution will take you far in dozens of other situations. In boating, remember that you are not out there to prove you are the fastest and toughest guy on the freeway, but rather to enjoy a few hours of leisure away from the rush.

Slow is good.

See another boat approaching from the left, which means you have the right of way, but he's not slowing down? You could speed up and cut him off, asserting your legal rights. But if he doesn't slow down, the legality of your actions and his might be left to the heirs and attorneys to sort out. Life is too short as it is—why take the risk? Besides, he's not really showing he's more macho than you, only more ignorant of the rules of the road.

Slow speeds are particularly apropos for docking in most situations. You never know when the motor will die just when you need it to slow down before plowing into a piling, so be wise and approach your slip with caution, with fenders over the side and boat hooks at the ready.

Even the most professional skippers goof by trying to be a bit too brisk in maneuvers at times. I was standing on the docks at Southwest Pass, near the mouth of the Mississippi River, when a brand new 50-foot sportfishing boat was brought into a slip bow-on by an old pro. The captain was fighting the current of the river, so he had plenty of power on, planning to use the torque of the big engines to stop the boat short.

The only problem was that something in the untested shifting mechanism let go. The bow hit the dock at about five knots, and proceeded to push up foot-thick timbers for about five feet before grinding to a halt. Only the boat's paint and the skipper's ego were damaged, but it could have been a lot worse.

All of this is not to say that there's no place for high-performance boats on the water. On the contrary, I enjoy mile-a-minute speeds as much as anybody—in the right place and at the right time. On open ocean or a broad lake or bay where traffic is minimal, there's no reason not to let your rig show its stuff on a calm, sunny day.

High-performance boats offer a fast, exciting ride with very little risk on open water during calm weather. Larger models like this one are easy to drive and not so touchy as smaller, lighter, high-speed rigs. (Photo credit: Frank Sargeant)

But in a winding residential canal or on the Intracoastal Waterway, in bad weather or after dark, a lot of unfortunate things can happen if one skipper can't keep his hand out of the carburetors.

Keep a Clear Head: Don't Drink and Boat

When the sun drops below the yardarm, many boaters like to enjoy an adult beverage or two aboard. Nothing wrong with that, as long as the boat is securely anchored or tied to the docks for the night. But *operating* a boat under the influence of alcohol or drugs is asking for big trouble. The majority of boating fatalities nationwide each year involve *boating while intoxicated* (BWI).

Look Out!
The majority of boating fatalities involve alcohol. *Never* operate a boat while under the influence of alcohol or drugs!

The designated-driver rule that applies ashore goes double afloat; while you may not mind if your passengers party on, the person at the wheel must be a teetotaler until the engines are shut down for the day.

All states have BWI laws, and it doesn't take a lot of alcohol to put you over the legal limits that range from .05 to .08. For most men, three to four beers will do the job, while two or three may do it for small-bodied women.

You don't have to be legally drunk, though, to be incapacitated as a skipper. Researchers say the effects of alcohol afloat can be more pronounced on the water than ashore. Dehydration from exposure to sun and wind, plus the rocking of waves and the tiredness that comes toward the end of a day of boating, can all contribute toward making you more tipsy for a given number of drinks than you might be back on shore.

The penalties for boating under the influence are as severe afloat as they are ashore, and the authorities can pull you over and check if you show any signs of BWI. In some states, Florida for one, any BWI conviction can result in points being added to your landside driver's license.

Don't take chances—steer clear of alcohol. The best policy is to keep your mind completely clear any time you may be called on to make decisions affecting the safety of your crew or your boat.

Running Out of Gas

Pretending to run out of gas might be a nice ploy to get cozy with a prospective mate, but the real thing is not very amusing when you're miles from shore with no other boats in sight.

As I've mentioned earlier, fuel gauges are notoriously inaccurate, and the safest course is to top off the fuel tank every morning before you head out.

If you know how far you intend to travel and about how many gallons per hour your boat burns, or what the miles-per-gallon figures are, you'll have a pretty good idea of whether or not your gas gauge is telling you tales. In general, fuel economy is likely to be best at near-idle speeds, as in slow-trolling at 1000 rpms, with a second peak almost as good somewhere between 3000 and 4500 rpms for outboards, 3000 and 4000 for inboards.

But one thing that some beginning boaters overlook is that proceeding at off-plane speeds can make your fuel gauge drop like the stock market in October. Some boats, when operated in a stern-down, bow-high position between 2000 and 3000 rpms, actually burn *more* fuel than at wide-open throttle, even though their speed may be only one-third as fast. As a result, if you plow along at this speed assuming you're saving fuel for the ride home, you may make a sad discovery while you're still many miles from the dock.

A fuel-flow meter is consequently a useful tool aboard—most offer both gallons-per-hour and miles-per-gallon readouts so that you can remain in the most efficient operating range.

Some boats come with an auxiliary fuel tank installed—when the main tank runs dry, you flip a lever and tap into several added gallons to get you home safe. If your boat doesn't have one of these tanks, consider carrying a spare portable fuel tank. The three-gallon size takes up little space and can save lots of headaches.

Getting Smart in a Hurry

Boating common sense is developed with years of experience, also known as trial-and-error. But one way for beginners to avoid a lot of mistakes is to take a boating course from the Coast Guard Auxiliary, U.S. Power Squadron, or a commercial provider like Sea School.

At this writing, only 19 states license boat operators and check their knowledge with some sort of test, but it's a great idea to let those with the know-how share it with you.

For boating classes near you, call (800) 336-BOAT.

The Least You Need to Know

➤ Make sure someone somewhere knows where you are and when you expect to return any time you're on your boat.

➤ Make your boat as storm-proof as possible, but never stay with it in a severe storm.

➤ High-speed driving has its place, but crowded waterways and harbors are not among them.

➤ For your safety and the safety of your crew and other boaters around you, never operate a boat while drinking alcohol or taking drugs.

Chapter 19

Common Emergencies (If There Are Such Things)

In This Chapter

➤ What to do if your boat becomes grounded

➤ Coping with hypothermia

➤ The items every skipper should have in his first-aid kit

➤ Rescuing a person who falls overboard

➤ Survival tips if you fall overboard

➤ Dealing with leaks, fires, and other onboard emergencies

➤ When to call the Coast Guard for help

You may go through your entire boating life without ever facing a single emergency worthy of the name. Most casual skippers do—boating is not a dangerous sport compared to many. And sometimes an "emergency" is in the eye of the beholder. Is running aground an emergency? Sort of, if the tide is going out, the sun is going down, and the mosquitoes are coming in.

On the other hand, some boaters take an unplanned visit to a bar in stride and have an oyster roast on the shells while they wait for the water to come back up.

But it's also true that a short hop across a quiet suburban pond can very quickly and unexpectedly become what everyone would agree is an emergency, a disaster in the making.

Note that having an emergency does not necessarily mean a tragedy. It's often your rapid response to the situation that determines the outcome. This chapter touches on both the mild and the serious forms of emergencies and how to deal with them.

You're Grounded—Now What?

There are times in every boatman's life when the bottom is too close to the top. You're grounded, for the first time since you were a teenager. It happens to everybody, from boat designers to skippers with 20 years under their belts, and sooner or later it will happen to you.

Boat Bytes
The first step when you go aground is to determine where the nearest water deep enough to float your boat lies. There's probably good water behind you, but there may be a drop-off just ahead or to one side, and sometimes it's easier to go forward than back if you've slid to the back side of a bar.

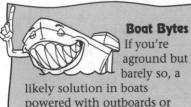

Boat Bytes
If you're aground but barely so, a likely solution in boats powered with outboards or stern drives is to tilt up the lower unit to the point where the prop is just beneath the surface and try to back off. Many times, this is all it takes.

One approach to the situation is to pretend it hasn't happened. Just tell your crew that this looks like a good place to drop anchor for a few hours and have lunch. Then assess the situation. How bad is it? If the motors sporadically started laboring, the boat bumped a few times and then slid to a stop, you're probably going to be fine. You're stuck, but not bad, and the bottom is soft. However, if the boat suddenly came to a halt and flopped over on one side of the bottom, this is not a good sign. You are up where only the flounder and stingrays can swim.

If there were loud crunching or grinding noises when you hit and you stopped with a jolt, you may have struck rock rather than soft sand or mud. There could be damage to the prop, lower unit, skeg, rudder, shaft, or even the hull itself. This is the worst-case scenario.

The tides are also a factor to consider. If it's low tide and you had a soft grounding, you're probably in luck. Just relax, do lunch, tell a few grounding jokes, and the tide will come back within a short time and float you off.

Props pull better in forward than in reverse. So, if the deep water lies behind you, you may want to try spinning the boat 180 degrees so that you can leave the bar with the gears in forward. On small boats, this can be done with muscle power, sometimes via a stout push pole or oar, but more often by going over the side and putting your shoulder to the bow.

Be sure to tilt up your lower unit far enough so that it does not touch bottom before you attempt to push the bow to one side or to force the boat backwards. The lower unit is the lowest part of the boat when tilted down, and it will block your efforts if not tilted up.

In fact, if the water is wading depth, it's best if everybody gets out—sometimes this reduction in weight raises the boat several inches and it floats free. (Get the largest folks out first! Sorry, but political correctness does not apply when you are grounded—specific gravity is all that counts.)

If you hit hard bottom at speed, check things out before you head for deeper water. Better to be grounded than sunk! A hard strike on rocks can put a hole in the hull. Open the bilge hatch and make sure no water is coming in.

Put out an anchor in the direction of deep water and keep tension on that line as the tide rises—often, this will pull you off. At least, it will keep the wind from pushing you farther up on the bar as you start to float.

Boat Bytes
Sometimes, just moving passengers from the bow, which is the deepest section of many boats, to the stern will bring you free. It's worth a try.

Tow, Tow, Tow Your Boat

Are seas rough, wind rising, or a storm coming? Is the tide falling? If so, you can't be casual about getting free. Use your cell phone or your VHF via channel 16 to contact a commercial towing service such as Sea Tow or TowBOAT/U.S. (for details, see Appendix B). These towing services will tow you clear for a price. Or flag down a passing boat—and do it quickly!

If you need a tow, use your anchor line for the tow line—it should be the strongest line on the boat. Dock lines won't do the job. And secure it to the bow eye (the ring at the bow to which a trailer's winch hook is attached), not to the cleats, which are held down by small screws—they'll be snatched out. (Ditto if you're ever called on to tow a boat—use the transom lifting eyes, which are through-bolted in the transom rather than screwed down like cleats.)

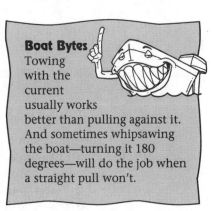

Boat Bytes
Towing with the current usually works better than pulling against it. And sometimes whipsawing the boat—turning it 180 degrees—will do the job when a straight pull won't.

With I/Os and outboards, tilt your drive up out of the water before a tow to prevent damage to the prop or skeg. With inboards, consider the damage that might be done by towing—you can't be pulled backwards without ruining the drive components, prop, shaft, and strut, and maybe allowing water to get in around the shaft log. And even a pull forward over a shallow bar may damage the running gear. You may have to wait for higher water.

Secure a heavy tow line to the bow eye of the towed boat. Note the bridle or yoke attached to the aft lifting eyes of the tow boat, rather than attaching the tow line to one of the cleats. (Photo credit: Frank Sargeant)

There are times when even the most inventive efforts will not get a grounded boat free. Waiting for the peak of an incoming tide then becomes necessary.

Sometimes, with big, heavy boats grounded on high tide in protected waters, the least expensive thing to do is leave the boat there until the monthly tide cycles peak, as they do every two weeks, bringing added water to the shoal and gently floating the hull free. (Don't try this as an excuse to extend your vacation a couple of weeks.) Secure the boat, take the dingy ashore, and forget about your little indiscretion until the full moon erases your mistake.

First Aid Afloat

Every boat should carry a basic first-aid kit for the cuts and scrapes that occasionally occur. Those who take longer voyages many hours from medical help ashore need more complete first-aid gear and the training in how to use it, but the following kit will do the job for most weekend boaters:

➤ A basic first-aid manual

➤ Antiseptic ointment

➤ Rubbing alcohol

➤ An assortment of bandages, gauze pads, and tape

➤ Tweezers

➤ Sunburn lotion

➤ Aspirin and other over-the-counter pain medications

➤ Pepto-Bismol or other diarrhea treatments

➤ Eye-drops such as Visine

➤ Plastic gloves and antiseptic soap

It's also wise for you, as skipper, to take a first-aid course that includes basic CPR and the Heimlich Maneuver to aid choking victims.

Person Overboard!

One of the most common potential emergencies is one of your crew going over the side. It happens sooner or later to just about everybody who spends a lot of time on the water, and whether or not it becomes an emergency depends on the conditions.

A fall from an anchored boat into calm water in the middle of a Georgia summer day by a good swimmer is an amusement, not an emergency. Give the swimmer a hand getting back aboard and no harm done. But falling off a sailboat during a fast downwind leg on a chilly fall evening in Maine when you're dressed heavily to keep out the cold can be deadly serious. Without fast action, it can become a tragedy.

Here are the steps in bringing someone safely back aboard:

1. *Don't lose sight of the victim.* If you can't find him, he's going to have to tread water a lot longer—maybe too long. Consequently, it's best if one crewperson does nothing but keep an eye on the swimmer, pointing at him steadily from the bow so the helmsperson knows where to steer for the recovery.

2. *Shut off the power immediately.* If you're on a sailboat, turn the boat into the wind to stop the forward motion. (There has to be some hasty sail handling here, to be sure, if the spinnaker is set.)

3. *If the person is within throwing range, toss a life ring or flotation cushion to him.* (If there's wind or a current, be sure to toss it on the upwind or up-current side so it drifts down to the person.)

4. *Swing the boat back to the person to make the recovery.* He knows you've seen him and he's got flotation, so he hopefully won't panic.

   In a shallow-draft boat like a houseboat or pontoon boat that tends to "kite" or blow sideways in the wind, it's probably best to come to the person from downwind. Coming in upwind may result in the boat being blown right past him, or even over him. With deep-vees and keeled sailboats less likely to be pushed around by the wind, coming in from upwind allows you to shut off the motor and drift close enough to throw a line to the swimmer. The hull creates a lee from wind and waves, as well.

5. *Draw the person in close, get a swim ladder over the side, and help him back aboard.* If the person is heavily dressed in waterlogged clothes, elderly, injured, or has been exposed to cold water, he may not have the strength to make it aboard himself. Haul him in with the help of two or three strong crew members, pulling on both arms and the back of the PFD he's hopefully wearing.

On sailboats with high freeboards, the boom's block and tackle (see Chapter 23) is sometimes used to hoist exhausted swimmers aboard, via a sling under their arms.

Hypothermia

Those who fall overboard in cold water and even those in warmer water for long periods may have their core body temperature reduced to the point where they lose strength and mental acuity—they are suffering from hypothermia. Longer exposure brings unconsciousness or death.

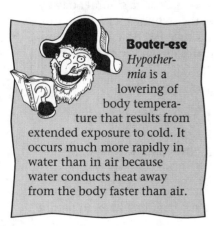

Boater-ese
Hypothermia is a lowering of body temperature that results from extended exposure to cold. It occurs much more rapidly in water than in air because water conducts heat away from the body faster than air.

What are the symptoms of hypothermia? They can be varied depending on the temperature and the length of exposure, but suspect hypothermia if the victim:

➤ Shivers uncontrollably

➤ Complains of being numb

➤ Complains of being dizzy

➤ Seems to be in a trance or not alert

➤ Goes to sleep suddenly

➤ Has an irregular or slow pulse

➤ Breathes irregularly

In water below 40 degrees, a person may become unconscious in as little as 15 minutes, according to the Coast Guard. Water from 40 to 50 degrees brings unconsciousness in 30 minutes to an hour, and from 50 to 60 degrees, in one to two hours.

In warmer weather, the prospects are much better. Water temperatures from 60 to 70 degrees can be endured for up to seven hours for healthy adults, and from 70 to 80 degrees, survival time can exceed 12 hours.

In short, in extremely cold water, rescues have to be nearly immediate to have much chance for saving the victim.

To treat a victim of hypothermia, follow these steps:

1. Strip off the victim's wet clothes and dry him thoroughly.
2. Cover the victim with blankets or a sleeping bag (but no hot baths; the body should be warmed slowly).
3. Give hot liquids if the victim is thoroughly awake.
4. Monitor the victim's heartbeat and breathing and be ready to give CPR if needed.
5. In cases where mental acuity, heart rate, or breathing are affected, get the victim to a physician as soon as possible.

Bet You Didn't Know

It doesn't even take a fall overboard to become hypothermic; getting wet from a rainstorm accompanied by howling winds can do the job, even when air temperatures are moderate. If you stay dry, you're much less likely to become chilled. Get your rain suit out sooner rather than later, even during a summer squall.

If You Fall Overboard

It's a horrible feeling to be left swimming in the open sea as your boat chugs off toward the horizon, according to those who have been there. Odds are huge that it won't ever happen to you, but there are several cases every year, and the larger the boat, the more likely it is that if you slip over the side, no one will notice. Having a boat sink out from under you can also force you to go for a swim when you'd rather not.

In either case, you're in immeasurably better shape if you've got on your PFD; you don't have to worry about staying afloat and can devote your attention to conserving body heat and to being found by rescuers.

Survival swimming experts suggest the following to improve your chances of survival:

➤ Don't take off your clothes so that you can swim better. Even wet clothes conserve heat. (If your clothes are so heavy you can't swim at all in them, however, shuck them.) Slip off your shoes, though—it will make it easier to kick.

➤ Use the Heat Escape Lessening Position (H.E.L.P) to conserve body heat. Basically, you pull your knees to your chest and hold them there with your arms.

➤ If you're in cold water, try to keep your head out of the water. The head is the body's radiator, and immersing your face will cause you to lose heat rapidly.

➤ If you're in the water due to a capsize, stay with the boat and try to climb out of the water onto the boat, if possible. Air transfers heat slower than water, so you'll maintain body heat longer on the boat. It also provides flotation and makes it much easier for rescuers to find you.

➤ If you're in warm water, use the survival floating technique, in which you allow yourself to float face down between breaths, to help to conserve energy.

➤ If you are tossed a life line by rescuers, make a loop around your chest and knot it securely. Your hands may not be strong enough to hold on when the line is drawn in.

➤ Stay away from the propellers if the rescue boat approaches with its engines running.

That Sinking Feeling

Recreational boats 20 feet and under are all equipped with full foam flotation that's supposed to keep them afloat in an upright position should the hull get a hole in it. Larger boats are not required to contain this flotation, and many do not—they can sink like stones. Obviously, when you buy a boat, you should give special consideration to those of whatever size that contain flotation to keep you and your crew safe no matter what.

Sinking is rare in any well-maintained boat. Leaks, however, are not. And when the water comes in faster than you can get it to go out, the boat fills up.

Even a boat with full flotation may not stay upright once it gets loaded down with hundreds of pounds of water. When buoyancy is lost, waves can roll over the gunnels and complete the swamping process—in rough water, the boat is likely to turn over.

If Your Boat Springs a Leak

Bilge pumps are the devices that stand between you and any leaks. A 2,000 gallon-per-hour pump costs only $50 more than a 500 gallon-per-hour pump, so it makes sense to check your bilge pump and if it's not a jumbo, replace it with a larger pump. It's very inexpensive insurance.

Pumps should be hooked to an automatic float switch that turns the pump on any time several inches of water gathers in the bilge. This way, you don't have to worry about a leak getting a big head start on you before you realize it, and just as important, you won't forget to turn off the pump, run it dry for hours, and burn it up.

Most leaks aboard fiberglass and aluminum boats result from malfunctioning through-hull fittings or hoses for bait wells and wash-down systems, and are not large enough to overcome the pumping ability of the bilge pump. However, for safety's sake, it's a good idea to carry some rubber stoppers that will plug your fittings in case something goes wrong with the valve or hose.

If you get a *big* leak, resulting from striking a submerged object, you may have to make some emergency hull repairs. Stuffing anything that will fit into the hull is the obvious and most practiced solution—PFDs and cushions do the job best, particularly when backed up with T-shirts and towels in the smaller cracks. You'll still have water coming in, but it may not flow so fast that the pump can't keep up with it. If the pumps can keep up with it, you can head for the boat ramp or marina. If they can't, head for the nearest beach or sandbar. And if the flow is too fast for that, break out the VHF and call for assistance, pronto.

> **Boat Bytes**
> Bilge pumps have to operate in the dirtiest part of any boat, the bilge, where all the sand, shells, busted screws, and other debris accumulate. As a consequence they can jam, and often do so at the worst possible time. Keep your bilge clean and clean out the pump strainer regularly.

> **Boat Bytes**
> Bilge pumps can burn out over time. If you're going on an extended cruise, particularly to a remote area, carry a spare or two for security.

Fire Aboard

Fires afloat are rare but scary, because the only solution for a serious fire is to go into the water and watch the burning boat drift away.

Although you're required to carry at least one fire extinguisher aboard almost any powerboat, the discharge time of that extinguisher will be less than 30 seconds. Clearly, if you have a fire, you have to attack it early and hit the base immediately or you won't be able to control it.

Fires in the engine room or anywhere near fuel lines or fuel tanks are particularly dangerous because a fuel explosion can take place at any time. A fire in proximity to fuel means everyone should put on PFDs immediately and prepare to jump overboard at a moment's notice.

Small fires in other parts of the boat are usually less critical—although they can get big in a hurry, particularly if strong winds are fanning them. If possible, turn the boat so that the fire blows off the boat, rather than into it. This will slow the spread of the flames and give you a few added minutes to fight them.

Cabin boats sometimes have galley fires. A handy flame retardant for grease fires is baking soda, a staple on most boats to keep the refrigerator or cooler smelling fresh. Throw loose handfuls of baking soda at the base of the flame. Don't use water—it can spread the flames.

Other cabin fires involving clothing or upholstery can be put out with your most abundant extinguisher on a boat, water brought below via a bucket or the boat's wash-down system.

Calling for Help

You can call the Coast Guard for advice or aid when you have problems, to be sure, but never issue the famous MAYDAY...MAYDAY...MAYDAY call to the Coast Guard unless you have a life-threatening emergency. (Running out of gas 20 miles at sea doesn't qualify.) The Coast Guard will help you in contacting other boats nearby to render aid, hook you up with a commercial towing service, or send members of the all-volunteer Coast Guard Auxiliary to assist you. They will also call the commercial towing services for you if you can't raise them yourself.

Getting caught in a storm that scares the bejeepers out of you is not an adequate reason to use the distress signal. However, a boat that is sinking rapidly, or drifting powerless toward a rocky shore and an enraged surf, or aflame in a fire so severe that abandoning ship will probably be required, all qualify as emergencies. So does a passenger who is severely ill with a heart attack, stroke, and so on.

Issuing the call for lesser problems will result in a very grim-faced encounter with Coast Guard officers when they arrive to find you alive and reasonably well.

The U.S. Coast Guard responds only to serious, life-threatening emergencies. Small problems like running out of gas are now handled by commercial tow services. (Photo credit: Frank Sargeant)

The call is issued on channel 16, which is constantly monitored by the Coast Guard. The proper format is to start with the MAYDAY call, repeated three times—this alerts any nearby boaters as well as the Coast Guard monitor that you have a very serious problem.

Don't yell, even if you're under duress—it will only make your transmission harder to understand. Speak loudly and clearly.

Be sure to include the following information in your call:

> **Boat Bytes**
> If you hear a MAYDAY call from another boat and you're close by, you're legally obligated to render assistance and stand by until the Coast Guard or other authorities arrive, as long as doing so doesn't endanger your own boat or crew. It's not uncommon for a Coast Guard helicopter to zoom in and wave nearby recreational boats to the rescue if they don't have a boat of their own in the area.

➤ Your boat's name

➤ A full description of your position, including latitude/longitude

➤ The nature of your emergency

➤ A description of your boat, including length and color, so the Coast Guard can spot you when they arrive

Other drastic emergency procedures are to make use of visual distress signals, lighting up flares, firing a parachute flare skyward, or waving down another boat using objects of clothing as a flag. The point is to do whatever it takes to get someone's attention promptly.

The Least You Need to Know

➤ Not all emergencies result in disaster—be prepared and you can come through most situations safely.

➤ Carrying appropriate emergency gear, including extra bilge pumps and a fire extinguisher, can save your boat in the event of a leak or fire on board.

➤ Knowing what to do in the event that you or one of your crew falls overboard can prevent a tragedy.

➤ Know the procedures for calling for help when your own remedies don't solve the problem.

Part 6
Boating Maintenance

Whether you own a house, a car, or a boat, you'll find that there's a bit of upkeep involved. Fortunately, boat maintenance is simple compared to some jobs, and most boaters find they can handle the majority of it on their own.

This section covers clean-ups essential to avoid corrosion and fouling, as well as tips on keeping your boat's gel coat gleaming. (Remember, the more shipshape you keep your boat, the more money you'll get back at trade-in time.)

And it's always smart to be aware of a few emergency repairs that can help your motor get you home when something goes wrong—you'll learn the basics in Chapter 22.

The Well-Equipped Nautical Toolbox

Maybe you don't like grease on your hands and oil in your hair—for reasons not understandable to those who love the noise, heat, and smell of an engine running right, some folks don't. But there are times in every boater's life afloat when a few repairs are needed, and you're the only "mechanic" in sight.

With the right supplies, good tools, and a bit of know-how, you can solve many common problems on the spot, without so much as resorting to your cellular phone to call your friendly marine mechanic ashore. (Although it's a very good idea to have a friendly marine mechanic ashore, and to keep his phone number written on the console just in case!)

Part of keeping things humming is having the right tools aboard to do the various jobs necessary to maintain your boat.

In this chapter, you'll learn what goes into the basic marine tool kit, as well as a bit about selecting boat batteries and the chargers that keep them well fed.

The Most Important Tool

The most important tool you can have for any boat is an engine repair manual dedicated to your particular year and model of motor. These shop manuals cost $25 to $35 each, and if they help you make one repair you couldn't have made without them, they've paid for themselves many times over. They're available through local marine dealers as well as large bookstores.

Gearing Up for Outboard Boats

Because of their two-cycle engines, outboards require extra oil and a way of getting it into the fuel mix. Small motors and a few larger economy models don't have automatic oil injection, so you have to measure and mix the proper quantity of oil each time you add gasoline. The usual mix is 50 to 100 parts gasoline per one part oil, by liquid measure.

You need aboard:

➤ A one-gallon (or more) container of TCW-3 oil, used to resupply the oil injection reservoir. Make sure to always buy extra oil when you refill the reservoir—you can't operate the motor without it, and if you run out miles from a marina you'll have a major problem.

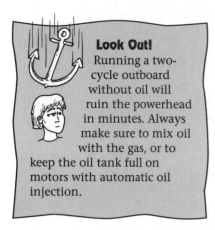

Look Out!
Running a two-cycle outboard without oil will ruin the powerhead in minutes. Always make sure to mix oil with the gas, or to keep the oil tank full on motors with automatic oil injection.

Most outboard manufacturers distribute their own brand of oil, but any National Marine Manufacturer's Association (NMMA)-approved TCW-3 oil, including the much less expensive brands you can get at discount stores, will work fine and will not void your motor's warranty. Buy it by the gallon to save money.

➤ A funnel to get the oil into the tank without spilling it down into the bilge. The bigger the funnel reservoir, the better. Those with flexible plastic nozzles are easiest to use in the tight confines of a hatch.

You can make a serviceable funnel by simply cutting the bottom out of plastic, one-quart oil bottle. Inverted, the small filler neck fits inside the oil-tank filler as you pour.

➤ Spare spark plugs. Make sure they're the same type used by the manufacturer.

➤ A spark plug wrench, including a soft insert to protect the ceramic insulator.

➤ On motors to 75 horses, a starter rope. Some larger motors can be pull-started, but only by rather burly mechanics. The starter rope is your insurance against a dead battery.

➤ On portable motors, a spare shear pin for the propeller.

➤ A spare propeller, prop nut, washer, and cotter pin.

➤ A wrench to fit the prop nut.

Some outboards make it easy to add oil to the injection system with a tank under the cowl. Others require a funnel and an exploration of the bilge. (Photo credit: Yamaha Outboards)

Inboard Supplies

Most inboards and I/Os, both gasoline and diesel, get their oil from inside the oil pan attached to the bottom of the engine and burn very little of it with their fuel. Consequently, you don't have to add oil as often—although a marine diesel will very likely want a small sip every morning, gasoline inboards are likely not to need a refill for weeks at a time.

Boat Bytes
Funnels used for oil create a sticky mess if not stowed properly. Wipe out the funnel with paper towels and stow it inside a gallon-sized plastic bag with an airtight locking seal to keep things clean.

Still, extra oil and a means to get it into the engine is necessary, as is some other gear. Here's a recommended list:

➤ At least a quart of oil for a gasoline engine and four quarts for a diesel. (Note that oil for diesels is not the same as oil for gasoline engines.)

➤ A funnel to fit the filler on top of the engine.

➤ Fuel filter elements and gaskets. Particularly with diesels, the filters have to be cleaned regularly.

➤ Spark plugs and wrench.

➤ A spare propeller, prop nut, washer, and cotter pin.

➤ Spare drive belts and a knowledge of how to install them.

A spare propeller is a good insurance policy, especially when boating in shallow areas. You also need a wrench to fit the prop nut and a spare cotter pin. (Photo credit: Frank Sargeant)

Universal Spares

There are some spare parts that are likely to be useful on almost any boat and in almost any situation. Make up a kit of the most common things to have aboard, and you'll be ready to fix many problems that crop up. Here's what I recommend every boater have:

➤ Nylon tie-wraps come in various sizes and are good for anything from securing a fishing reel to a rod to fixing a broken radio antenna.

➤ Stainless-steel screw clamps are handy. Get them in several sizes to fit everything from fuel hoses to bilge-pump connections.

➤ An assortment of screws, washers, nuts, and bolts, preferably in stainless steel, carried in a plastic divider box that keeps them sorted by size, is invaluable. Marine stores sell kits that contain the most common sizes, all sorted in plastic bins.

➤ Wire coat hangers can come in handy—the wire can be bent into all sorts of useful tools for retrieving dropped gear, securing loose stuff, hanging up other tools, and so on. Keep several on board.

Sticky Stuff

Something is always coming loose, flying around the cockpit or springing a leak on a boat. You need an assortment of "sticky stuff" to take care of these little annoyances. Here's what I recommend:

➤ A large roll of duct tape is handy for taping a chart to a table, fixing a water hose, even repairing a hole in a rain suit—always keep some aboard.

➤ A tube of marine sealer, particularly the tough, stick-to-anything type known as 5200 Sealer from 3M, can be used to patch holes in the hull as well as fix all sorts of other leaks, glue things together, and so on.

➤ Several sticks of "hot-glue" are also useful. You can melt it with a cigarette lighter (careful—the sticks will burn!) and let it drip on things you want to stick together.

➤ Epoxy-resin–based auto-body filler has endless uses. I once fixed a busted exhaust manifold with it, and the stuff stayed in place for over two months without cracking! It can patch holes in the hull, glue things together, and so on.

Tool Time

Some guys believe you can never have enough tools, but it's probably more accurate to say that a few tools that you know how to use and that you keep where you can find them are more helpful than a 200-pound chest full of unsorted equipment.

One Size Fits All—Adjustable Tools

If you're not into owning large tool sets, adjustable tools can go a long way toward solving most mechanical problems.

Adjustable tools allow one tool to do the work of a half-dozen, so they take up less space and add less weight to your tool kit than conventional tools, plus they save you money.

The first tool you'll want in your basic one-size-fits-all box is probably the venerable locking pliers, which works both as pliers and a wrench when necessary. Get two of them, a nine-inch and a five-inch, and you'll be ready to tackle most anything.

Crescent wrenches are equally useful. Get a 12-incher, an eight-incher, and a six-incher and you can cover most jobs, down to tightening the nut on your trailer hitch.

Third in your one-size-fits-all box is a slip-joint pliers, about 10 inches long, that allows you to lock on to pipes and large nuts.

Other Tools You'll Need

One of the first tools any boater should buy is a magnetic "wand" designed to retrieve bolts or other tools that fall down into the bilge under the engine. It's worth its weight in gold at times, and available at most automotive parts shops.

You'll also need large and small Phillips-head and flat screwdrivers. It's a good idea to get an extra flat driver with a 12- to 14-inch shaft if you own an inboard or stern drive; the extra reach is often handy in the tight confines of the engine box.

It's also useful to carry a set of ratcheting socket drives (U.S. or metric, depending on the nuts and bolts on your engine) in $^3/_8$" drive.

A set of hex keys, ideally all fitted together into a single tool like a locking knife, will often come in handy.

Boat Bytes

A tool most anglers will want is a pair of stainless-steel side-cutter pliers. These are used for making wire leaders for toothy species, cutting monofilament lines, and removing fish hooks. Wear them in a holster on your belt so they don't get misplaced.

A claw hammer is occasionally useful, as well—fiberglass-handle models give fewer problems around the water.

A pair of electrical pliers, including wire strippers and screw cutters, will pay for themselves dozens of times.

A torque wrench is a tool with a meter for measuring the amount of pressure put on the bolt or nut being tightened. Torque wrenches are essential for adjusting cylinder head bolts because uneven tightening can cause leaks and/or damage.

You can get most of these tools in a fitted plastic kit for $50 to $80, and the kit has slots so you can always keep everything in place.

Slippery Subject

If you tow your boat on a trailer, you *must* have a grease gun and plenty of waterproof grease. If you don't shoot a few shots of grease to the wheel bearings after every long trip, you will absolutely, positively, have fried bearings before long, possibly resulting in a locked-up wheel, resulting in a flat tire...you get the idea. It's a lot easier to grease the bearings.

The grease gun is also useful for lubing your outboard motor, steering cables, and all other moving, mechanical parts aboard. The best way to handle this messy job is with a cartridge-type grease gun—it keeps the worst of the mess off your hands. Even at that, though, you need plenty of paper towels, and the gun should be stowed inside a sealed plastic bag so that it doesn't ooze grease all over the compartment.

Electrical Extras

Electrical wiring causes frequent problems aboard. Carry several fuses that will fit each of the circuits you have on your boat (many newer boats have circuit breakers that do not require fuses), insulating electrical tape, and several spare pieces of insulated wire in various sizes.

The All-Purpose Swiss Army Knife

If you own a canoe, rowboat, kayak, or other simple craft, it's possible that the only tool you need is a multipurpose Leatherman or a Swiss Army knife hanging on your belt. These handy devices cover a multitude of situations, and after you've worn one a while you don't feel quite fully dressed without it. The basic Leatherman includes pliers, two types of screwdrivers, knife, hole punch, bottle opener, and file. The Swiss Army knife includes everything except the pliers, and some models include scissors.

If you don't carry a Swiss Army knife, at least make sure to carry a quality lock-back pocket knife with a blade that's three to four inches long. And keep a sharpening tool aboard—the diamond-edged hones are most effective.

Bet You Didn't Know

Bolts and screws used around water have a habit of freezing in place, and when you try to remove them they break off. The solution to getting the broken section out of the hole is a tool called the "EZ Out," which allows you to get leverage on the offender. It's available at some marine dealers and all auto parts stores.

It also happens that you will ruin the threads on engine parts by overtightening a bolt, particularly in aluminum heads. You can make emergency repairs with an epoxy material that is rubbed on the threads. When it sets, it has enough strength to let the bolt grab once again. (Long-term repairs are better made by inserting a metal coil that will remake the threads.)

Tool Quality

There are two theories on boat tool quality. One says buy the best tools you can afford, take good care of them, and keep them for life. The other says buy the cheapest tools that will do the job, don't worry about them, and toss them away when they break and get others.

Which theory is best for you? That depends on whether you like to mess with tools. Both wind up costing about the same over your boating life, because you'll likely buy three sets of junkers to make up for that one quality set—but you won't feel nearly as bad when a $1 screwdriver goes over the side as when a $10 screwdriver goes over the side.

Tool Care

Tools and water don't mix. Even if you never get your tools wet, water and salt mist will find a way to reach them, rust and corrode them, and eventually make them useless unless you take special care.

The best way to keep tools bright is to wipe them down after every use with an oiled rag. My favorite corrosion-resisting oil is a thin blue liquid called Corrosion-X, but there are many good ones, including Bo-Shield and others. All are available at boating supply stores and many hardware stores.

It's also a good idea to store your tools inside a watertight box, and put that box inside a dry-storage box aboard. Also, take a tip from professional mechanics: Always put your tools back into the box in the same exact slot you took them from. You'll save endless time sorting through the mess looking for a particular wrench or driver this way, and you'll know immediately if you left your favorite $5/8$ boxend wrench under the oil pan.

Current Events—Marine Batteries

There are two types of batteries used for boats:

➤ The basic starting battery, which is much like the battery in your car, is designed to provide a lot of power for short periods of time. Starting batteries don't do well if drawn below 50 percent of their amp capacity repeatedly. (The amp capacity is a way of measuring the available electrical energy of a battery.)

➤ The "deep-cycle" battery is designed to provide long-term power to low-amp draws like trolling motors and boat lights. These batteries have thicker plates, which allow them to survive many complete discharges without damage.

Most batteries of both types are filled with a liquid acid that can spill out if the battery turns over. Sealed batteries avoid this problem; they cost a little more, but they can't spill and you never have to add water.

Marine batteries come in both high-output versions designed for short bursts of power to start the engines, and deep-cycle models that produce their power slowly and steadily and can survive repeated discharges to near zero, used to power electric trolling motors and other accessories. (Photo credit: GNB Batteries)

Gel cell batteries, which replace the liquid with a thick jelly-like acid, last about twice as long as conventional acid-filled batteries, but they cost three times as much. A typical 85-amp gel cell goes for around $200, compared to about $75 for the same thing in a standard battery. But if your batteries are in a tough-to-reach spot where installation and removal is tough, the gels are worth considering.

Getting a Charge Out of Chargers

Alternating current (AC) battery chargers aren't exactly tools in the sense of being used to fix something that has gone wrong, but they're an extra most boaters want sooner or later to give their boat's alternator an assist. You'll find the charger particularly useful if you make use of your boat for overnights, have a lot of electrical accessories, or use an electric trolling motor.

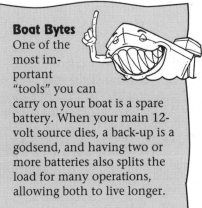

Boat Bytes
One of the most important "tools" you can carry on your boat is a spare battery. When your main 12-volt source dies, a back-up is a godsend, and having two or more batteries also splits the load for many operations, allowing both to live longer.

A basic 10-amp single or 20-amp two-battery charger is adequate to keep trolling motor batteries charged, and some of these units are so compact they mount inside the boat and stay there. To use them, you simply fit a special plug into the trolling motor panel. They're inexpensive, ranging from $40 to $100.

For jumbo boat accessory batteries, you need a marine charger. Many of these have a special "amp boost" feature that gives a short jolt of added power if your engine is balky to starting, and they put out lots of power, up to 50 amps, to keep all your accessories operational.

The best chargers are "multi-stage"—they charge the battery rapidly up to about 50 percent of full charge, then reduce the flow to gradually finish off the job without danger of over-charging. They're also shock-proof, which many chargers designed for automotive use are not. Prices range from $200 to $500.

Solar panel battery chargers are useful for keeping batteries topped off while you're on the water or at the dock. They lie flat on a cabin roof, are unobtrusive, and you never have to do anything to them. They do need a controller to prevent overcharging, though. They range in price from $100 to $300, plus an added $100 for the controller.

Got a Light?

Without being able to see what you're doing down in the engine box, all the rest of your tools are worthless. Thus, several good flashlights should be standard equipment. These should be waterproof, plastic, rubber-coated, or stainless steel. The "Krypton" bulbs used in some models put out a lot more light than the standard, although they burn up the batteries somewhat faster. (Even waterproof flashlights should be protected from salt spray—keep them in the console, or in a plastic bag in "dry storage" until needed, and store fresh batteries with them.)

A spotlight can be worth a lot when you're looking for an unlighted marker on a dark night. They come in sizes from small up to what are called "owl-roasters," which can send a blaze of up to 750,000 candlepower into the night. This is a laser, and you don't want to shine it in your eyes, or in the eyes of another skipper, but it's tremendous for seeing at night. They're surprisingly inexpensive—from $30 to $75. For big boats, you can also buy remote-controlled spotlights to mount on the bow. These cost about $300 to $400.

The Least You Need to Know

➤ An engine repair manual is the most important tool you can have aboard.

➤ A basic kit of adjustable tools should be kept aboard every boat.

➤ Tools and water don't mix—protect your tools from corrosion by wiping them after use and storing them properly.

➤ Without a flashlight, all your other tools can sometimes be useless. Keep several good-quality flashlights aboard.

Chapter 21

Keeping Your Boat Shipshape

In This Chapter

➤ Keeping your boat clean

➤ Mildew-busting strategies for the cabin

➤ Protecting your bottom from algae, barnacles, and other marine growth

➤ Hull repairs in fiberglass and aluminum

Fiberglass boats don't take a lot of care. In fact, if you're not so inclined, you can pretty much leave the cleanup chores to the rain and the wind and still have a serviceable boat, year after year.

Of course, it will look like heck and it won't be worth much when you want to sell it. But there's very little that you *have* to do to keep a fiberglass boat working.

Most of us, however, take a certain pride in a clean boat kept new-looking, and a clean hull actually runs better and saves fuel. And the hours of elbow grease spent keeping a boat clean are often repaid when it's time to sell the boat—appearance is everything when it comes to moving a used boat.

In this chapter, you'll learn tricks for cleaning and polishing your boat, some tips on the use of anti-fouling paints, and a bit about patching small holes or leaks that might develop in your hull.

Washing Down

Although boats live in water, they get dirty. Those used for fishing get *very* dirty. To keep a boat looking new and functioning well, it has to be washed regularly—and those used in salt water must be washed after every day on the water.

Boater-ese
The *gel coat* is the outer layer of a fiberglass boat, the "skin" that gives the hull its shine and color. It's a hard resin, thicker and more durable than paint.

The standard wash-down is with soap and fresh water. Wash-and-wax–type car-wash soaps do a nice job and leave a protective coating on the gel coat, but plain old dish soap is okay, too.

A large sponge or wash mitt works best on flat surfaces, but use a scrub brush on skidproof decking and around the crevices and screws on metal work. (Washing all metal parts is particularly important on coastal boats, because just a bit of salt left in place will cause electrolytic corrosion—that green crud.) A scrub brush with a telescoping handle is handy for use on larger boats to reach areas below the waterline.

Fishing offal (or *awful*, as it's better termed) comes off best with a bleach solution—use about a cup of bleach per gallon of water. Remember, bleach will eat your clothes and your bare feet and hands; wear old clothes and use a long-handled scrub brush. Wash it off thoroughly with plenty of fresh water.

Boat Bytes
Got a green scum line on your hull? Spray it with straight bleach. The stuff vaporizes algae, so that you scarcely have to scrub—just hose it off with fresh water. (This doesn't work if there's oil or other goop in the line, however.)

You can pour undiluted bleach into the live wells to get rid of the fishy smell—but be sure to rinse it out very thoroughly, or you'll come up with some very white but very dead baitfish next trip.

Kitchen cleansers with bleach, in a spray bottle, are very handy for spot cleaning (Clorox Clean-Up is the best I've found). Spray it on any dark spots on the finish, let it set a few minutes, and wipe the spots away. (Remember, bleach can corrode metal, so keep it off the engine, cleats, and any other metal parts.)

It's a good idea to apply a fiberglass cleaner about twice a year to remove chalking caused by the sun. This brings back the shine, which can then be preserved by using a fiberglass wax.

Although it may be tempting to try an abrasive cleansing powder on a dulled fiberglass finish, don't do it. The stuff eats right through the gel coat, making it impossible to ever get a shine again. Micro-abrasives or cleaners like Soft-Scrub do the job with gentle pressure but don't destroy the gel coat.

Biodegradable cleaners like this one from Iosso won't harm marine organisms if the cleanser is washed into the harbor. Still, it's best to wash boats on shore when possible. (Photo credit: Jerry Martin & Associates)

Sailboat Rigging

Sailboat rigging takes special care because there are a lot of complicated metal parts that trap salt and may rust or corrode over time, weakening gear that must endure tremendous loads when the boat is under sail.

After use in salt water, all the rigging should be hosed down thoroughly with fresh water, and at least weekly all metal parts of the rigging should get a soap-and-water bath. A soft-bristled scrub brush is the best tool for getting salt out of crevices.

Get Waxed

Once a boat has been thoroughly washed and allowed to dry, it's wise to add a good paste wax designed for gel coats, at least twice yearly. The wax cuts down on ultraviolet oxidation and also causes some dirt to slide off, as well as making your gel coat look brighter.

Special formulas for glass, such as Rain-X and Rain View, are well worth buying for offshore boaters who regularly get water on their windshields. The products make the glass so slippery that most water simply slides off, giving much better visibility even without windshield washers. (Salt crusts on the shield when it dries, though, so you still have to wash it down later.)

Boat Bytes
Many soaps and cleaners can be harmful to marine life. Use biodegradable cleaners and avoid letting phosphates run into the water by washing your boat on shore when possible.

Look Out!
Fiberglass remains shiny longer if waxed regularly—but never put wax on walking surfaces. With a bit of water added, this becomes as slippery as an ice rink. Soap and water only on decks and walk-on gunnels, please.

Rain-X is so slippery that some boaters apply it to their boat bottoms to keep algae from forming a scum line. Just rub it on and wipe it off—a treatment once a month helps a lot.

Cabin Cleanups

If your boat has a cabin, it's probably got mildew. The best way to keep mildew out of a cabin is with a low-powered heater like the "Golden Rod," which dehumidifies the compartment. (These heaters only work when attached to 110-volt AC, however.)

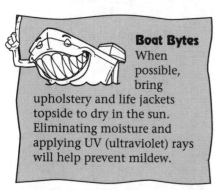

Boat Bytes
When possible, bring upholstery and life jackets topside to dry in the sun. Eliminating moisture and applying UV (ultraviolet) rays will help prevent mildew.

Mildew preventives such as Damp-Rid and No-Damp are chemical dehumidifiers that help a lot in compartments that are closed tightly. And mildew-killing sprays such as Lysol will also help keep the black crud from getting started.

If you have vinyl sleeping pads below, treat them with a vinyl preservative once a year. This keeps them looking new and retains their flexibility. Use the stuff monthly on any upholstery such as cushions in the cockpit, too, because vinyl exposed to the sun dries out and starts to crack quickly without it. It's a good idea to stow your cockpit upholstery in the shade of the cabin or your garage when the boat is not in use.

The Bottom Line

The most significant cleaning job on any boat is the bottom. If the running surfaces are not kept clean and smooth, performance suffers.

So what's to make them dirty down there in the water, you ask?

In fresh water, there's algae, scum, and over the last 10 years, zebra mussels. Along the coast, a variety of sea life attaches itself to boat bottoms, but barnacles are the fastest-growing and most tenacious.

In warm weather, barnacles large enough for you to see and feel will grow on a boat left in the water just one week. The growth slows as the water cools, stopping completely in areas where water drops into the 40s in the winter. But in warmer climates like Florida, the little critters are down there digging in year-round—it takes them a couple weeks to show in winter, but they'll be there. Growth can be amazingly rapid, particularly on boats left at the docks for long periods of time.

Small shellfish are no problem to remove—they can be scrubbed away with a light chlorine solution (about a cup in a gallon of water) and a medium bristle brush. (Better wear rubber gloves if your hands are not barnacle-tough.)

If left until they become the size of a dime, barnacles become unbelievably difficult to get off. Scraping and power-sanding is then the only solution, and the sanding knocks off the gel coat so you then have to paint the bottom. So clearly, it's wise not to let the growth go past the initial stages. In warm weather, 10 days is about the max.

For larger boats that must be left in the water, it's a good idea to don a mask and fins and go over the side to give the bottom a monthly scrubbing with a firm brush (do this in the summer). If you wait too long, the hull will have to be hauled out at considerable expense and scraped down.

The easy way to avoid problems is not to leave your boat in the water for more than a few days at a time. Although the larval forms may latch on to your hull if it sits still for only a few hours, they quickly die and fall off if the boat is pulled out and allowed to dry.

Paint Your Bottoms

Another solution, most common for large boats that have to be left in the water, is to use "anti-fouling paint." This is a paint that contains elements toxic to barnacles and other marine organisms. The most commonly used anti-fouling paints include copper as the toxicant.

There are leaching paints, in which the copper leaches through the paint but leaves the surface itself fairly intact, and ablative paints, which wear away in layers, revealing fresh copper as the top layers disappear.

With either type of paint, a layer of gel-coat primer, applied after a thorough fine-grit sanding, is usually needed to make the anti-fouling paint stick. Not all types are compatible with each other—check with your dealer or read the cans for advice.

Anti-fouling paints like Unepoxy keep marine growth from latching on to your hull. Most types of growth-inhibiting paint are best applied yearly. (Photo credit: Pettit Paints)

Take your checkbook with you when you go shopping for anti-fouling paint—it's horrendously expensive compared to conventional paints. Prices of $75 to $100 per gallon are typical, and you need about a gallon to do the bottom of a typical 24-footer.

Bottom-painting is definitely one of the nastier jobs in boat maintenance, and if you can afford it, you may want to have the boatyard do the job. But having the bottom of a large boat painted by a boatyard can be an expensive proposition—many hours of labor plus the cost of the materials add up. Shop around and get several estimates, in writing, before you make a choice. Be sure the estimate includes the cost of hauling your boat—lifting it out of the water and setting it on blocks so the work can be done. Also include the approximate time when the job will be done. You may be thinking weeks while the yard owner is thinking months.

However, if you're a do-it-yourselfer, here are the basic steps from Pettit Paints, one of the leading suppliers of anti-fouling paints:

1. Make a waterline mark around your hull. The easiest way is to get in the water and mark it with a crayon.

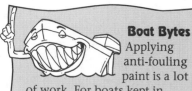

Boat Bytes
Applying anti-fouling paint is a lot of work. For boats kept in freshwater lakes, it's much easier to use a growth-repelling bottom wax like Easy On, which keeps zebra mussels and algae from taking hold. (Unfortunately, it's not effective against saltwater barnacles.)

Look Out!
Some types of anti-fouling paint lose their effectiveness if allowed to dry out while the boat is out of the water. Keep the boat in the water if you use one of these types of paint or you'll have wasted your painting effort.

2. Dewax the hull. Newer fiberglass hulls often have leftover mold-release wax that will also cause your paint to release. Use a fiberglass solvent to get rid of the wax.

3. Sand the hull to a dull finish with 80-grit sandpaper. (Pettit Paints makes a "sandless primer" that forms a chemical bond with the gel coat and eliminates the need for sanding before applying bottom paints—it saves a lot of time and effort.)

4. Rewash the hull with the solvent.

5. Apply two coats of the paint, allowing each coat to dry according to the instructions on the can.

6. Wood hulls gets the same treatment, except you start with a wipe-down with a tacky rag with thinner, then make the first coat of anti-fouling paint with 25 percent thinner so that it penetrates the wood. Finish off with more coats unthinned.

Anti-Fouling on Aluminum

Aluminum gets a different paint, usually one with copper thiocyonate, which does not cause electrolysis as does the standard cuprous oxide used in most anti-fouling paints. (Tin-based paints are also used for metal boats, but must be applied by specialists because they are considered hazardous materials.)

The surface is sandblasted (you can rent a sandblaster and try this yourself, but beware, too much pressure or too long in one spot, and you'll need to know how to repair holes in aluminum boats!), then coated with metal primer, then epoxy primer, sanded, more epoxy primer, and then two finish coats of tin-based or other aluminum-type anti-fouling paint. Whew! This definitely sounds like one for the boatyard.

Teak Treatment

Teak is a lovely, durable wood that is a tradition in fine boat building. But teak is, to put it mildly, a pain in the stern to care for. For that reason, a lot of modern builders have eliminated it completely, replacing fittings such as rod holders and cup holders with composite plastics. They don't look nearly as good, but they never require care.

If you have teak aboard, however, you do have to take care of it to keep it from looking like driftwood.

Teak cleaners are strong acids or corrosives designed to bleach away oils and dirt. They have to be applied while wearing rubber gloves. You let them set on the wood for a few minutes, brush them down, and then rinse with fresh water.

Once the teak dries after this treatment, it turns almost white. To restore the golden glow, you add teak oil, available at all marine dealers. Just rub it on, let it dry, and then rub on a second or third coat. The oil makes water bead up rather than penetrate, helping to keep the wood clean.

Keeping Stuff Dry

There are "dry boxes" on most boats, distinguished by the fact that everything you put into them gets soaking wet. They're sort of like those "water-resistant" watches that work fine until they get anywhere near water.

Dry boxes or storage compartments that are truly dry are almost non-existent. Most makers don't build hatch lids that are adequately guttered, and fewer still are gasketed. This means rain, spray, and wash-down water gets in.

Condensation is also a problem, gathering on the inside of the lids during the cool of night, dripping into the compartment as the sun rises. (This is avoided on a few well-made boats with insulated lids.) And a bit of salt on anything stowed in a box will draw water out of the air, making everything else in the box damp.

The solution? Put a truly watertight box inside the dry box. Plastic boxes with snap-on lids are the ticket. And with sensitive stuff like toilet paper that you really want to keep dry, it's not a bad idea to put the item inside a Ziplock bag, then place the bag inside a plastic box, then place the plastic box inside the dry box. It's sort of like those trick birthday presents that come in a very large box, inside of which is a smaller box, inside of which is an even smaller box, and so on, but it works.

Basic Hull Repairs

With fiberglass, when you get a hole, you fill it with more fiberglass. In fact, tiny holes can be repaired with filled polyester resin putty, which contains a thickener and small glass fibers.

It spreads like peanut butter (but smells worse) and hardens to about the same density as the glass. You then sand it smooth, finishing with 600-grit sandpaper, and spray on gel coat, feathering it in at the edges. Finish with rubbing compound.

Patching Bigger Holes

It's not easy to punch a big hole in a fiberglass boat, but it can be done. Boatyards sometimes manage the trick by dropping boats off fork lifts. At sea, running into a submerged post or rock will do it—and give you a lot more problems than simply how to patch it so it looks nice. (See Chapter 19 on emergency procedures for suggestions. Quick!)

Bigger holes require a patch be inserted from inside the hull. You may have to cut a hole in the floor to insert the patch, and then patch that as well (it's one of those deals where you start out to tighten a drip from a pipe under the sink, and then you find that to get at that drip you have to remove the sink, and then the sink molding breaks when you're taking it out...been there?).

Patching small fiberglass holes on your own is potentially a home-handy-person type of job because the stuff is relatively simple to work with. However, larger holes may or may not be something you want to tackle. Here's the drill—read and decide for yourself:

1. Grind away the broken glass, leaving a smooth hole that tapers inward all around at least 1/8 inch. (You don't want any sharp edges because then the patch can't be sanded in smoothly with the surrounding surfaces.) The inside of the hole is also tapered slightly to give the patch a better grip.

Boater-ese
The two most common types of fiberglass cloth are flat, thin *mats* of random-direction fibers or threads, and *woven roving*, which has thicker threads of glass fibers woven like a wool scarf into a heavy fabric.

2. Wet the patch—glass mat rather than woven roving—with resin and put it into place. Allow the patch to harden, then back it with a thin layer of putty for waterproofing, then several more layers of glass mat, to the thickness of the original bottom.

3. The first piece of fiberglass cloth should be at least two inches larger than the hole all around to allow for a good grip all around. Make each succeeding layer a little bigger, to tap into the strength of the surrounding glass. Don't sand the inside part—it won't show and you'd be taking away strength. In a large boat that's used offshore, it's common to back a couple layers of mat with a layer or two of woven roving, which is stronger but less waterproof.

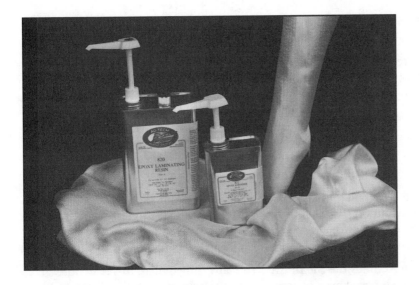

A fiberglass patching kit like this one from Ad-Tech includes resin, hardener, and fiberglass cloth. These are the same materials used in making fiberglass hulls originally. (Photo credit: Ad-Tech Corp.)

4. Add the resin putty filler on the outside, sand it smooth with progressively smaller grits from 00 working down to 600-grit paper, and finish it with sprayed gel-coat resin. Polish it with rubbing compound.

That may be more than you ever wanted to know about patching a boat. Sounds like a lot of work, doesn't it?

It is.

Fiberglass dust up your nose, little pieces of glass in your arms, resin under your fingernails for weeks. If you're not into this sort of thing, just do what the pros do—send your boat down to the nearest boat hospital and hope your credit card won't melt down over the bill. (Boat-repair guys don't get quite what heart surgeons do, but they're not far behind.)

Look Out!
Acetone, the best cleaner for polyester resin-coated tools, is extremely flammable and hazardous if inhaled in high concentrations. Keep this product well clear of heat and flames and use it only in open, well-ventilated areas.

Patching Aluminum Boats

In truth, most patches in aluminum fail sooner or later. It's very difficult to get anything to stick to aluminum permanently, and the different flex rates between the patch and the expanding and contracting metal eventually cause those tiny leaks to start again.

However, the same epoxy/fiberglass compounds used for fiberglass boats also offer good initial adhesion to aluminum, as long as the parts are thoroughly roughsanded and wiped down with acetone, the standard solvent for epoxy resins.

So-called "liquid aluminum" patching material that comes in tubes also works, but it's basically epoxy resin with an aluminum and/or fiberglass filler.

Aluminum hulls more than .025-inch thick can be repaired by heli-arc welding at an aluminum shop, but the thinner material on most jon boats and canoes simply burns into a larger hole if welding is attempted.

Hull Painting

It's usually not necessary to paint fiberglass boats because the gel coat lasts for decades, particularly if you apply UV-inhibiting polish once or twice a year.

There are a few paints designed for fiberglass, though, that can make an old hull look like new, and that will stay put on the smooth surface. It's not something most boaters can do for themselves and come out with a respectable finish, however, because the paint is best sprayed to lay properly, and on smooth, vertical surfaces spray-painting can be a challenge.

If you truly feel the need to restore the finish on a badly dulled boat, this is a chore that's best left to the pros. Your best course of action is to regularly perform the clean-up duties on your hull to make sure painting will never be necessary.

The Least You Need to Know

➤ Time spent cleaning your boat is repaid in less maintenance and better resale value.

➤ Keeping your boat's bottom clean is a continuous chore for boats left afloat.

➤ Simple hull repairs of small holes are easy to do at home, but larger holes take more work and might be better left to the pros.

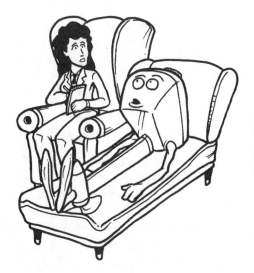

Keeping Your Engine Happy

Modern marine engines don't take a lot of care, but they do need a bit of attention from time to time to keep them purring. A few minutes of engine care before every boating day will be repaid with reliable starts, longer engine life, and much less chance of trouble when you're far from land, so it's time well spent. And it can save you a boatload of money—it's a lot cheaper to add a quart of oil today than to rebuild the engine tomorrow.

This chapter looks at general engine maintenance, and also includes a few tips for minor troubleshooting when something goes wrong. (Thankfully, the tinkering that used to be a part of many outings is starting to disappear with ever-more-reliable marine engines.)

Let's Get Oiled

The most obvious but probably most forgotten part of engine care is keeping oil in the tank of two-cycle engines with oil injection. Although there are warning horns and speed-limiters to prevent you from overlooking this duty for long, many boaters have learned that by the time the horns go off and the limiters kick in, it's too late—your next cruise is to the $40-an-hour repair shop.

> **Boater-ese**
> A *speed-limiter* (or "rev-limiter") is used on many marine engines, both to prevent winding past the redline or recommended top limit for revolutions-per-minute, and to slow the engine to near idle speed if anything goes wrong with the lubrication or cooling systems.

Two-cycles engines, unlike four-cycles engines, rely on delivery of lubricating oil with the gasoline to control friction and heat in the cylinders and bearings, so if you don't make sure there's always oil available to mix with the gas, your engine will have a short, unhappy life. (Four-cycles have a pool of oil in a pan at the bottom of the engine, and don't require it to be mixed with their fuel.)

Most outboards of four cylinders or more have protective systems to prevent damage resulting from operation without oil. Most have warning horns (electronic beepers mounted in the dash or throttle box) that give an audible signal when you need to add oil or when the engine is running hot.

On stern drives and inboards, both gas and diesel, check the oil dipstick religiously before every trip, and at each stop along the way on longer cruises. A four-cycle engine kept full of oil is a happy four-cycle.

Tighten Your Belt

When the belt on your trousers gets loose, it's good. When your engine's belts get loose, it's bad. Outboards use rubber and fabric belts to drive their alternators, and inboards and I/Os use them to drive water pumps, the alternator, power steering, and more. The heat and vibration of operation on the water causes these belts to gradually go slack, and when they do they begin to slip. The more they slip, the faster they wear and the looser they get in a vicious circle that eventually sees them break.

Keep the belts tight (most have an idler arm—a moveable pulley—or other adjuster) and you'll eliminate this potential problem. Also, at least yearly, look at the underside of the belts for fraying or missing pieces. Any damage at all means it's time for a replacement.

The belts on stern-drive engines like this one drive several critical systems. Check the belts for tightness and wear regularly. (Photo credit: Outboard Marine Corp.)

Torque Time

At 5,000 revolutions per minute, there are a lot of vibrations in a marine engine. Vibration makes nuts, bolts, and screws work loose.

To keep something unfortunate from happening, it's wise to check your engine every four or five trips for anything that might be coming loose and retighten all suspects.

In engines with aluminum heads and blocks, including all outboards, it's easy to strip the threads by putting too much pressure on a stainless-steel bolt or screw. A torque wrench is needed, along with the shop manual suggesting how many foot-pounds can safely be applied to each fastener.

Lube Job

Because the steering systems on outboards and stern drives are constantly exposed to water and to salt in coastal areas, they require frequent lubrication. The fittings and brackets support a lot of weight, and if that weight is moved over dry surfaces the steering becomes very difficult.

The throttle cables can also use a shot of lube regularly to allow for easy speed adjustment.

Hydraulic and power steering systems are filled with oil (not motor oil, but hydraulic steering fluid), and unless they leak, you'll rarely need to add any oil. If you open the system to add oil, you may have to bleed air from it—a job better left to a pro if you're not inclined to tinker.

While you're examining the steering system, check it for any binding or excessive play, grating noises, or loose fasteners. Any problems in this system can lead to disaster, obviously, so if you even suspect problems, take the boat to a shop.

Check the Oil, Please

The lower unit of outboards and stern drives is filled with gear oil, and this should be checked regularly. Do so by opening the upper inspection hole, sealed with a flush-mounted screw. A slight amount of the oil will run out when you pull the screw if the unit is properly filled.

The oil should be dark and clear. If it's milky-looking, there's water in the lower unit and you need to visit the repair shop promptly to find out why. (Usually it's a prop-shaft seal, but sometimes it's a crack in the housing, the result of striking an obstruction.)

If the unit needs oil, it has to be added from the bottom. Oil added from the top traps air, creates bubbles, and makes a mess.

The oil filler screw is on the bottom side of the gear housing, just above the skeg. Don't remove it until you put the upper screw back into place unless you want to drain the unit and refill it completely. The air lock formed by the airtight housing will keep most oil from running out when you remove the lower screw.

Check the oil that comes out of the bottom hole for metal particles. If you see any, it's a sign that something is coming apart inside—have a mechanic take a look. If you don't see any, put the filler tube into the filler hole, and then slightly loosen the upper screw so that air can escape as you pump or squeeze oil into the lower tube.

When oil comes out the upper hole, tighten that screw to recreate the vacuum, then quickly remove the filler tube and plug it with the lower screw. Now tighten both securely and wipe off any excess oil with paper towels.

Another hidden spot that may need a refill once a year is your tilt/trim reservoir. Check your owner's manual for location and access to the filler tube, and use only the recommended fluid.

Sparking Your Relationship

Without lots of fire, marine engines don't run well. On outboards, the spark plugs and the wires that lead to them stick out where they can be bumped or loosened by contact with the cowl or by careless work on some other part of the engine.

Check the plug wires and connections regularly. Particularly on older motors, the connector insulation sometimes goes soft and sticky due to long exposure to gas fumes and loses its insulating capability. Replace any plug wires that are not firm and dry, and make sure the connectors snap securely on the spark plug contacts.

With diesels like this Yanmar, you can be sure that the spark plugs are not the problem. Diesels function without them. (Photo credit: Yanman Diesels)

It's not a bad idea to pull the spark plugs before the start of the boating season. Clean them with a wire brush, check the gaps and adjust according to the manual, and then reinstall.

Use a torque wrench to tighten the plugs. It's *very easy* to strip the threads in the aluminum heads by over-tightening spark plugs—don't try to do this by "feel" unless you've been a mechanic for 20 years.

When you fit the cowl back in place on an outboard, make sure that it doesn't hit any of the plugs or wires and cause problems.

The powerhead of an outboard runs in a mist of wet air, with lots of salt along the coast. This soon corrodes or causes electrolysis if the metals are not protected. Spray down your powerhead monthly with a water-replacing oil spray like Corrosion-X or WD-40 to keep corrosion away. The same products also help to keep rust and corrosion off inboards and stern drives.

Look Out!

Any time you take the cowl off an outboard, make absolutely certain that the rubber seal at the bottom fits back into the casement around the powerhead. Any misfit here or any failure to properly clamp the cowl back into place will let water into areas where it shouldn't be, particularly if you use the boat in big, following seas.

Prop Problems?

Check the propeller several times a year, or immediately after you brush bottom. Any bent or damaged blades can cause vibration that may eventually ruin the seals in an outdrive or stuffing box and lead to lots more problems. (A *stuffing box* is the sealing system that prevents water from entering around the hole where the drive shaft of an inboard passes through the bottom of the boat. A similar system is used around the post that supports the rudder on inboards and sailboats.)

It's not possible to correctly reshape the blades of a bent propeller without templates and other gear, so the best thing to do when you see damage is to send the prop to the shop.

Also, watch for fishline on the prop shaft, next to the seals. If not removed, this can eventually work its way between the seal and the shaft and cause leaks.

Follow all these maintenance tips and your engine problems will be rare. However, there will be times when even the best cared-for motor will be balky.

Why Won't It Start? Basic Troubleshooting

Considering that V6 outboards and stern drives now cost more than a Saturn car—and almost as much as a Saturn rocket—you'd think they'd start right up, first time, every time.

Some do, some don't. Carbureted motors are particularly cranky at times, which is why more and more builders are going to fuel injection. Especially with older motors in used rigs, there may be a bit of gasping and wheezing and sometimes, nothing at all.

The loudest sound in the world is when, 20 miles from the nearest land, you turn the starter key and hear…nothing.

Before you face that situation, let's review some of the most common reasons why an engine may not start and how to fix the problem.

Nothing Happens When I Turn the Key

This could be the simplest of all problems, in that you don't have the shift lever in neutral. Most marine engines have a lock-out that prevents them from starting in gear. And some shift levers don't have a neutral detent that's all that obvious. Always check this first when you get no response, moving the shifter to reverse, forward, and then feeling for that center position.

Silence might also mean that wires have come loose, either those to the ignition key or those to the battery. Check the battery first—shifting of the batteries due to boat motion sometimes makes wires come loose, and corrosion building up on the terminals can also be a culprit.

Wiggle the large black and red wires attaching to the terminal post to see if anything is loose. Look at the connectors and the post to see if there's any sort of blue-green build-up that indicates corrosion. If so, remove them and scrape the inside of the connectors with a knife until they're bright, and then reattach securely.

If the wires are tight and clean but the engine won't turn over, it's possible that the battery is dead. If you have auxiliary batteries aboard (those used for trolling motors, cabin lights, and so on) you can tap into these to get things going by using jumper cables.

Another possibility on many engines is that a main fuse has blown or a breaker has tripped. The fuses are usually found in a waterproof connector near the starter. Check and replace or reset as needed. (You'll want to carry a spare fuse of the proper amperage, obviously.)

Look Out!
Working on the wiring is a likely source of fire, if not explosion. Because direct current doesn't shock, there's a tendency to treat boat wiring with a lack of caution. But a 12-volt battery can generate instant, red-hot metal if you cross connections or drop a wrench that lands across both terminals. Burns and boat fires can happen very quickly to the careless, so always use caution when working on wiring.

It Turns Over But It Won't Start

The most obvious solution here is that there's no fuel reaching the firing chamber. To get it there, you hit the choke or "prime" button. About 98 percent of the time on cold-start with an engine that's not fuel-injected, the problem is too little fuel.

With outboards, it might simply be that the motor was stored in a position that let the fuel run out of the carburetor bowl—storing a motor at the full-tilt position will cause this to happen in some motors. First try tilting the motor down, so that it's upright in the running position.

Look Out!
Using jumper cables causes sparks, so always make sure there's no gas leak in the engine compartment before you use them. And remember, black goes to the negative post, red to the positive posts—otherwise you'll get some real fireworks!

Then choke the engine, most commonly done by pushing in on the ignition key as you crank the starter. On manual-start motors, you pull a choke lever. The choke puts an air restricter across the carburetor, reducing the amount of air that gets in, making the fuel/air mix richer. Some motors have a "primer" that squirts a shot of fuel into the intake manifold.

In either case, you're enriching the mix, getting explosive fuel into the air inside the cylinder, so that when the spark plug fires, the motor starts.

Look Out!
If a cold motor stumbles, pops, or belches smoke, even for a second, the fuel is there—*so stop choking it*! If you continue, it will flood—get too much fuel for the amount of air—and not start because the spark plug won't fire liquid fuel nearly as well as vaporized fuel.

Look Out!
Never choke or prime a hot engine, because the fuel is already where it needs to be, and the motor will flood immediately if you add excess fuel.

The normal routine is, the motor stumbles, then you stop choking, turn the starter one more time, and it starts. You may need to press in on the key, in short blips, to keep it running after the first start-up, but after 15 to 20 seconds, it should smooth out.

If the motor coughs and runs for a few seconds and then quits with a lot of smoking, don't choke it again just yet. Open the throttle a little and crank the motor once more. Often, it will pop right off.

If you crank 10 seconds more and don't get another cough and don't smell gasoline, give the engine another blip of choke until it coughs again, and then repeat the procedure.

I Flooded the Engine—Now What?

You can tell when your engine is flooded because you'll smell gasoline and the motor will sound "wet" when you crank it. To fix this problem, you have to add more air and cut off the fuel.

Make sure the choke is "off." Don't squeeze the prime bulb, but do open the throttle. (On outboards and stern drives, you do this by pushing a button on the bottom of the throttle lever, which disengages the shifting rod and allows you to open the throttle without putting the motor into gear.) Then crank for 10-second bursts, with 30 seconds in between, until the motor coughs or sputters. (If you're hand-cranking, do it until *you* cough or sputter.)

Don't keep the starter cranking for long periods—it will simply overheat and burn up. Crank the motor for no more than three or four 10-second bursts, then rest it for several minutes to let the starter cool before you crank it again.

In a worst-case scenario, you might have to unplug the fuel hose, take out the spark plugs, crank the engine a bit with them out to blow out the excess fuel, dry off the plug elements, and then reinstall the spark plugs.

Don't choke the engine after this procedure—it should pop right off. (If you have a chronically troublesome engine, a shot of Quick Start or other fuel vapor into the spark plug hole will help.)

Most of the time when your motor won't start, it's the fuel/air mix. Each motor has a particular starting procedure that works best. Learn the idiosyncrasies of your motor and these problems will go away.

Uh-Oh, I Pulled the Kill Switch

The kill switch or emergency stop connector is found on a red lanyard near the ignition switch on most outboard powered boats and many performance inboards and stern drives. If this switch is tripped by pulling the cord, no matter how long you crank, the motor can never start.

On bass boats and high-performance rigs where it's the norm to clip the kill switch lanyard to the life jacket, the classic goof is to stand up with the jacket on and jerk the switch free. When you try to restart, you wonder what suddenly happened to your brand new $12,000 outboard, never realizing that the $1 gizmo that will make it work is dangling from your vest.

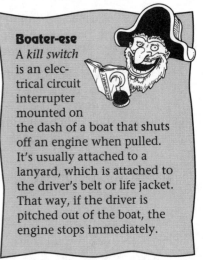

Boater-ese
A *kill switch* is an electrical circuit interrupter mounted on the dash of a boat that shuts off an engine when pulled. It's usually attached to a lanyard, which is attached to the driver's belt or life jacket. That way, if the driver is pitched out of the boat, the engine stops immediately.

Put the switch connector back in the "run" position by snapping it over the nipple attachment on the dash, if needed. (Of course, if you've turned the motor over very long with the kill switch detached, you've probably flooded it—see "I Flooded the Engine—Now What?" on the previous page.)

Could I Be Out of Gas?

Dumb as it sounds, your boat may simply be out of gas. Never trust fuel gauges on boats. Because the floats bounce around so drastically, fuel gauges often get out of whack. So whenever you have the slightest doubt that you may be low on gas, add more. (It's a good idea to keep the tanks topped off, anyway, to prevent water condensation inside, which eventually builds up enough to cause rust and maybe even running problems.)

To avoid low fuel problems afloat, the general rule of thumb is, use no more than $1/_3$ of a tank for the trip out, no more than $1/_3$ for the trip back, and save $1/_3$ for reserve. Why so much? Because currents, wind, and waves working against you can suddenly convert your five-miles-per-gallon motor into one that gets only two miles per gallon. (Anglers who troll for hours must reserve plenty for that, as well.)

I've Tried Everything and the Motor Still Won't Start!

If you've done everything right and still can't get the motor to start, check for loose fittings in the fuel line. At times, the quick-release connector on hoses for portable outboards pops loose at the engine cowling. Check for secure attachment here, and at the entry to the portable tank, if you have one.

The fuel hose could also be pinched—maybe someone set a heavy tackle box on top of it. Check the length of the hose, particularly if it's exposed in the cockpit.

On portable tanks, the vent may be closed. It's designed to prevent fuel spillage during transport, but it forms an airlock if left screwed shut when you try to start the engine. (Suspect this one in particular if the engine starts briefly but then shuts down and won't start again.) The vent is a small screw located on the filler cap.

The culprit could also be dirt in a fuel filter. Modern fuel-injected outboards and diesel inboards have several filters built into their fuel systems. If any of them clog, the motor won't start (or it will stumble when it does). Check the filters if simpler remedies fail.

Water in the fuel is another problem. It sometimes results from condensation in older tanks, or it can come from contaminated fuel at a gas station or marina. It's not a common problem, but it can happen. Keep a can of dry gas handy to add to your tank, just in case. (You may have to shoot Quick-Start down the air intake of your motor or through the spark plug holes to get the contaminated fuel clear.)

When the Motor Overheats

Boat Bytes
All outboards have a "telltale" spout on the cowl that squirts a thin stream of water out to the side when the cooling system has proper pressure. Check this spray regularly, particularly when you pass through weeds, to head off overheating problems.

When the warning buzzer comes on, it's usually because of weeds in the water intake, found on the lower unit housing slightly above the bullet or gear housing on most outboards. Plastic bags can also cover these intakes. And if you run aground, soft mud can jam them.

It's also possible, on outboards and stern drives, that you have the lower unit—the part that sticks down into the water—tilted up too high, as you might when crossing a shallow area. If the water intake comes above the surface, the motor will get hot.

The third possible cause of overheating is a bad water pump—not a fun repair on most engines. See your owner's manual and break out the wrenches, or have the water pump repaired by a professional. (It's a good idea to carry a spare water pump impeller, just in case.)

It Runs But It Doesn't Move

If the motor runs fine until you shift it into gear, then it dies, you could be looking at some major surgery, as in broken shafts, gears, or other parts. But more often, it's a rope, wire crab trap, or other obstruction wrapped around the propeller.

The solution is to tilt up the lower unit on outboards and stern drives and work on the offending tangle with a knife, pliers, or wire cutters. On inboards, you have to put on your dive mask to get at the source—no fun at all in winter!

It's also possible that the shaft is turning but the propeller is not—indicating a broken cotter pin in small motors, a spun rubber impact hub in the prop on larger outboards and stern drives. To replace the pin, remove the propeller, tap out the old pin, and then insert the new one. You can also use a stout nail cut to size if you don't carry a spare pin.

If the prop has a spun hub, you can't fix it yourself. However, most propellers will operate at idle speed, allowing you to get back to the dock. (If you speed up, the load is too much for the minimal friction in the hub and the prop won't turn.) Carrying a spare prop is the best way to deal with a spun hub.

The Least You Need to Know

➤ Many engine problems can be avoided with proper maintenance.

➤ Some apparent problems can be solved without ever touching a tool—think things through before you act.

➤ Fuel and air problems are the most common reasons why engines fail to start.

Part 7
Sailing, Sailing...

Sailing offers a curious combination of peace and quiet and laid-back lifestyle with intellectual and physical challenge, depending on how you go about it.

This section details the language of sailors as well as the remarkable variety of types of sailing vessels, ranging from fly-weight sailboards to giant schooners big enough to take on transoceanic voyages.

And although getting started in sailing usually requires a bit of hands-on instruction, you can learn the basics through reading this section—from attaching and hoisting the sails to steering through all the points of sail from close-hauled to a downwind run.

Now repeat after me: ARRRR...

Chapter 23

How to Tell the Main From the Jib: A Sailor's Vocabulary

In This Chapter

➤ Sailing schools give you the basics, but hands-on instruction is best

➤ The names of all that stuff

➤ Learning the points of sail

Sailing is an art almost as old as boats themselves, and those who take the time to learn (it doesn't take much) are rewarded with voyages that offer peace and grace and blessed silence that many feel is more at one with the watery environment than the noise and the fumes generated by powerboats.

Sailing is a thinking person's mode of transportation, employing physics, geometry, and ergonomics. It's not for those who simply want to step aboard, turn the key, and take off. But with a bit of study, anyone can learn the basics of sailing in a long weekend. After that, it's a long path you can follow as far as you like toward becoming a master.

And although sailing can be among the most tranquil of sports, it can also be among the most exciting and challenging. It holds a life-long attraction, both for those who race avidly in competition, and for those who only race avidly for the best sundown anchorage.

In this chapter, you'll become familiar with the names of all the parts of a sailboat and its rigging; the masts, sails, and lines that make it sail; as well as the points of sail and an assortment of other terms that will make sailing easier. It's a simple language, and one you'll pick up quickly as you spend a bit of time aboard.

Sailboat or Powerboat?

Powerboats are a means to an end, useful tools to go fishing, picnicking, water skiing, or gunk-holing. In sailing, the sailing itself is often the end, as in flying a sailplane or an ultra-light.

And because you rarely have to visit a fuel dock, larger sailing craft and "motor-sailers," sailboats equipped with dependable diesel engines and spacious cabins, are often the choice of those who make long-distance voyages to the remote corners of the world.

Here are some good things you can say about sailboats that you can't about powerboats:

➤ You never have to change the oil.

➤ They always start. (At least, if the wind is blowing.)

➤ You never have to buy gas.

➤ The captain gets to give lots of orders.

➤ You don't have to deal with smelly exhaust fumes.

Getting Started

It does take a bit of application to get started in sailing, but in retrospect, those who have learned feel it's almost intuitive. I once wrote in my newspaper column that sailing was a technical sport that took a fair amount of instruction. An avid sailor wrote back in a huff that sailing is *not* a technical sport. "Give me three full days and I can teach anybody to sail," he wrote.

I guess he meant it wasn't technical in the sense that nuclear physics is technical. But compared to powerboating, it's pretty complex.

Boat Bytes
The American Sailing Association, (310) 822-7171, and the U.S. Sailing Association, (401) 683-0800, both offer listings of sailing schools nationwide. See Appendix B for more information.

Note that there are hundreds of "sailing schools" throughout the world, but almost no "powerboat schools." This should tell you something.

The biggest part of the difficulty is in the vocabulary. If you know what to call all the parts of a sailboat, instructions suddenly become much clearer.

I learned to sail at Steve Colgate's week-long Offshore Sailing School and recommend it strongly, but there are many other good schools that can get you going, some over a weekend.

You can't truly learn in a classroom, however, and all the good schools feature on-the-water instruction after a brief period of book learning.

Sailing requires some know-how and practice, but the rewards are well worth it. This family uses a single-masted sailboat known as a sloop to visit an island in Lake Erie. (Photo credit: Frank Sargeant)

The Absolute Basics of Sailing

You don't have to know the difference between a mizzenmast and a shroud to put up the sail and go for a turn around the bay.

Pick a day with just a little wind for this, under 10 knots—otherwise, you may have to learn a little more quickly than you want to. And make your first attempts in a small, basic sloop-rigged sailboat—no twin-masted ketches to start, please. (See Chapter 24 for details on the types of sailboats.)

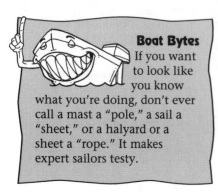

Boat Bytes
If you want to look like you know what you're doing, don't ever call a mast a "pole," a sail a "sheet," or a halyard or a sheet a "rope." It makes expert sailors testy.

Here are the absolute basics of sailing in 35 words or less:

1. Hitch the white sheet to the pole.
2. Raise the white sheet up the pole by pulling on the rope.
3. Tension it off with the ropes along the edge.
4. Hang on—you're sailing!

To say the least, this may be a little oversimplified, but these are the steps that everyone from former America's Cup champion Dennis Connor on down go through when they use the wind as their engine.

Learning sailing is like learning German, not so tough if you're in-country with people who speak it, and, when they hand you a cup of coffee, tell you it's "eine tasse caffee." Sailing is like that. It's easier to learn by doing than by reading about it.

Go do it first, with a patient instructor, then learn the terms. You can learn to get around the buoy and back in an hour. Doing it in style or with any hint of speed can take months and years of study and practice.

From A to Z: Parts of a Sailboat

However you learn to sail, though, there are a considerable number of terms that you will eventually want to know, and the sooner you know them, the easier learning will be. Check the figure that appears after this list for an idea of what is located where.

Let's define these parts of a sailboat one by one:

1. *Mainsail.* The large sail on the back side of the main mast.
2. *Jib.* The sail set on the front side of the main mast and supported by the head stay.
3. *Mast.* The vertically mounted pole used to support the sails and rigging.
4. *Boom.* The horizontal pole along the foot of a sail.
5. *Main sheet.* The line used to control the mainsail via the boom.
6. *Jib sheet.* The line used to control the jib sail.
7. *Halyards.* Lines used to hoist sails up the mast.
8. *Luff.* The front edge of a sail. (When a sail is "luffing," it is flapping and loose, not creating lift.)

9. *Leech.* The back edge of a sail.

10. *Head.* The top corner of a sail. (Not to be confused with the marine toilet, which goes by the same name.)

11. *Foot.* The bottom edge of a sail.

12. *Clew.* The bottom rear corner of a sail, where the sheet attaches.

13. *Tack.* The bottom front corner of a sail. (To "tack," however, is also a term meaning to work back and forth into the wind.)

14. *Backstay.* A tensioned support cable that runs from the top of the mast to the stern of the boat.

15. *Forestay.* A tensioned support cable that runs from the top of the mast to the bow of the boat.

16. *Battens.* These are stiffeners that insert into pockets in a sail's leech to improve the shape and the lifting ability.

17. *Keel or Centerboard.* The keel is the fin on the bottom of the sailboat that keeps the boat from slipping sideways. It's usually ballasted or weighted to help prevent a capsize. The centerboard is a moveable keel, unballasted, that's used on smaller boats. The swing-up keel makes it easier to beach or trailer the boat.

18. *Boom vang.* This is the line used to control boom position. It sits closer to the mast than the main sheet, which is also attached to the boom.

Run through this list a few times while studying the figure on the following page. When you know the names of all the parts without sneaking a peek at the key, you're ready for some on-the-water instruction.

1. Mainsail
2. Jib
3. Mast
4. Boom
5. Main sheet
6. Jib sheet
7. Halyards
8. Luff
9. Leech
10. Head
11. Foot
12. Clew
13. Tack
14. Backstay
15. Forestay
16. Battens
17. Keel or Centerboard
18. Boom vang

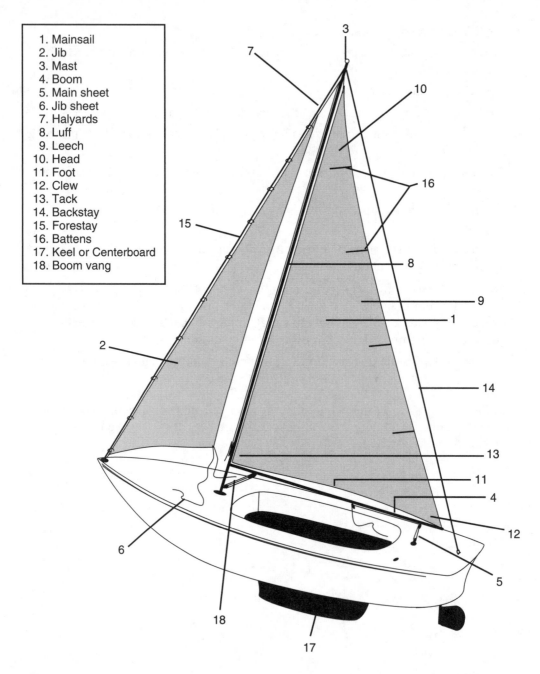

The parts of a sailboat's rigging or sailing gear have specialized names that you'll want to become familiar with.

The Points of Sail

A sailboat's heading in relation to the wind is everything in sailing. No boat can sail directly into the wind, and going directly downwind is, surprisingly to initiates, not the most efficient course unless you break out a special sail called a "spinnaker" (which we'll talk about in Chapter 26).

The headings in relation to the wind have a set of names (doesn't everything in sailing?) that you will want to be familiar with. They're shown in the following figure.

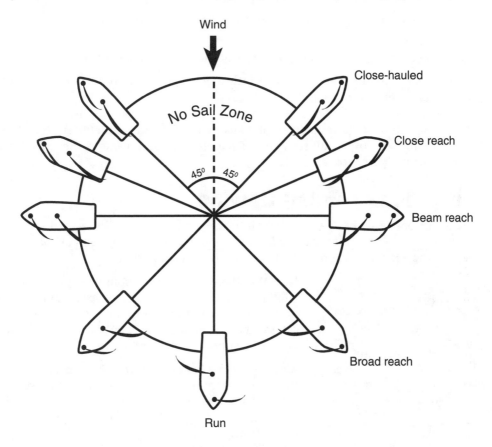

The terms for the points of sail, the boat's heading relative to the wind, are shown in this diagram. Note that all points crossing the wind are known as "reaches," while points heading into the wind at 45 degrees or less are known as "beats." Note too the position of the boat's sails in each heading.

Here's the rundown on each of these terms:

➤ *Run.* This is a downwind leg, usually sailed with the main and the jib on opposite sides of the mast (also called sailing wing-on-wing).

➤ *Reach.* To sail across the wind at any angle.

➤ *Broad reach.* To sail downwind at an angle greater than 90 degrees from the wind direction.

➤ *Beam reach.* To sail across the wind at 90 degrees.

➤ *Close reach.* To sail upwind at an angle less than 90 degrees but not directly into the wind.

➤ *Close-hauled.* To sail as nearly into the wind as the boat will allow.

➤ *Beating.* To sail at an angle of as little as 45 degrees into the wind. No sailboat will beat directly into a wind.

Each point of sail requires a different adjustment of the sails for efficient travel (you'll learn more about these adjustments in Chapter 25). But in general, the reaches are the most efficient points of sail.

Sailing Magic—Going Upwind

Sailboats obviously can't sail directly into the wind, but they can easily reach upwind locations by beating into the wind. This is sailing a series of legs or tacks back and forth across the wind, as shown in the figure on the following page.

Boater-ese
Tacking is sailing back and forth on a series of beats to work toward an upwind objective.

Note that there's an area of about 90 degrees going into the wind (45 degrees on either side of straight upwind) where most sailboats can't function. A few specially designed boats can sail a bit nearer the wind, but for most, close-hauling fails at just under 45 degrees.

Also note that a boat on a *port tack* (bearing to the right of the wind direction) has the wind coming in over the port side. On a *starboard tack*, the boat is steered to the left of the wind direction so that the wind comes from the starboard or right side.

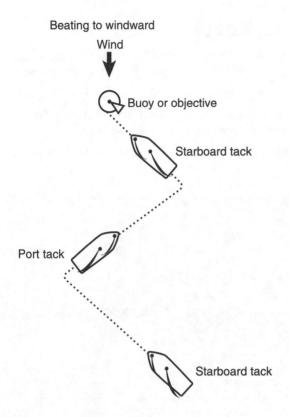

Beating to windward

Wind

Buoy or objective

Starboard tack

Port tack

Starboard tack

Beating into the wind in a series of direction changes is slow going, but it's the only way short of breaking out the kicker for a sailboat to reach an upwind location.

Terms for Downwind

When sailing on a beam reach, broad reach, or a run, it's also necessary to turn downwind across the wind at times, which is called *jibing*. In this maneuver, the bow swings through the direct downwind position, the exact opposite of changing tacks on an upwind beat. Note the position of the sails in the following figure.

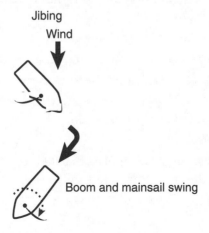

Jibing

Wind

Boom and mainsail swing

To jibe is to turn away from the wind, swinging the bow through the downwind position and back out the other side. Because the boom can swing rapidly (and sometimes unexpectedly) on this maneuver, caution is required.

Other Handy Terms to Know

There are a number of other components on most sailboats, as well as sailing terms, that may someday be useful to know as you become more practiced. Here are some of them:

➤ *Apparent wind.* The wind as it affects a sailboat in motion. Apparent wind on a downwind run is minimal, while on a close reach the felt wind is near maximum, combining wind speed with the forward motion of the boat.

➤ *Bosun's chair.* A sling used to hoist a crewperson up the mast to inspect and repair rigging.

The bosun's chair allows a crewperson to be hoisted aloft (carefully!) to clean the standing rigging. (Photo credit: Frank Sargeant)

➤ *Cam cleats.* These are cleats that depend on eccentric or off-center wheels to lock lines in place—they are faster to use than conventional cleats, so they are favored for sheets.

➤ *Coming about.* To change direction or change tacks.

➤ *Genoa.* A large jib sail that actually overlaps the mast.

➤ *Heeling.* Leaning to one side, often from the force of the wind on the sails.

➤ *In irons.* A boat is said to be in irons when it is stuck pointing directly upwind and the sails cannot be filled to begin sailing again.

➤ *Leeward.* Away from the wind.

➤ *Life lines.* A safety rail usually made of plastic-coated steel cable that circles the deck of larger boats to keep the crew from falling overboard.

The life lines or safety rails on this Irwin 52 protect the crew from falling overboard. Note the neat handling of sheets on this yacht. (Photo credit: Frank Sargeant)

➤ *Outhaul.* A line used to tension the foot of a sail along a boom.

➤ *Reefing.* To reduce the sail area by partially lowering the sail and rolling or tying it to the boom.

➤ *Roller furling.* A system of storing sails by winding them on a rotating spool.

➤ *Running rigging.* Refers to all the lines and gear used to raise and tension the sails. It is adjusted frequently as winds and course change.

➤ *Shrouds.* Support wires that run from the mast to the sides of the boat, part of the standing rigging.

➤ *Slot.* The space between the headsail and the mainsail, where much of the lift or propelling force is generated.

➤ *Spinnaker.* A lightweight, three-cornered sail with a parachute-like shape used for adding speed on downwind runs.

➤ *Standing rigging.* The stays and shrouds that hold the mast upright. It is more or less fixed rigging.

➤ *Telltales.* Small bits of yarn or other lightweight materials that are attached to the sail or other readily visible spot to indicate wind direction and flow.

➤ *Windward.* Toward the wind.

All the terms listed here may seem a jumble as you read them, but take this book with you aboard and think about the names of each piece of gear as you rig it, and about the names of the maneuvers as you perform them, and you'll have it locked within a trip or two.

The Least You Need to Know

➤ The easiest way to get started in sailing is with hands-on learning from a good instructor.

➤ Learning the sailor's vocabulary helps communication between teacher and student.

➤ The best way to learn the vocabulary is aboard a boat.

A.   B.   C.

Chapter 24

Types of Sailboats

In This Chapter

➤ How to tell the difference between a sloop and a schooner

➤ Sailboats with single, double, and triple hulls

➤ Types of sails

➤ Taking care of your sails

It doesn't matter, in terms of your success and enjoyment of sailing, whether you ever learn the names of the types of rigging, hulls, and the categories of sails. Plenty of very happy and very good sailors never do.

But as your experience grows, it's likely that you'll want to be able to converse with others who do know these terms, so this chapter presents a brief review.

What Do You Call It?

Sailboats are generally classified according to the number and position of the masts. The size doesn't matter in this case, simply the way the mast or masts are put on the boat, and it's possible for a catboat to become a sloop if someone goes to the trouble and expense of changing the position and rigging of the mast.

Single-Mast Sailing

Most modern sailboats are of one type, the single-mast stepped or set into the deck and/ or hull a bit forward of amidships, and supporting two sails, a main on the back side of the mast and a jib in front. These sailboats are known as *sloops* and range in size from under 10 feet to more than 40 feet long.

If the mast is stepped amidships and carries two sails forward of the mast, the boat is known as a *cutter*.

And if the mast is stepped well forward and carries only a mainsail, it's known as a *catboat*.

Single-mast boats are generally smaller, less expensive, and easier to sail than two-mast boats—your first sailboat should be a single-master, even if you are Bill Gates' only heir.

Single-mast sail-boats include sloops, cutters, and catboats. The location of the mast is the determining factor in how the boat is categorized.

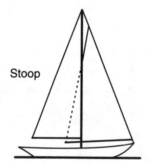

Stoop

Cutter

Catboat

Two-Mast Sailing

Larger boats can handle more sail power, and need it for reasonable performance. Two masts can support more sail area than one, so two-mast rigs are common among offshore voyagers. Two-masters begin at around 40 feet and stretch out to over a majestic 100 feet long.

A *ketch*-rigged two-master has the taller or main mast in front, and a smaller "mizzen" mast aft, but in front of the wheel or tiller.

A *schooner*, once the most common rig for island traders and other large sailboats, has a foremast that's shorter than the mainmast, which sits well aft. Large schooners can have more than two masts, but as long as the foremast is shorter than the main, it's still a schooner.

A *yawl* is like a ketch except that the mizzen or aft mast is stepped behind the wheel or tiller. It's a rare rig these days.

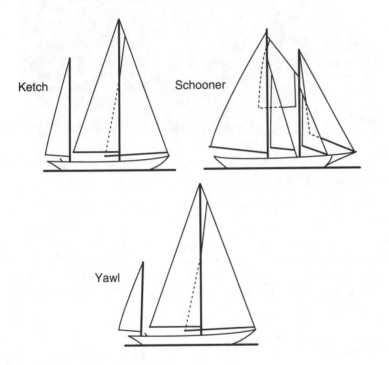

Ketch

Schooner

Yawl

Two-masted sailboats include ketches, schooners, and yawls. Both ketches and yawls feature a taller main mast forward and a shorter mizzen mast aft, while schooners have the tallest mast aft.

One Hull or Two?

If one hull is good, can two be better? How about three? It depends on what you want to do with the boat, and what you can afford.

The vast majority of sailboats are *monohulls*, which means they have a single hull—they look like a boat is "supposed" to look.

Monohulls have the grace of line that appeals to many, and they're sometimes easier to afford than a catamaran of equivalent size, particularly in cruising sailboats, because it takes far less fiberglass to build one hull than two. The narrower beam of a monohull also makes it easier to trailer and easier to fit into your garage (with the mast folded down).

However, *catamaran* or two-hull sailboats ("cats," not to be confused with catboats) and even *trimarans*, with three hulls, are becoming increasingly popular. One reason is that they're tremendously stable, even without a ballasted keel. The broad spread between the hulls creates powerful leverage to help keep the boat upright.

Catamarans like this Endeavour 34 offer remarkable stability plus an enormous amount of space below decks. This particular boat has a 15-foot beam, far wider than the typical monohull. (Photo credit: Endeavour Yachts)

Cats are also noted for a soft ride in rough head seas, and in cabin rigs, the great span of the beam allows space below decks that makes any monohull seem like a tunnel.

When operated on auxiliary power, catamarans are also highly fuel-efficient, another advantage for long-range cruising.

Are there any negatives about catamarans? Maybe a few—some say that the cabin space divided by the bridge between the sponsons is inconvenient on some models. And cats are somewhat less graceful to the eye than a sleek monohull, and some models cost more at a given length. But there's enough to like about cats that you should give them a try to see if they suit you and your family.

Daysailers, Cruisers, and Racers

Daysailers are the most popular and affordable of all sailboats, and include everything from the tiniest dinghy to 30-footers that can handle a crew of a half-dozen. They have no overnight accommodations, however—just a cockpit where the crew can sit. (That's why they call them *day*sailers.)

Sailing *cruisers* are the largest and most comfortable of sailboats, distinguished by overnight accommodations below decks. These can range from nothing more than a vee-berth to very plush multi-stateroom digs. Cruisers usually have full-length keels that make the boats very stable.

Ocean-*racers,* like those used in the America's Cup and many other series, are much like oversized (and unbelievably expensive) dinghies. They have no accommodations, not a pound of extra weight devoted to creature comforts, but they're loaded to the gills with high-tech sails, winches, and navigational gear. They sport a fairly flat bottom, with a short but deep keel that is heavily ballasted.

Beautiful motorsailing cruisers like this one are a match for the world's finest powerboats, and are seaworthy enough to take on all the world's oceans in competent hands. (Photo credit: Endeavor Yachts)

Bet You Didn't Know

The America's Cup Race is the world's oldest international sailing race, named for the U.S. yacht *America*, which won it from English competition in 1851. For most of its history (until 1983) the cup has belonged to U.S. sailors, but in recent years Australia and New Zealand have taken it home. The America's Cup takes place every four to five years, with the next race slated for the year 2000. It's always sailed in the home waters of the defending champion. For details, contact the America's Cup Challenge Association at (401) 847-2707.

It's a Surfboard...No, It's a Sailboat... No, It's a Sailboard

Combine a surfboard with a sail and you have a *sailboard* (also known as a *Windsurfer*). This is an extremely lightweight and inexpensive boat that can be transported on the tops of the smallest cars. It's also very, very fast. In fact, sailboards are among the fastest sailboats in the world, with speeds exceeding 50 mph on special boards in the hands of experts. These boats can literally fly, traveling many yards through the air, when sailed off the tops of big rolling waves or "rollers."

Sailboards have a single mast and a single sail, and they depend on the rider to keep the mast erect—there are no stays. The mast and boom fold down for compact transport.

They also have a "wishbone"-type boom that has a spar on each side of the mainsail. The boom attachment is adjustable to suit the varying heights of users.

Boat Bytes
Sailboards are about performance and exercise and exhilaration. If you don't like getting wet and want to go for a leisurely sundown cruise with your significant other, they're not quite what you need!

Sails are usually a lightweight laminate of Mylar and fabric, which is waterproof and won't become soggy and heavy when wetted repeatedly. The sails also have a PVC window in them (a section of clear plastic) so that the user can see the course ahead through the sail.

Footstraps on top of most boards help you to stay put and to gain leverage in sharp turns.

Although many sailboards have a centerboard, they have no true rudder, only a skeg to help stiffen the boat against blowing sideways. Steering is accomplished by tilting the sail and mast forward to turn into the wind, aft to turn away from the wind.

Every ride starts with pulling the wet sail and mast up out of the water, and you'll use muscles you never knew you had as you try to keep the thing upright. You'll fall—a lot—while you're learning. Maybe even more than sailing a conventional sloop, sailboarding is best learned with an instructor.

Bet You Didn't Know

The most challenging of sailboard riding is known as "shortboarding," with the boards under 10 feet long and designed for high-speed performance in the surf and in extreme winds. Most of the spectacular jumps and tricks you see on video are done by skilled shortboarders. Riding these boards takes lots of experience, though—they're not for beginners!

Boat Bytes
It's a good idea to buy one of the popular models of sport cats, because most who try catamaran sailing sooner or later get interested in racing, and those with lots of boats nationwide offer "class" races everywhere against identical boats.

Sport Cats

Also very fast are sport catamarans, twin-hulled boats that can actually plane like powerboats, jumping up on top and skimming along at white-wake speeds in winds of as little as 15 mph.

The Hobie Cat is the most famous of the breed, but there are many other well-known builders, including G-Cat, Prindle, and Nacra.

Sport catamarans have no cockpit, only a "trampoline" of mesh fabric or rope over the water where one or two can sit. The wide spread between the hulls gives the boat great stability and resistance to heeling, and makes it possible for the crew to use their weight to leverage the boat flat against powerful winds.

Larger sails can be used on catamarans because of this, adding to their potential speed without making it so likely that they will be knocked down as a monohull with the same weight and sail area. And, because the hulls are very narrow, there's very little drag.

Sport catamarans are light enough to be launched off the beach and offer great performance, although there are minimal creature comforts aboard the trampoline between the hulls. (Photo credit: Frank Sargeant)

Sport cats are light, easily trailered, shallow in draft so that they can be sailed off any beach, and reasonably economical.

Some have no centerboard, depending on sharp keels to hold them stable against the sideways push of the sails. Others use a "daggerboard"-type centerboard, which is pushed straight down through the center of the boat.

The smallest Hobies and some others are "cat-rigged," which refers to their use of a single sail, rather than their hull configuration. Others use a jib in front of the mast and are therefore "sloop-rigged."

Flying on Water

One of the most spectacular forms of sailing, called "flying the hull," is available to catamaran sailors. It takes place when the upwind hull is actually raised off the water by the heeling force on the sails. If allowed to go too far, flying can result in a capsizing, and you've got a long way to fall from the upwind side of a cat. But kept under control by steering slightly into the wind and hiking out on the windward side, it's an effective tactic for balancing a catamaran. (*Hiking out* is hanging off the high side of a sailboat when it heels to help keep the hull upright through moving the center of gravity to windward. "Hiking straps" across the trampoline secure your feet so you don't fall overboard.)

Cats with big sails sometimes call for "trapezing" in strong winds to keep them upright. This is done by attaching a cable from the mast to a harness around the helmsman, allowing him to stand on the rail with the body extended almost horizontally over the water—one of sailing's biggest rushes!

Sail Shapes

In addition to the names for different configurations of boats, there are also names for various types of sails—not something you have to drop into conversation when you're stepping aboard for the first time, but something you will want to know somewhere down the road.

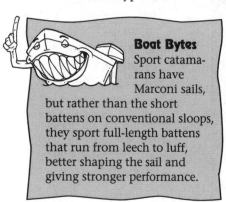

Boat Bytes
Sport catamarans have Marconi sails, but rather than the short battens on conventional sloops, they sport full-length battens that run from leech to luff, better shaping the sail and giving stronger performance.

The most common type of sail is the triangular "Marconi" rig, which is the sail you see on virtually all modern sailboats. Allegedly, it was originally named because the stays and shrouds holding up the mast reminded Depression-era sailors of the first radio towers set up by the Italian inventor.

Lateen sails are spread by two spars, a lower boom that extends past the mast and a second that runs at an angle from the forward end of the boom to the top of the mast. It's the rig for some popular "board boats" such as the Sunfish.

The very popular Sunfish class boats sport a lateen sail. (Photo credit: Frank Sargeant)

Gaff rigs are still seen on classic catboats here and there along the east coast—they include a spar or "gaff" extending out along the sail's upper edge from about two-thirds of the way up the mast.

One of the most thorough and interesting books on sail design, function, use, and care is *Sails* by Jeremy Howard-Williams (J. de Graff, 1983). It's been through umpteen editions since the first in 1967, but it's still the definitive work for those who really want to get the best from sail-power.

Sail Care

Whatever the type of sail, it should be folded neatly at day's end. The accordion fold is most common, starting at the foot and working toward the head. Storing a sail via the accordion fold is called *flaking* and is designed to keep the sail neat without bending the fibers excessively.

Fold the sail over on itself several times or roll it up and store it in the bag it came in. Sails should be stowed out of the weather and kept away from excessive heat. Store them in an air-conditioned building when possible to assure long life.

Most sails are made of Dacron, a tough, low-stretch synthetic. Dacron sailcloth doesn't rot and has tremendous resistance to tearing. However, Dacron and all other sails should be washed with fresh water, then dried thoroughly before winter storage to prevent mildew.

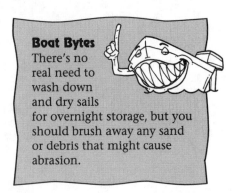

Boat Bytes
There's no real need to wash down and dry sails for overnight storage, but you should brush away any sand or debris that might cause abrasion.

It's not necessary to take the mainsail off the boom for overnight storage. It can be rolled up or flaked, with alternating folds on each side of the boom, then secured in place with bungee cords so it's ready to go in the morning.

Get Caught Up in the Race

Most sailing fans turn to racing at least a bit as their skills develop and they want to know just how good they are by competing with others.

To measure skill, there are "one-design" classes that pit boats of exactly the same length, weight, and design against each other—some classes are so carefully defined that they require all boats to be of the same color! Most one-design classes are comprised of the same model boat from a single builder. This puts all the weight of winning on the skill of the crew.

Some boats race in "formula" classes, which use a complicated set of parameters to rate the sailing efficiency of completely different designs against one another. It's a form of the handicapping system, but no time allowance is made—the rating system is intended to equalize hulls racing in the same class.

True handicap classes give time allowances, permitting larger, slower boats to compete against smaller and/or faster ones.

The U.S. Sailing Association in Portsmouth, Rhode Island, maintains a complete list of addresses and phone numbers for all the dozens of one-design racing classes (see Appendix B for contact information).

The Least You Need to Know

➤ Sailboats are categorized by height, placement, and number of masts.

➤ Sailboats can have one, two, or even three hulls. Each type has its own advantages.

➤ Sailboards and sport cats offer some of the most exciting and demanding types of sailing.

➤ Modern sails are tough, but take a bit of basic care to stay in top shape.

The Mechanics of Sailing

By now you have some idea of the sailor's vocabulary and the different types of sailboats that are out there. But before you jump on board and sail off into the wild blue yonder, there are a few basics you need to know.

In this chapter, we'll tackle the nitty-gritty of sailing, including the basics of rigging the sails, and leaving the dock and going for a sail across the bay under the power of the wind. You'll also learn the basics of turning under sail, going both upwind and down.

Why Sailboats Sail

A sailboat sails on the same principle that allows an aircraft to fly. Air passing over a rounded or convex section, be it a wing or a curved sail, goes faster than across a flat or concave section because it has to travel a greater distance to the aft edge. This creates a lower pressure on the convex side than on the concave side, according to Bernoulli's principle. So, there's less pressure on the convex or leeward side of the sail than on the concave or windward side, and a lifting force is exerted toward the convex side.

Lift is created in sails when air flows faster over the convex, leeward side than over the concave, windward side.

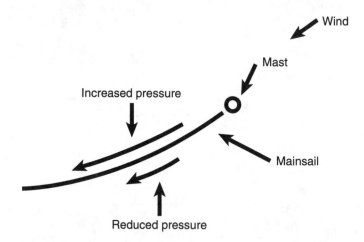

This gives lift in an aircraft wing and thrust in a sailboat. But in a sailboat, no mechanical power is required—you travel on the power of the flowing air alone.

A keel in the sailboat "stiffens" the boat, holding it from blowing sideways or even over on its beam ends with the pressure of the sail. (A boat rolled on its *beam ends* is flipped up on its side, on the verge of capsizing.) The keel acts on somewhat the same principle as the sail—it's a rounded "hydrofoil," and when directed slightly to windward by the rudder, it generates lift in that direction.

The force acting on the sail is balanced by appropriate steering with the force acting on the keel, and the boat goes straight ahead.

Many larger sailboats have weighted keels that function as "ballast," a righting force when winds threaten to capsize the boat. Smaller boats depend on movement of the crew from gunnel to gunnel to act as ballast.

These are the most basic principles of sailing—there are endless volumes on the finer points, but you don't need to know those now and you probably won't ever want to know them unless you become a serious racer or sail maker.

Your First Sailing Trip

Step aboard a fully rigged sloop and you'll see it looks like a marine rats' nest of ropes, cables, winches, pulleys, and other unidentifiable stuff that could have come from the insides of a computer, and is just as expensive. Do you have to learn what all this does to go sailing?

Sort of.

All of this equipment is used to keep the sails at an efficient angle to the wind and extract the most thrust or lift to push the boat forward.

But it's not as hard as it looks (of course, that's what your calculus teacher told you), at least not until you get to the competitive level. A couple of hours on a boat is adequate to get you started.

It's much easier if you have an instructor, either a pro who teaches for money, a friendly sailing club member, or a neighbor from the next slip. It's generally not a great idea to try learning sailing solo—too many things can go wrong, causing frustration, disappointment, and maybe even a bit of danger. It's much easier, faster, and more fun if you have experienced sailors around you.

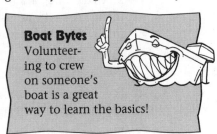

Boat Bytes
Volunteering to crew on someone's boat is a great way to learn the basics!

The basic steps to getting started are not quite as simple as indicated in Chapter 23, but they're not a whole lot more difficult, either. Here they are, without any of the subtleties you'll learn as you gain experience:

1. With the boat in the water and tied to the dock, lay out the mainsail on deck next to the boom.

2. Locate the clew of the main (the rear corner that will go out to the tip of the boom) and feed it into the fittings in the track on top of the boom or into the groove designed to hold it. This is easier if one person fits the foot of the sail to the track while the other works it toward the outer end of the boom.

3. If the sail has batten pockets along the leech or trailing edge, insert the battens or sail stiffeners. They're often tapered—put the thinner end in first. They're not all the same size, so be sure to fit them to their proper pockets.

4. Straighten the leading edge (the luff) of the sail and get out any twists, then secure the tack of the sail (the bottom front corner) to the fitting on the front or inside of the boom, near where it attaches to the mast. Pin the tack through the brass grommet in the corner.

5. Attach the clew to the outhaul at the other end of the boom. You've now got the foot of the sail secured and can put a bit of tension on the line to stretch it out. Cleat off the outhaul.

6. Now you're almost ready to hoist the sail. Check the main halyard to make sure it's not twisted around one of the stays (a common problem). Attach the halyard to the head of the sail through the brass grommet via the shackle provided.

7. Attach the luff of the leading edge of the main sail to the mast via the slide attachments spaced along its edge.

8. If your boat has only a mainsail, or if you're only using one sail for your first trip—a very good idea—you can now lower the centerboard and make sure the rudder is secure and functioning.

9. Before you raise the sails, point the boat into the wind so that the sails can't fill when first raised. You want the boat to sail, but not until you're ready. By pointing directly upwind, you put the boat "in irons"—unable to move due to a lack of lift on the sails—and it can't go anywhere.

   Go for it—go ahead and raise the main at this point, feeding the slides into the groove in the back of the mast as you pull on the main halyard. (Make sure the mainsheet—the adjustment rope that controls the mainsail—is slack so the sail can't fill until you want it to.)

   Cleat off the halyard on the mast, coil the leftover line neatly, and hang it below the cleat.

10. If your boat has a jib, the tack is first attached to a fitting near the bow, adjacent to the forestay, which supports the jib in the way the mast supports the mainsail.

    You can identify the jib tack because the angle there is wider than at the clew. On your own sails, it's not a bad idea to mark the tack in indelible ink.

    When you're sorting through a pile of sail looking for the tack and the clew, it can be hard to tell which is which. The best way to find the tack is to look for the corner where the bolt ropes that attach to the boom and the mast meet. If there's only one rope, it's the clew.

11. The jib is now attached to the forestay via the hanks or snaps along its luff. Start from the bottom of the sail up, not vice versa—that way the bottom section will be easier to attach.

12. Attach the jib sheets, using a bow line or shackles, and run the sheets through the pulleys (known as "blocks" to sailers) provided back to the cockpit—one goes to each side. Put a stopper knot, a figure eight, in the end of each so they don't slip back through the pulleys.

13. Attach the jib halyard to the head of the jib. On a windy day, it's very easy for the jib to be blown off the front deck. Have a crewperson sit on the jib until you're ready to hoist it.

That's it—you're ready to go, at last. Before you move the boat away from the dock, though, make one final check to make sure both jib sheets and the mainsheet are slack, so that the sails won't fill immediately when you push off.

Getting Underway

To get started sailing, raise the main first, if you haven't already done so, as in step 9. Then raise the jib. Pull both taut to the top of the mast and cleat them off, coiling the halyards neatly. Never tie the halyards in a knot that could be difficult to release quickly, and always make sure the end coils are orderly. This is so that you can quickly lower the sails—your only way of stopping short of turning up into the wind—in an emergency.

Since the boat is still pointed directly into the wind, the only thing that happens at this point is that the sails start to flap fast and loud if there's a lot of wind.

If you're in a crowded harbor, it's not a bad idea for the crew to man the paddles and make your way out before the sails are trimmed. Once the boat starts sailing things can get pretty busy, and it's best to have open water ahead.

To make the sails fill, push the bow off the dock or paddle so that it turns a bit away from the wind, which will bring the bow beyond the "no-sail" area (where the boat is pointed almost dead into the wind and the sails have no lift). This will allow the wind to strike the sails at an angle greater than 45 degrees.

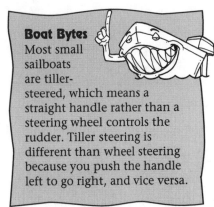

Boat Bytes
Most small sailboats are tiller-steered, which means a straight handle rather than a steering wheel controls the rudder. Tiller steering is different than wheel steering because you push the handle left to go right, and vice versa.

Backing the jib is using the jib sail to turn the boat enough to catch the wind, and is the usual course of experienced sailors for getting under way. It's done by a crewperson holding the clew of the jib out to one side of the bow, while the tiller is put over to the opposite side. The breeze catches the jib and swings the bow in the desired direction.

In close quarters, such as passing under a draw-bridge, even the most experienced sailors often use their engines to assist the sails and maintain steerage. (Photo credit: Frank Sargeant)

Boat Bytes

How do you know where the wind is coming from? Keep an eye on the *telltales*, those bits of yarn or other lightweight material that are attached to the shrouds. They fly like flags, streaming away from the wind. Telltales are also sometimes stitched through the luff of the jib to check for the best sail trim. When the sail is trimmed at its most efficient angle for a given heading, the yarn on both sides of the sail streams directly aft.

Trimming the Sails

Now you can tighten up the sheets, the main first. The sail will balloon out but will flutter at first. Draw in or *trim* the mainsheet until the fluttering stops and the sail stiffens—you're sailing!

Trim the jib similarly to the main with the lee-side sheet and your speed will begin to increase.

The sails will remain properly trimmed as long as you hold this heading or as long as the wind remains steady from the same direction. If you turn, the sails will begin to flutter again and must be adjusted. Your first courses should be beam reaches, basically sailing across the wind (see Chapter 23).

To try a close reach (at an angle between 45 and 90 degrees from the wind direction), turn up into the wind slightly. The sails will begin to flutter, but will tighten again as you draw in the sheets slightly.

As you point up even farther, you sail "close-hauled" to the wind, as near as you dare without going into the no-sail zone and losing power. As you do, the boat heels over. If the boat leans enough to make you nervous, turn a few degrees back away from the wind and the hull will straighten up.

For a broad reach, (at an angle of more than 90 degrees but less than 180 degrees from the wind direction) turn away from the wind slightly, and let out the sheets a bit.

Safe Downwind Turns

Turning across the wind on a run is known as a *jibe,* and it requires coordination between skipper and crew.

As long as the wind comes from the side of the boat opposite the side that the boom is on, even at a modest angle, the boom is under control. When you turn directly downwind and then back to the other side, putting wind and boom on the same side of the boat, the boom is going to swing.

On larger boats, the boom vang serves as an added safety line on the boom when properly rigged, preventing it from swinging uncontrolled across the boat to whack unsuspecting crew members during an unplanned jibe.

A controlled jibe requires you to warn the crew that you're about to turn across the wind, by saying "Ready to jibe." This tells them that the boom is going to come across the cockpit, although hopefully it will come slowly and under control of the mainsheet, which you or an assigned crew member will control.

When everybody is paying attention, you issue the command "Jibe ho" and make the turn, while a crewperson first draws in the mainsheet to start the boom swinging, and then gradually lets it back out as it crosses to the other side of the boat and begins to fill.

To anyone in the cockpit, the "Jibe ho" command should be a signal to duck their heads, because many booms swing across at just about head level.

For more on jibing, see Chapter 23.

Look Out!

Don't turn directly downwind or anywhere close to it at first, because a downwind run can cause an unintentional jibe, or crossing of the wind, which makes the boom swing across the cockpit at great speed if winds are strong and the sheet is loose. The boom can seriously injure crewpersons as well as knock them overboard.

Tackling Tacking

Tacking, as you'll recall from Chapter 23, is the procedure for sailing or beating toward an upwind objective. It's done in a series of close reaches, just greater than 45 degrees from being directly into the wind.

By running a zig-zag course, the boat eventually gets to the upwind target that it could never reach by sailing straight into the wind.

Tacking upwind is much like jibing downwind in terms of sail-handling. Again, you make sure the crew has their heads up (down, that is) by issuing the command "Ready to tack" or "Ready about." The crew uncleats the jib sheet and gets ready to slack it, and responds "Ready" to signify they know what's coming.

Boat Bytes

If your hands are not used to manual labor, you'll regret a day spent handling the sheets aboard a sailboat in strong winds unless you wear gloves. Sailing gloves are thin so you can work with the lines, and sometimes they are fingerless. A leather palm patch prevents sliding sheets from burning your skin. They sell for around $20.

The helmsperson then commands "Tacking" or "Helm's alee" and turns the rudder to make the bow swing across the wind.

The sails begin to flap or luff as you come into the 90 degrees where there is no lift available, and the boom swings across the cockpit. It doesn't make the big, fast swing that it might on a jibe because it's controlled by the shortened mainsheet, so this is usually not a problem for the crew.

Come about smartly when tacking—if you let the boat lose forward motion, it may not complete the turn and you'll wind up in irons, with no sail power.

At this point, the crew lets go the jib sheet and switches sides to put their weight on the new windward side as the boat comes out the opposite side of the no-sail area and the sails begin to fill again. They then take in the new windward jib sheet and adjust it to stop the sails from luffing. The main is also readjusted, and the tack is complete.

The Least You Need to Know

➤ Understanding sail rigging from a book is harder than understanding it from a friendly teacher, so get some hands-on experience.

➤ When sails flap or luff, they have no lift and the boat will sit still.

➤ When sails fill and tighten, the boat starts to move—be ready to let go of the sheets if you're not quite ready.

➤ Always be wary of the boom on downwind runs, because a uncontrolled jibe can send it violently across the cockpit and endanger your crew.

Handling Your Sailboat

Sailboats present some unusual challenges in handling under sail, because if you're not careful about how you maneuver, you can suddenly lose power just at the moment you need it most.

Of course, you can duck the issue by paddling, hanging an auxiliary outboard off a bracket on the stern of most small sailboats, or by starting the inboard on larger rigs—and that's the way most people do it.

But serious sailors sometimes like to do it the "right" way, which is sometimes the hard way. And being able to handle your boat in tight situations under sail gives you a backup for the day when your auxiliary won't start. In this chapter, I'll direct you around some of the potential problems.

Sailing to the Dock

The major difference between sailboats and powerboats in docking is that in sailing, you have no real brakes except the wind. With a powerboat, reversing the propeller can bring the boat to a halt in less than a boatlength, but sailboats keep going for some distance after the sails are doused or lowered and the boat headed up into the wind.

The trick in coming to a dock is to plan your landing so that you turn up into the wind at the last moment. This allows the momentum of your turn to push you sideways close enough to toss a line ashore or hook onto something with a boat hook, or to have a crew member step onto the dock and secure the bow line. The person should be at the bow ready to step on the dock with the bow line the instant the boat is within safe distance. With any amount of wind or current, the boat won't stay in position long, so the crew will need to look lively.

> **Look Out!**
> A large sailboat coming to the docks has a lot of momentum, and it can't be stopped by the casual push of a foot. Keep feet and hands out of the space between the rail and the pilings or injuries can result.

So, depending on the wind, you may come to a dock in a number of different ways and you may have to dock on a particular end of the structure, whether you want to or not, due to conditions. You can then walk the boat to where you'll tie it up while you have lunch or stay overnight.

Three typical situations are shown in the following figures.

Docking with the wind to the dock is best accomplished by approaching with only a small jib flying. Turn the boat parallel to the dock and loose the jib sheet so the sail begins to luff as the hull swings sideways. Momentum from the turn carries the boat forward while the wind pushes it sideways to reach the dock. Fenders should be put over the side in advance to protect the hull.

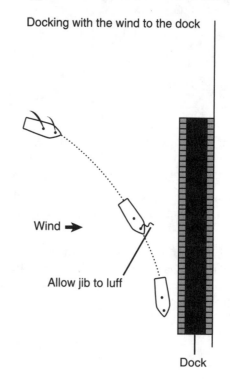

Docking with the wind to the dock

Wind ➤

Allow jib to luff

Dock

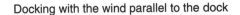

Docking with the wind parallel to the dock

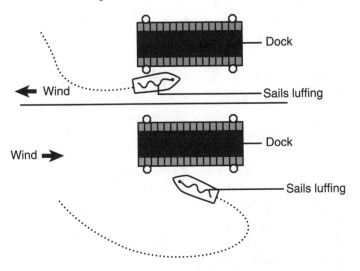

Docking with the wind parallel to the dock is not difficult if you remember to head up into the wind as you near the landing point. Be sure to maintain your motion to maintain steerage—approaching too slowly may leave you dead in the water before you can heave a line to the dock.

Docking into the wind

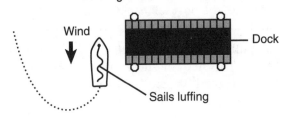

Docking into the wind is risky if there's no area where you can shoot past the dock, because your speed has to be calculated just right to stop the boat before it hits the dock. A sharp turn while still a boatlength or two off the dock may bring you in just right, but have a hand ready to heave a line in case you're too far out, and have the fenders over the side in case you're closer than you think.

319

Anchoring Under Sail

It's by far easiest to anchor under power, and if you have an auxiliary engine that's what you should do. However, if not, here's the procedure to do it the way that Captain Cook and Magellan did it:

1. Drop the jib before you approach your selected anchorage. If you don't, it's going to be in the way of the person handling the anchor on the bow.

Boat Bytes
To anchor in a harbor crowded with both power and sailboats, choose a spot near the other sailboats. They are more influenced by current than wind due to their deep keels and will all swing at about the same rate, while the powerboats will swing mostly based on the wind direction.

2. Select the spot where your anchor needs to go to allow lots of scope and hold you in place. If you're picking an overnight spot in a cruising sailboat, choose an area where the boat can swing 360 degrees with any changes in wind and tide without going aground or bumping another boat.

3. Sail toward your drop spot and turn directly into the wind as you get within two or three boatlengths. The sails will luff and the hull will coast to a stop.

4. Lower the anchor and pay out the rode as the wind pushes the boat backwards. (If there's not much wind, you may want to "back" the mainsail by pushing the boom out to one side so the sail fills and makes the boat sail backwards.)

5. When you've released adequate scope (three to five times the water depth or more, as you'll recall from Chapter 8), pull on the rode and see if you can help the flukes to work their way into the bottom. This step isn't necessary in a powerboat where the engine puts pressure on the rode, but it's a good idea in a sailboat under light winds.

6. Cleat off the rode.

7. When you're ready to leave the spot, push the bow off the wind, trim the sails, and sail past the spot where the anchor is set while leaving the anchor line slack. Cleat the line when you're well past the anchor and it should turn over, come out of the bottom, and be ready to hoist back aboard.

Getting to a Moored Boat

With large fixed-keel sailboats, it's common to leave the boat at a mooring well away from the dock, avoiding the handling problems of docking in a tight spot. The *dinghy,* or "dink," is a small boat used to travel back and forth from shore to the boat.

The dinghy is also a mobile fishing and diving platform that allows you to poke into shallows where the mother ship can't go. It's also useful for setting out a second anchor where necessary for overnights. (The anchor is lowered into the dinghy, and the rode payed out as the smaller boat moves away from the mother ship.) And there are times when it can serve as your tow boat, as well; even with a 4-horse outboard, a dinghy can tow a 40-footer out of the harbor, slowly but surely.

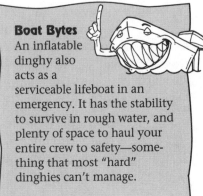

Boat Bytes
An inflatable dinghy also acts as a serviceable lifeboat in an emergency. It has the stability to survive in rough water, and plenty of space to haul your entire crew to safety—something that most "hard" dinghies can't manage.

Inflatables like this Zodiac make excellent dinghies because of their great load capacity and stability, and the soft sides don't mar the surface of the mother ship. They're also light enough to hoist aboard easily. (Photo credit: Zodiac of North America)

A Route You Can Root For

Wind, tides, and seas control where you can go and how fast you can go there in a sailboat much more than in a powerboat, so a day-long voyage to an offshore island, for example, takes a bit of advance planning. Before embarking on the trip, you should do the following:

➤ Check the tidal currents for the area you'll be cruising. If the tide will be coming in when you're going out or vice versa, it would be better to leave earlier or later to have the tides in your favor. See Chapter 16 for more on tides.

➤ Study the weather forecast (see Chapter 15). If the winds are going to force a long beat in one direction, it might be better to select another destination where you can go and come on a reach.

➤ If you'll be sailing to windward on one leg, remember that this will take far longer than the run in the opposite direction. Allow plenty of time so that you can get home before sunset unless you feel experienced enough to try sailing after dark.

➤ Check the charts for tricky water with lots of shoals (see Chapter 11 for more on charts). It's often best to plan a much longer route that will avoid the shoals rather than try to pick your way through. The longer route will take less time if you figure in a couple of hours for working off a sandbar on the short route.

The Sailing Right of Way

The rules of the road for sailboats under sail are a little different than for powerboats. In general, a sailboat under sail has the right of way over a powerboat, no matter what the angle of approach between the two craft. This is because the sailboat can't maneuver as rapidly as the powerboat. (When a sailboat is operating under motor power, it's considered a powerboat and must obey the same rules as all powerboats.)

In fact, powerboats are supposed to stay well clear of boats under sail. A large powerboat wake hitting a small daysailer can literally "knock the wind out of the sails" and cause the boat to lose steerage, and maybe even broach or make a rapid turn sideways to the sea, with some danger of swamping.

Look Out!
The passage of a large ship to windward of your boat can block your wind and make your sails luff. The wake of a fast-moving ship can also shake the wind from your sails as the boat hobbyhorses back and forth. Give these sea monsters plenty of space!

Sailboats on a run dead downwind can be forced into an unexpected jibe, complete with wildly sweeping boom, if forced to bear off by the close pass of a powerboat off the bow.

For these reasons, powerboats must give way to sailing boats unless the powered vessel is dead in the water, or is a deep-draft vessel with limited maneuverability due to water depth in a narrow channel.

For sailboat meeting sailboat, there are three basics rules:

1. With two boats on the same tack, the leeward boat has the right of way.

2. With two boats on opposite tacks, the boat on a starboard tack has the right of way.

3. When one boat overtakes another, the one ahead has the right of way.

Powerboaters who see a boat flying a spinnaker can be sure it's sailing on a run or a broad reach and will have a hard time safely maneuvering if they pass too close on the bow. (Photo credit: Endeavour Yachts)

Dealing With the Draft—and the Drift

Keeled sailboats draw a lot of water compared to powerboats of similar size. Typically they have twice the draft at a given length; that is, it takes twice the depth to keep them from going aground. The deeper the keel sits in the water, the better it works, because the greater the leverage to hold the boat upright when it begins to heel.

However, deep draft means that you will go aground in areas that even some fairly substantial powerboats cross with impunity. And when you sink a fixed keel deep into a mud flat under the power of full sail, it will be very difficult to get it back out under the power of the typical auxiliary engine on most sailboats.

A sharp lookout, polarized glasses to cut the glare, and good local knowledge can help you avoid most groundings. However, nobody, not even the most seasoned skipper, stays off the bottom all the time.

If you go on slowly in soft mud, you might be able to sail free, or to crank up the kicker and back off. Or if you have a moveable keel (a centerboard), just raise it up far enough to clear the bottom and go on your way.

If you're stuck hard, however, you'll have to apply other methods.

One is to raise the keel through heeling the boat—move everybody to the leeward side and you may gain a few precious inches of clearance so that you can sail clear. You might consider sending an athletic crewperson crawling out along the winged-out boom, with the mainsail down, to provide more heeling leverage.

Boat Bytes
The best way to prevent your sailboat from grounding is chart study. If you know the waters ahead and your exact draft, and keep track of where you are at all times and watch your depth finder, you can avoid any risky areas.

If that doesn't work, you may have to get some weight off the boat. In calm, shallow water during the summer, the crew can simply hop overboard for a swim while the skipper stays aboard to steer for deeper water. PFDs should be worn by the swimmers, just in case the boat gets off quicker than expected. The crew can then swim to the edge of deeper water to be picked up on the next pass.

In high-current areas such as passes (where groundings are frequent) getting crew off the boat is not an option unless you have a dinghy. Make sure the dinghy is secured to the boat if the flow is strong, or your crew may take a fast ride downtide toward a nasty inlet.

Look Out!
If you hit really hard on a rock bottom, under strong winds or rough waves, check your bilge for leaks before trying to get back to deep water. It's better to be grounded than sunk!

It's also possible to use the anchor to "kedge" or pull your boat off a bar. The trick is to get the anchor well away from the boat, the full length of the anchor rode, so that holding power will be maximized. (Remember that the more scope, the better the anchor holds.) You can then use one of the winches aboard to inch the boat off via cranking in the anchor line.

A more time-consuming but often essential possibility is simply to sit and wait for the next high tide, unless, of course, you went aground on high tide. If you did, you're going to have to flag down a tow quickly or endure a very long wait through an entire tidal cycle.

Heavy-Weather Sailing

Although sailors love wind, there's such a thing as too much of a good thing. But getting caught in a squall is a part of sailing; the moderate speeds available in most sailing craft mean there's no chance you can run for the docks in time to avoid a storm once the black clouds blot out the sun, as you sometimes can in a powerboat.

The basic response to a serious blow is to reduce sail, but when the first blast hits, it may be too late to inform your crew of your plans in time to avoid a capsize.

Any time the weather seems iffy, it's a good idea to review the basic heavy-weather plan, which should be followed in progressive order as the winds become more severe:

1. Before the storm arrives, make sure the sheets and halyards are clear and ready to run free as needed.

2. If the crew are not already wearing PFDs, they should put them on. Foul-weather gear is also a good idea, even in warm weather—the wind chill can be fierce with a 50-knot wind after you're soaked by rain or spray.

3. If you have an engine, get it started. You'll have more options than facing the storm under sail alone.

4. If the wind lays the boat over on its side, ease the sheets immediately and turn up into the wind.

5. If it's a major storm, drop the mainsail. If the boat is still heeling excessively, drop the jib as well. The idea is to get all that wind-catching sail area down on the deck so that the boat isn't pushed over on its side. (Lash the sails down to the boom or deck hardware—the wind may catch and tear them otherwise.)

6. You may find that you can't beat up into the wind, even under engine power, because the wind and seas stop all forward motion. If this is the case, turn downwind enough to take the seas on your stern quarter and head for the nearest protected area.

7. In a worst-case scenario, all sails down and the boat blowing down on a shoal, put the anchor over the bow, let the entire length of the rode run out, cleat it, and hope it catches!

Riding the Waves

Sailboat handling is a bit different than powerboat handling in large waves because of the minimal power available from the sail and/or auxiliary engine.

It's best to sail close-hauled into oncoming seas, letting the bow take the seas at an angle. This prevents the boat from rolling in the troughs and stabilizes the ride.

Going downwind in a strong storm can make the boat go out of control because the waves from aft may throw the stern sideways. Sailboats that venture offshore should carry a "drogue" or sea anchor that can be trailed from the stern to keep the boat straight.

A drogue or sea anchor behaves like a parachute to create drag and keep the stern from rolling into the trough in following seas.

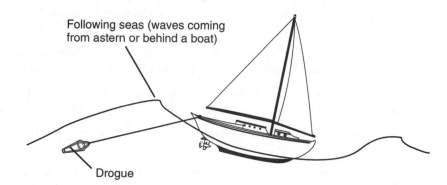

Following seas (waves coming from astern or behind a boat)

Drogue

Righting a Capsize

Whoa! This isn't supposed to happen, but it's not uncommon for sailboats under 20 feet without weighted keels to be knocked down by a blast of wind that comes so fast no corrective action can be taken. Sailing a bit beyond the edge of your skill is also frequently to blame—if you wait a moment too long to ease the sheets as you enjoy the foam and noise of a boat practically on its beam ends, you may find yourself in the water.

This is a fairly predictable "emergency" in dinghy-class boats (small one-designs such as the Sunfish) designed to be righted by their crew, and it's one you should practice dealing with in calm winds and seas.

The drill is basically this:

1. Get on the centerboard with your feet as quickly as possible, before the boat rolls completely upside down.

2. Loosen the sheets (which you should have done a few moments earlier to avoid the capsize but didn't!) so that when the mast comes up, the sails can't fill and knock you down again.

Boater-ese
The *coaming* is a raised edge or lip on the gunnels, designed to prevent spray from dripping into the cockpit.

3. Put both hands on the gunnel or coaming and pull it to you while you push down with your legs on the centerboard. It takes a major pull to make the sail come clear of the water—don't be delicate.

4. If the boat goes completely upside down, reverse your position compared to the above, grabbing the centerboard with your hands and standing on the rail until you roll it on its beam ends. Then proceed as in step 3.

5. As the boat rolls back to its upright position, climb right over the rail and into the cockpit—you're saved!

6. Help any other crew back aboard. Make sure nothing important (like the rudder!) came loose and floated away during the spill.

7. Bail out excess water and go back to sailing—but this time ease the sheet! (If the boat is full of water to the gunnels, you may have to bail it out before you or anyone else gets back aboard. Tie a gallon bucket somewhere in the cockpit to be sure it's there when you need it.)

Boat Bytes
Small sailboats often get very wet, even if they don't capsize. If you carry equipment abroad that can be damaged by water or that could sink if the boat turns over—cameras, portable GPS or VHF, and so on—protect it in sealed, watertight bags tied to the boat or secured in latched compartments.

Obviously, capsizing is anything but routine in larger sailboats, and there's no way you're going to manually right a 25-footer that goes bottom-side up, but for the smallest sailing craft, it's a fairly common procedure.

The Least You Need to Know

➤ Sailboats can't be maneuvered quickly or stopped like powerboats, so more care is required when docking and anchoring them.

➤ Boats under sail have a different set of rules of the road than powerboats.

➤ The deep draft of many sailboat keels makes grounding frequent—know the tricks for getting free.

➤ Sailboats can handle rough weather easily if the crew prepares in advance.

Glossary

adrift   Loose from moorings or anchor, without power.

aft   Toward the rear section of a boat.

aground   When a boat is stuck on bottom.

amidships   Near the middle of the boat.

anchor   A device for securing a boat in place in open water, attached to the boat by an anchor rode or line.

anchorage   A harbor or protected area where waves can't normally reach.

anchor light   A white light displayed on the highest point of a boat at anchor, visible 360 degrees.

anchor rode   The rope or line leading from the boat to the anchor.

astern   Toward the back of a boat, or sometimes behind the stern of a boat.

autopilot   An automatic steering device designed to hold a compass course despite wind and current.

backstay   A supporting guywire running from a sailboat mast to the stern area.

barometer   A meter for measuring atmospheric pressure, indicative of weather changes.

battens   Thin strips of plastic used to stiffen or flatten the leech of a sail.

beam   The width of a boat.

bearing   The course in degrees toward a distant object.

beating   Sailing to windward via tacking.

bilge   The lowest area inside the bottom of a boat.

bitter end   The cut end of any line.

block-and-tackle   An assembly of pulleys and ropes to multiply force.

boat hook   A hook with rounded ends set on a long handle, designed to pull in or fend off other boats; distinguished from a gaff hook, a sharp-pointed hook designed to boat large fish.

boom   The horizontal pole that secures the bottom of the mainsail.

boom vang   Lines and fittings that secure the boom.

bosun's chair   A seat used to hoist sailors aloft to work on rigging on the mast.

bow   The forward part of a boat.

bowline   One of the most useful of boating knots, used to make a secure loop.

bow line   A line attached to the bow of a boat, used to secure it to a dock or mooring.

breakers   Waves rolling over on themselves to create white, disturbed, and often dangerous water.

bulkhead   A frame member or wall that lies across the beam of a boat.

buoy   A floating navigational aid.

capsize   When a hull turns upside down.

cast off   Set free or loose, as in "cast off the dock lines."

catamaran   A twin-hulled boat.

cavitate   When a propeller loses its bite on the water and spins rapidly while losing forward thrust.

centerboard   A pivoting keel board that can be lowered to keep a sailboat from being pushed sideways by the wind.

chafing gear   Protective material secured around a dock line to prevent abrasion.

channel   The deeper portion of a waterway, often marked for navigation.

charts   Nautical road maps describing depths, aids to navigation, and so on.

chine   Where the sides of a boat meet the bottom. Hard chines are nearly square, while soft chines are rounded.

chock   A U-shaped fitting designed to keep a line in place.

cleat   A two-horned fitting that allows one to rapidly secure lines without tying knots.

clove hitch   A tie-up created by using two loops crossed over each other on a piling.

coaming   A raised edge or lip on the gunnels, designed to prevent spray from dripping into the cockpit.

cockpit   The working area of a boat, aft of the wheel.

come about   To change directions, turn around.

compass   A magnetic navigational tool.

cotter pin   A wire or fastener used to secure nuts on bolts or to keep turnbuckles in place.

Cunningham   A line used to control tension along a sail's luff.

davits   Stout lifting arms designed to hoist a boat onto a seawall or to bring a dinghy aboard a larger boat.

dead reckoning   Determining position based on distance, time, and speed.

deadrise   The angle between one side of the bottom and the horizontal, usually measured near the transom. Boats with a high degree of deadrise—deep vee hulls—perform well in rough water.

deck   The floor or walking surface inside a boat.

dinghy   A small boat, also known as a "dink," that is used to travel back and forth from shore to a larger boat.

displacement   The weight of water displaced by a boat.

displacement hull   A boat that maintains a consistent draft while moving. The speed of displacement hulls is limited mostly by their length, with longer boats traveling faster.

douse   To drop a sail quickly.

downwind   With the wind.

draft   Vertical distance from the waterline to the lowest point on a vessel.

ease   To let tension off a line gradually, as in adjusting a sail.

ebb   An outgoing flow of water, falling tide.

fathom   A unit of measurement that equals six feet.

fathometer   An electronic instrument used to measure depth.

fender   A cushion placed between two boats or a boat and a dock to prevent damage.

fetch   The distance over water the wind blows, which affects wave height.

flare   The outward curve of a boat's sides near the bow. Also, an emergency distress signal.

flood   An incoming flow of water, rising tide.

following seas   Waves that come from astern or behind.

forward   Toward the front section of a boat.

freeboard   The distance from the surface of the water to the gunwales.

gaff   A spar to support a sail. Also, a hooked tool to land fish.

gel coat   The outer layer of resin, usually colored, on a fiberglass boat.

gunwale   The upper edge of a boat's side, also spelled "gunnel."

hatch   Deck openings, usually fitted with watertight doors.

head   The upper corner of a sail. Also, a marine toilet.

heading   The direction in which the bow points.

heel   To tip to one side.

helm   The wheel, tiller, or steering control.

hull   The body of a boat, not including interior liner, decks, cabin, and rigging.

in irons   A sailboat headed into the wind with sails luffing and unable to make headway is said to be in irons.

inboard   A powerboat with the engine inside the hull and the prop shaft running through the bottom of the boat.

inboard outboard   Also known as an I/O or stern drive, this propulsion system combines an inboard engine with a drive unit on the transom. The drive can be trimmed up or down to improve running attitude.

Intracoastal Waterway   The protected, marked, and often dredged inland waterway that runs along the U.S. coast from Maine to Florida and around the Gulf of Mexico.

jib   The triangular foresail.

jibe   To change directions on a sailboat on a downwind run so that the boom swings across the cockpit.

keel   The bottom center of the hull, bow to transom. Sailboat keels often project below the bottom of the boat.

ketch   A two-masted sailboat with the foremast taller than the aft mast, and the aft mast stepped ahead of the rudder post.

knot   One nautical mile per hour, equal to 1.15 miles per hour.

latitude   A measure of geographic distance north or south of the equator. Latitude lines on a chart run east and west.

lee shore   A shore lying downwind.

leeward   Away from the wind.

line   Rope or cord used aboard a boat.

longitude   A measure of geographic distance east or west of the prime meridian which runs through Greenwich, England. Longitude lines on a chart run north and south.

lubber's line   The line on a compass indicating the boat's direction.

luff   The leading edge of a sail. When a sail flaps because it's improperly trimmed, it's said to be luffing.

mainsail   The sail on the back side of the main mast.

mast   An upright spar to support rigging and sails.

mizzen   A smaller mast set aft of the main mast.

mooring   A permanent anchor attached to a buoy, allowing tie-ups without dropping the boat's anchor.

nautical mile   One minute of latitude, or 6,076 feet.

neap tides   The quarter-moon periods when tide movement is minimal.

outboard   An engine and drive system that attaches to a boat's transom.

painter   A line attached to the bow, usually of a dinghy.

piling   A support post for a pier.

piloting   Navigation by use of visible references.

planing hull   A hull designed to lift to near the surface, decreasing drag and increasing speed.

port   Left, facing forward on a boat. Also, a harbor.

port tack   When a sailing vessel has the wind coming over the port side.

prop   Short for "propeller," used to push a boat through the water via mechanical power.

quartering seas   Waves that come from aft of amidships.

radar   An electronic navigation system used to "see" via reflected radio waves.

Radio Direction Finder   Also known as RDF, this is a radio with an antenna that can be tuned to locate the geographic position of distant stations and thus to locate a vessel's position.

reach   Sailing across the wind.

right of way   The boat with the legal right to continue course and speed in meeting situations. The other boat is said to be the "burdened" vessel.

rode   The anchor line and chain.

rudder   A vertical plate near the stern for steering a boat.

running lights   Lights on a boat that are required by law to be shown between sundown and sunup.

running rigging   The adjustable lines on a sailboat, used to control spars and sails.

schooner   A vessel with two or more masts, with the forward masts shorter than the last aft mast.

scope   The ratio between the depth of water and the length of the anchor rope. A scope of 3:1 is the minimum for anchoring in protected water, and scopes up to 7:1 are recommended in exposed conditions.

sea anchor   Also known as a drogue or drift anchor, this is any device that is streamed to act as a drag from bow or stern and slow the drift of a boat.

sea cock   A through-hull fitting that controls water flow; a valve.

shackle   A U-shaped metal fitting used to bind together anchor and rode or sail and line.

shear pin   A soft metal pin designed to break when the prop hits an obstruction, thus preventing damage to prop or gears.

sheet   A line used to adjust sail trim.

shipshape   In clean, orderly condition.

shrouds   Fixed rigging that supports the mast from the sides of the boat.

slip   A berth for a boat with pilings and finger piers on both sides.

sloop   A sailboat with a single mast set slightly forward of amidships, usually equipped with a mainsail and a jib.

spars   The masts and booms of a sailboat.

spinnaker   A three-cornered, parachute-like sail, usually brightly colored, for sailing downwind.

splice   To permanently join two ropes by tucking strands of each over the other, creating a smoother joint than any knot.

spring line   Lines used to control fore and aft motion of a boat tied up in a slip.

spring tides   Periods around the new and full moons when high tides are higher than usual and low tides are lower than usual.

squall   A sudden storm accompanied by strong winds.

standing line   The main part of a line, the part not used in a knot.

starboard   Right, facing forward on a boat.

starboard tack   When a sailboat has the wind coming over the starboard side.

stays   Wire rigging used to support the mast fore and aft.

stepped   Secured to the deck or keel, used in referring to sailboat masts.

stern   The rear part of a boat.

stern drive   Same as inboard/outboard or I/O.

stern line   A line from the stern cleat to the dock.

stow   To put an item in a secure spot.

swamp   When a boat fills with water over the gunnels, often prior to sinking.

tack   The legs of an upwind beat in sailing. Also, the forward lower corner of a sail.

tacking   Changing the heading of a sailing vessel so that the wind comes over the opposite rail.

tackle   Pulleys and lines used to gain mechanical advantage. Also used to describe anchor gear and fishing gear.

telltale   A wind indicator mounted on sail or stay.

thwart   A brace running laterally across a boat.

tides   The vertical rise and fall of sea water caused by the pull of the sun and moon.

tiller   An arm or lever for steering.

transom   The squared-off section of the stern.

trim   To adjust the running attitude of a powerboat through moving the drives up or down or adjusting trim tabs. Also, to adjust sails for most effective sailing.

trimaran   A boat with three hulls.

trip line   A line attached to the lower part of an anchor so that it can be easily pulled free of bottom.

true wind   The actual direction and force of the wind, as compared to "apparent wind" felt aboard a moving boat.

underway   When a vessel is in motion, not at anchor.

upwind   Toward the direction from which the wind is blowing.

v-bottom   A hull with a sharp or v-shaped bottom, designed to split the waves and soften the ride. Also spelled "vee-bottom."

variation   Compass error caused by the difference between geographic north and the magnetic north pole.

ventilate   To pump fumes out of the bilge via an electric blower. Also, when a prop draws in air and loses its grip in the water.

VHF radio   Very High Frequency radio, the most common boat-to-boat and boat-to-shore communication system on recreational boats.

wake   The waves created by boat movement.

walk-through   A passageway through the windshield via a folding section, most often found on bow-rider powerboats.

waterline   The line where the surface of the water meets the sides of the boat, sometimes marked with a trim strip.

weather shore   A shore lying upwind.

whipping   Securing the loose ends of a cut strand of line with cord. Sometimes applied to securing the ends with heat, tape, or glue.

winch   A circular drum used to provide a mechanical advantage when hauling in line or cable.

windward   Toward the direction from which the wind is blowing.

yawl   A two-masted sailboat with a forward main mast and a smaller aft mast stepped behind the rudder post.

Resources

Boating School Sources

U.S. Coast Guard Boating Safety Hotline:
(800) 368-5647

U.S. Coast Guard Auxiliary:
(800) 336-2628

U.S. Power Squadron:
(888) 367-8777, (888) 828-3380

United Safe Boating Institute:
(800) 336-BOAT

Sailing School Sources

American Sailing Association
13922 Marquesas Way
Marina del Rey, CA 90292
(310) 822-7171

National Sailing Industry Association
200 E. Randolph Drive, Suite 5100
Chicago, IL 60601-6528
(800) 535-SAIL, (312) 946-6200

Marina Sailing (six California sailing schools):
(800) 262-7245

Offshore Sailing School (eastern U.S. and British Virgin Islands):
(800) 221-4326

U.S. Sailing Association
P.O. Box 1260
Portsmouth, RI 02871
(401) 683-0800

Sources of Charts and Publications

U.S. Coastal Waters and Great Lakes, NOAA:
(301) 436-6990

Coastal waters of other nations, NOAA:
(301) 436-6990

Mississippi River, U.S. Army Corps of Engineers maps:
(800) 537-7962

Tennessee Valley Authority lakes and rivers:
(423) 751-6277

Guide Books

The *Waterway Guides* are a series of books that have long been the bibles for Intracoastal Waterway cruisers from Maine to Texas and throughout the Bahamas. The books feature complete maps of the routes plus descriptions of the approach to every harbor, attractions along the way, and more. They are priced at about $37 each. For information, contact *Waterway Guides*, 6151 Powers Ferry Road NW, Atlanta, GA 30339; (770) 955-2500.

The *Embassy Boating Guides* are remarkably detailed, spiral-bound, full-color books on coastal boating, fishing, and diving. They include color charts of coastal areas, suggested GPS fishing hotspots, aerial photos of many harbor entrances, and even a list of fishing guides and their phone numbers. They sell for about $40 each. For information, contact *Embassy Guides*, 35 Hartwell Avenue, Lexington, MA 02173; (888) 839-5551.

The *Chart Kit* series features full-scale color nautical charts in book format—much easier to handle than loose sheets. The price is $110 per area. The data is also available on CD-ROM and floppy disks for $199.95. For information, contact the Better Boating Association, Riverside Drive, Andover, MA 01810; (781) 982-4060.

For a wide variety of navigational guides and charts, try Bluewater Books & Charts, 1481 SE 17th Street, Fort Lauderdale, FL 33316; (800) 942-2583.

Towing Services

Sea Tow offers memberships for $95/year with unlimited free towing in many coastal areas nationwide. Contact Sea Tow, 1560 Youngs Avenue, Southhold, NY 11971; (516) 765-3660.

TowBOAT/U.S. is a service associated with BOAT U.S. It includes nationwide towing 24 hours a day. Contact TowBOAT/U.S., 880 S. Pickett Street, Alexandria, VA 22304-4606; (800) 888-4869.

Other Resources

BOAT U.S. is the nation's largest recreational boating club. It lobbies for boating interests in state and federal legislatures and publishes a monthly newsletter. Club members get discounts on fuel and dockage at many marinas. The company is also an excellent source of all sorts of economically priced marine gear via a mail-order catalog. The club loans life jackets to kids via yacht clubs and marinas nationwide. For information, contact 880 S. Pickett Street, Alexandria, VA 22304-4606; (800) 395-2628 or (703) 823-9550; Web site: **www.boatus.com**.

Another Web site, **www.allaboutboats.com**, by Trader Publications, not only lists thousands of boats for sale privately, but provides links to boating magazines and information on weather, tides, fishing sites, and lots more.

BUC Information Services publishes the *BUC Used Boat Price Guide*, which is the "bluebook" for buying or selling a used boat. The company also has a Web site at **www.buc.com**. For information, contact BUC Information Services, 1314 NE 17th Ct., Fort Lauderdale, FL 33305; (800) 327-6929.

Tidemaster produces a computerized yearly tide listing that's very handy for trip planning. Contact Zephyr Services, 1900 Murray Avenue, Pittsburgh, PA 15217; (412) 422-6600.

Index

D

N